Faces of Aging

Faces of Aging

The Lived Experiences of the Elderly in Japan

Edited by Yoshiko Matsumoto

Stanford University Press
Stanford, California

Stanford University Press
Stanford, California

Printed in the United States of America on acid-free, archival-quality paper

Library of Congress Cataloging-in-Publication Data

Faces of aging : the lived experiences of the elderly in Japan / edited by Yoshiko Matsumoto.
   p. cm.
Includes bibliographical references and index.
ISBN 978-0-8047-7148-1 (cloth : alk. paper) — ISBN 978-0-8047-7149-8 (pbk. : alk. paper)
1. Older people—Japan. 2. Aging—Social aspects—Japan. I. Matsumoto, Yoshiko, 1954–
HQ1064.J3F33 2011
305.260952—dc22
                    2010039804

Typeset by Bruce Lundquist in 10/14 Minion

To the memory of my father,
and the strength and cheerfulness of my mother

Contents

Illustrations

Acknowledgments

I would like to express my most sincere gratitude to the contributors to this volume. Their unfailing support and patience during the long process of publication gave me the energy and motivation to continue pursuing our project. Needless to say, without their intellectual and moral contributions, this volume would not have come into existence.

This book has roots in a conference, "Faces and Masks of Aging: Implications from the Lives of Japanese Elderly," held at Stanford University in May 2005. The conference was held with the generous support of several units within Stanford University: School of Humanities and Sciences; School of Medicine; Center for East Asian Studies; Stanford Society of Fellows in Japanese Studies; Department of East Asian Languages and Cultures (formerly Department of Asian Languages); Division of Literatures, Cultures, and Languages; and Stanford Humanities Center. Their funding was also of great assistance in the preparation of this publication. I am indebted to Sharon Long, former dean of humanities and sciences, whose encouragement of my research on the topic of aging first gave me the idea of holding a conference. I am also grateful to Laura Carstensen, director of the Stanford Center on Longevity, and to Arnold Rampersad, former senior associate dean of humanities, for their intellectual support and thought-provoking keynote and introductory addresses at the conference. Thanks are also due to the speakers whose valuable contributions were presented at the conference but not included in the volume: Sachi Hamano, Akiko Hashimoto, Hazel Markus, Nancy Morioka-Douglas, and Haruo Yanai. Dr. Yanai and his colleagues' statistical research on lifestyle habits of the Japanese elderly based on the data of 300,000 people is comparable to the research supported by the MacArthur Foundation in the United States, the Midlife Development in the U.S. (MIDUS). I hope their findings will become available to a wider audience sometime in the near future.

Many people extended their assistance and moral support in the process of preparing this volume for publication. I will not be able to mention everyone here, but in particular, I am grateful for editorial and research assistance offered by Beth Carey, Susan Mast, Molly Valor, and Mamiko Yamashita. Thanks are also due to Stacy Wagner at Stanford University Press for her incisive advice. Michelle Li gave me valuable suggestions for improvements. My husband, John Ryan, gave me constant moral and intellectual support. The faith that Mona, my daughter, has that I can do something useful for others kept me going. I am thankful for their encouragement. Last but not least, I am grateful to my late father, Yoshiji Matsumoto, and my mother, Gyoko Matsumoto, for all the love and education they provided me. As I live across the Pacific from them, I was mostly not there when my father was ill and when my mother was caring for him. This volume is dedicated to the memory of my father, and the strength and cheerfulness of my mother.

Yoshiko Matsumoto

Faces of Aging

Introduction

Yoshiko Matsumoto

For me—and for those of us who are older and hence "different"—a shifting self-image is based not only on the changed person I see in the mirror, but also on the behavior of those around me. "Let me help you cross the street." "Why don't you take my seat?" "Would you like to take a nap?" The solicitude is always heartfelt, but it reflects a stereotype.

    We are characterized on the basis of a number of assumptions: we're fragile, our memory is spotty, our energy is low, we're anxious about the next DMV license exam, we fall more often. And to some extent, all of that is true.

Herbert L. Abrams, "How It Feels to Get Old,"
Stanford Magazine **July/August (2004, 53)**

WE AGE AS LONG AS WE LIVE, so issues of aging should be everyone's concern. But despite the large number and the longevity of older people in developed countries such as the United States and Japan, the elderly as individuals are in many ways still invisible. They tend to be perceived as recipients of health care, consumers of social security savings, and the passive targets of scientific research and public policy; their faces and voices seem hidden behind statistics of the elderly population at large. Except for the fortunate who in their early years had intimate contact with old people, younger people may find it difficult to understand or appreciate the experience of the elderly. Even those with such contact may not fully comprehend what it is like to be older since it is not yet their experience. The perceived distance of the lives and concerns of older people from those of younger generations seems also to affect scholarly research, and may

1

engender stereotyping (Eckert 1984). Young and middle-aged researchers without the direct experience of being elderly, as many of us are, need to be aware of the possible discrepancies between commonly held views about old age and the actual lives of the elderly. We need to be aware that preconceptions about older people may influence the process of selecting among multiple interpretations of what we observe.

Faces of Aging

Defining old age itself is a complex issue. Researchers, including the contributors to this volume, who work with old people in developed countries often refer to individuals over 65 years of age as old, but they are also aware that this chronological characterization is too simplistic. The perception of one's age is not necessarily defined by chronological age (Boden and Bielby 1986) and can be "disjunctive" (Coupland, Coupland, and Giles 1989). Age is also felt in terms of one's physical facilities ("functional age") and the rites of passage one takes ("social age") (see Counts and Counts 1985; Hamilton 1999). The chapters in this volume make a concerted effort to put a human face on aging issues, and consider multiple dimensions of the aging experience.

As with other groups of people, older persons live under diverse economic, regional, and health conditions. Some live in an urban environment and some in rural areas; some are in nursing homes, while others live independently or with families; some are women and some are men. Heterogeneity, in fact, is perhaps more pronounced among the elderly. One person can also have multiple faces—an image of oneself, a face that is given by others, a face or faces one presents to others, and a face one sees as one's own. I have used the word "face" here to refer to the human aspect of the aging experience and to the various dimensions of that experience. The concept of "face" has also been used in the sociology of interaction, notably by Goffman (1967), to mean "the positive social value a person effectively claims to himself by the line others assume he has taken during a particular contact" (5). The epigraph to this introduction suggests various "faces" of aging in the way I have used the word, but also evokes Goffman's "face" especially in the sense of individuals being "in wrong face," that is, experiencing a mismatch between who they think they are and who they are considered to be. According to Goffman, "a person may be said to *be in wrong face* when information is brought forth in some way about his social worth which cannot be integrated, even with effort, into the line that is being sustained for him" (8). However, the situation of aging is complex. The image that others have of the elderly is not completely wrong, as the epigraph suggests, but it is not how the elderly see themselves all the time. In other words, there are definite physical and social changes associated with aging, but they do not completely alter the person.

The chapters in this book are written with an awareness of the multilayered conditions associated with the lives of elderly persons. They attempt to reveal the experience of aging with close attention to the point of view of the persons who undergo the process, going beyond the interpretations assigned by the broader society or appropriated by the elderly themselves. Giving more attention to the individual experiences of the aging population should make it possible to shift the perception of aging issues from "their" problems to matters of our own concern, and help us attain a fuller understanding of the complex issues of aging and the well-being of the overall population.

Multidisciplinary Perspective

The volume is designed specifically to present a spectrum of elder-centered issues on aging rather than narrowing to one topic or one discipline. The choice of a multidisciplinary perspective reflects, first of all, the multifaceted nature of aging issues. It is intended to encourage future interdisciplinary investigations, which in turn will form a crucial basis for effective public policies. The importance of multidisciplinary and interdisciplinary studies that diverge from the previous trend of biology-centered research has been repeatedly advocated, particularly in the domain of aging studies (e.g., Johnson 2005; National Research Council 2005; Majeski and Stover 2005). The Gerontological Society of America held its 58th Annual Scientific Meeting in 2005 with the main theme "The Interdisciplinary Mandate," in which gerontologists, including experts in the biological and medical traditions, encouraged their professions to take a step toward cross-fertilization.

An additional motivation for compiling a volume with chapters representing multiple disciplines is to respond to a challenge noted in gerontological studies, namely, a "lack of broad training" (National Research Council 2005, 89). Ryan and Norris (2001) lament that, although "gerontology is a multidisciplinary field, . . . as knowledge about aging grows in depth and complexity . . . the crossover of even related subspecialities has become less likely" (286). They draw attention to the trend of journals becoming so specialized that a specialist in one field has no chance of accidentally "tripping over" an article in another and they observe that "given this rigid and powerful disciplinarity, it is little wonder that older adults and their families feel challenged and frustrated by their interactions with health care professionals" (ibid.). While it is undoubtedly challenging to pursue successful interdisciplinary studies, exposure to a variety of research agendas and disciplines will help individual researchers gain a fuller background and understanding of the nature of the research topics, and enable them to produce more textured observations. A commonly shared view may emerge from different disciplines and topics of investigation, which in turn can help to form a basis for effective public policies. This book offers an opportunity for the interested eye to "trip over" studies in specializations of others.

By providing access to different aspects of studies on aging, the chapters in this book are also designed to offer qualitative studies of aging for researchers in any discipline or for anyone who has personal or professional interests in issues of aging. As we age, or as we have increasing contact with older people, all of us, including those who are not gerontologists, may become interested in issues of aging. Considering the significant impact that the increasing number of old people has made and will be making in many countries, the more investigation in a wide range of disciplines is mobilized, the better our understanding will be. It is not easy, however, to find scholarly introductory literature that provides a broad background on aging issues. Available publications are almost entirely discipline specific and are frequently written to support a particular agenda. The chapters of this book showcase qualitative studies by specialists of various disciplines—medicine, nursing, gerontology, psychology, sociology, anthropology, film studies, gender studies, communication, and linguistics—in an attempt to keep a balance of depth and breadth of investigation, and to encourage contributions from a variety of fields.

Lives of the Elderly in Japan

While this book covers topics of aging from multiple disciplinary perspectives, all the chapters approach their questions with the Japanese situation in mind. Japan leads other developed countries in its proportion of elderly members of the population. People over 65 years of age amounted to 20 percent of the nation's population in 2005, a figure that is expected to reach 30 percent by 2025 (Statistics Bureau of the Ministry of Internal Affairs and Communications 2006). With average life expectancy at birth in 2007 reaching 85.99 years for women and 79.19 years for men (Ministry of Health, Labor, and Welfare 2008), the population of elderly in Japan is likely to continue to grow for some time, while the birth rate has declined in 2006 to the rate of 1.25 children born to a woman. It is predicted that in the year 2050 the median age of Japanese will be 53.4 years and that the population pyramid will be top-heavy, resembling the shape of an ice cream cone or an urn (National Institute of Population and Social Security Research 2002).

Detailed statistics of Japan's demography are found in reports by government agencies such as the Ministry of Health, Labor, and Welfare and the National Institute of Population and Social Security Research. In general, Japanese elderly "reap the fruits of a busy life, enjoying relatively carefree years of retirement in good health and without economic worries" (Coulmas 2007, 2). Because of the trend of the population structure, establishment of a better pension system, and other factors, Japanese people's attitude toward old age has been changing. In a 2001 survey by the Cabinet Office the percentage of the elderly who desire to live always with their children and grandchildren was 43.5 percent and dropped by 10.7 percent compared to 1986 (Coulmas 2007, 28). The largest portion of people (33 percent) in 2003 responded that they wished to spend their old age "leisurely to suit their tastes and hobbies" in contrast to only 24 percent who wanted to live "peacefully with their children and grandchildren," while the ratio was opposite in 1973 (Coulmas 2007, 28–29).

The Japanese situation offers a wealth of resources for research—not only a large number of older people, but also a culturally and socially interesting setting for considering the implications of aging in the modern world. There are commonly held views, of varying relations with reality, including the notions that Japan is a society where the elderly are respected, families have close ties, harmony is prized, and women are subservient. A number of chapters of this volume discuss how these understandings compare with the current lives of older people in Japan, and consider the implications of such findings for general issues of aging.

Since the Japanese situation offers a convenient point of cross-cultural comparison, there have been several notable works on aging in Japan as well as elsewhere in East Asia that investigate specific social and anthropological questions. Topics investigated include the social conditions of caregiving in Japan (Long 2000; Wu 2004), the implications of the Confucian concept of filial piety in the modern world (Ikels 2004), social and family support of the elderly (Kendig, Hashimoto, and Coppard 1992; Hashimoto 1996), end of life (Long 2005), aging interpreted as psychological maturity (Plath 1980), and aging in a rural environment (Traphagan 2000; 2004). As we will see more clearly in the following sections, this volume also includes topics that have not been discussed in existing books, such as verbal interactions, sexuality represented in film, lifestyle, and the psychology of communication. In offering such a diverse view of the lives of the elderly beyond statistics, it is hoped that this volume will complement the existing literature and extend our understanding of elders' lives.

Background of the Volume

The majority of contributors to the volume were also speakers at a three-day conference, "Faces and Masks of Aging: Implications from the Lives of Japanese Elderly," held at Stanford University in May 2005. The conference was open to the public, and had the participation of people from both Stanford and outside communities. The conference focused on qualitative investigations of the lives of old people from a cross-cultural perspective, drawing examples from various scholarly research projects and from an artistic depiction of the lives of Japanese and American elderly. The conference was intended to promote conversation and collaboration on qualitative aspects of the lives of the elderly among researchers in Japan and the United States who work in various academic fields. It was also intended to create and sustain a dialogue on aging issues in Japan and the United States, and to encourage greater attention to the latter part of the life span by illuminating the richness of the language and lives of the elderly and offering evidence against the simple decrement-based "ageist" view. Fourteen specialists from Japan and the United States in the fields of psychology, medicine, nursing, gerontological health care, sociology, anthropology, communication, film, and linguistics presented their research. Laura Carstensen, director of the Stanford Center on Longevity, delivered a keynote speech, and the award-winning film *Yurisai* (Lily Festival) was screened, followed by a public discussion with the director, Sachi Hamano. This volume is an outgrowth of those presentations and the conversations that continued after the conference. The chapters represent contributions that were particularly pertinent to exposing multiple aspects, or faces, of the lives of old people, with particular attention to the situation in Japan. After the conference, additional contributions were solicited for the purpose of this publication.

Varied Experiences and Varied Representations:
Preview of the Chapters

The ten chapters, excluding the Introduction and the Afterword, are organized in two parts. The chapters in Part 1 present varied life experiences of old people depending on their personal and social backgrounds. They lead us to the clear awareness that lumping together people who have varied health and living conditions in a single category of the "elderly," and assuming that their lives and needs are similar because of their advanced age, is utterly meaningless. For example, an important factor for successful aging in one group, such as being in close contact with younger family members (Doba et al., this volume), may work against successful aging in another context, in rural Japan (Traphagan, this volume). Contrasts such as this are perhaps more apparent in the context of chapters juxtaposing different lives. A further benefit of such juxtaposition is that we are also presented with various possibilities and resources that may be available to old individuals. Issues of gender and sexuality, which may often be avoided if considered taboo, are also discussed in Part 1.

The chapters in Part 2 focus on verbal communication involving old people, and on considering how old individuals verbally represent themselves, how they may be interpreted by others, and what we learn from such interactions. While there have been notable studies in communication and aging, especially in North America and Great Britain (e.g., Nussbaum and Coupland 2004), this is an area of study that has not been well represented in the field of gerontology on either side of the Pacific Ocean. For instance, no independent chapter on communication or linguistics is included in the 744-page handbook on age and aging (Johnson 2005), despite the apparent and unarguable importance of verbal communication to human life. Linguistic studies of discourse by Japanese elderly have appeared only recently (e.g., Hamaguchi 2001; Matsumoto 2005; 2007; Backhaus 2009). The chapters in this section discuss verbal communication of the elderly from the point of view of human interaction rather than from the viewpoint of decreased biomedical ability, and reveal a complexity of self-expression in verbal interactions with and among older people. Aging from the perspective of communication is further discussed in the Afterword by Jon F. Nussbaum and Carla L. Fisher.

Part 1: Varied Lives and Experiences of the Elderly

The first chapter presents a case study on successful aging through participation in the activity of photography. Through their interviews with elderly people who took up photography as a post-retirement hobby and joined photography clubs, Keiko Takahashi, Makiko Toroko, and Giyoo Hatano find that enhancing social relationships with others and having flexible and accepting attitudes toward aging are significant factors in remaining engaged and leading a meaningful life.

The findings of the first chapter are echoed in the second chapter, which introduces the "New Elder Citizen Movement," a rapidly growing movement that promotes the enriched physical and mental quality of later life. The movement has been led by Shigeaki Hinohara (who will be a centenarian in 2011), the honorary president of a teaching hospital in Tokyo, and a co-author of this chapter with Nobutaka Doba. The lifestyle variations of the members, who are predominantly over seventy-five years of age, are examined in detail to provide a general picture of how they live. Through investigation of a relatively large number of elders, this study focuses on quality of life issues and initiatives taken by the elderly themselves.

The first two chapters present the elderly as resilient and self-reliant. This picture runs counter to the stereotypical image of the elderly as defeated and discouraged. While some elderly defy stereotypes by leading active and engaged lives, others also defy stereotypes in very different ways, as other chapters in this part illustrate. In Chapter 3, Susan Orpett Long discusses the strained relations between older spouses when one must care for the other. Long points out how caregiving relationships have changed, noting that adult children, who traditionally provided care for their parents, no longer live at home and so the responsibility falls to one's spouse. Taking a case in which the husband cares for his ill wife, Long discusses tension, dependency, and sacrifice as experienced by the elderly couple and the reality of the caregiving situation. In interviews, the multiple public and private faces of the old couple, or *soto-zura* (public mask) and *uchi-zura* (inward-facing representation), are revealed, adding texture to the image of the husband as a good family caregiver.

Tension among family members is also clearly felt in the rural families discussed by John W. Traphagan in Chapter 4. Unlike in urban environments, elders in rural areas can be more isolated from other elders and have to depend on their younger family members, whose life experiences are far different from their own. Traphagan focuses on such rural elders' experiences and voices, which he relates to the increased number of suicides among the elderly in rural Japan. The chapter makes us realize that close contact with young family members, which can be beneficial in certain situations (Doba and Hinohara, this volume), does not necessarily ensure happiness in either generation, and in fact, could cause more tension. It also makes us wonder about reasons for the difference between the experiences of the elderly in a photography club in the midsize city of Ueda in mountainous Nagano Prefecture (which is far less urban than Tokyo) and experiences of the elderly in rural Iwate Prefecture.

If those in Traphagan's study had an independent means of transportation to gather with others of their age, could they also become like the "shutter bugs" studied by Takahashi et al.? Doba and Hinohara's study also shows that older individuals wish to remain useful and relevant in the world. Is there a way for the elderly in rural Iwate to feel useful to others? Many questions arise when contrasting their conditions and experiences with those of elders in other situations.

Calling our attention to a topic rarely discussed in the arena of aging and the aged, Chapter 5 concerns an area in which a gap exists between widespread social expectations and the elderly's subjective experience, namely, sexuality. Hikari Hori discusses aging, failed virility, alliances between a "good wife" and a "fallen woman," and lesbianism, all of which are depicted in the award-winning romantic comedy *Yurisai* (Lily Festival). Hori argues against the common stereotypes of the elderly, especially of elderly women, by analyzing the film and addressing women's participation in the production of films regarding aging.

Part Two: Understanding and Misunderstanding the Verbal Behavior of the Elderly

In Chapter 6, Anne R. Bower, a sociolinguist and gerontologist who has been observing American nursing homes, cautions against importing cultural and generational bias into the study of elders' speech practices. The emphasis on capability of verbal communication may be culturally or generationally motivated and may not be shared by other cultures or by the elderly themselves. More specifically, as taciturnity is known not to be regarded as a sign of poor communicative ability in Japan, we should recognize that a similar view may be held by the elderly even in America, where talk is highly valued. Bower's chapter offers the alternative perspective of a culturally sensitive model that can be used to understand elders' speech practices in both countries.

In a similar vein, Chapter 7, by Natsumi Morita, a scholar of nursing, questions the assumptions of healthcare professionals and advocates the use by doctors and nurses of lay terminology that patients themselves use to describe their varied inner experiences. This suggestion opposes the use of objective technical terms from medicine in communicating with dialysis patients, the majority of whom are elderly. The chapter supports the elderly centered perspective even, or especially, in the medical environment, and promotes a closer understanding of the experiences of the people whom healthcare professionals encounter.

In Chapter 8, Yoshiko Matsumoto turns the focus of attention from institutional settings to discourse practices in informal peer settings. A linguistic examination of naturally occurring conversations among elderly Japanese women—a type of data that has rarely been studied—reveals that, in contrast to the often negative assessments based on younger speakers' (or analysts') perspectives, peer conversations were lively and often humorous, even on topics of distressing life experiences such as a husband's death or a speaker's own illnesses. The conversations also refute other commonly held perceptions about elderly women and their verbal behavior, such as the images of being submissive and unconcerned about physical attractiveness, as discussed in greater detail in Hori's chapter. The peer conversations studied in this chapter thus offer alternatives to the common view of the discourse practices of the elderly as negative, self-pitying, and dependent, and suggest attention to multiple dimensions of a seemingly simple phenomenon.

Natural conversations are also the topic of investigation by another linguist, Toshiko Hamaguchi, in Chapter 9. Based on a longitudinal study of intergenerational family conversations among the author, her grandmother, and her mother, Hamaguchi argues that solidarity among family members is enhanced through co-construction of narratives and that elderly people's apparent overuse of pronouns whose reference is not immediately clear within family conversations should not be interpreted as a sign of decreased linguistic and cognitive ability, but as an expression of intimacy. Family members, or those who have an intimate relationship with one another, are privileged to be able to fill in each other's thoughts and references, and can rely on and be assured of such close ties. This chapter, like the one by Matsumoto, reveals an alternative understanding of a phenomenon that has often been subject to negative interpretations.

The importance of enhancing opportunities for the elderly in Japan for communication within and across generations is also advocated in Chapter 10 by communication specialists Hiroshi Ota and Howard Giles in their study of inter- and intragenerational verbal communication. While there is a "good story," i.e., the stereotypical view of the young respecting the old, as Traphagan also shows in his chapter, the elderly in Japan are also perceived negatively by their own and younger generations, a fact that hinders close communicative relationships between them. Ota and Giles advocate balanced and "mindful" accommodation in society, and suggest that mindful communication may help honor the identities desired by the other party in the interaction and allow older adults to pay greater attention to the positive aspects of aging.

Concluding Remarks

This volume presents a multidimensional picture of aging with a focus on Japan. It also attempts to provide an opportunity for researchers to become aware of a broader research agenda and to think in interdisciplinary directions, while furthering knowledge in each discipline represented. Shared insights may emerge from the variety of studies presented in the volume. For instance, it seems clear that the "standard view" based on stereotypes of the elderly in Japan or elsewhere should not obscure the complexity of real aging experiences, which vary depending on living conditions and the perspectives from which individuals view their lives and interactions. Several chapters suggest that opportunities to interact verbally or nonverbally with people with whom one can sustain a positive relationship are indispensable for the well-being of the elderly. The danger of isolation, while not confined to the elderly, is a critical issue. As is true for other generations as well, an old adult can be completely isolated even when surrounded by family members, as illustrated by cases of elder suicide in rural Japan and tension in spousal care. In contrast, interactions with younger people outside the family or with friends and peers close in age who may share interests and similar experiences can contribute to positive relationships and encounters. While the life of the elderly is enhanced by fruitful *inter*generational relationships at home and beyond, many chapters also suggest an additional, rewarding direction, namely *intra*generational interaction. Among peers and friends, older adults engage in verbal and nonverbal activities that may not fit with the images and standards held by younger people. The elderly may feel free to keep their "old" values or talk about topics that younger people may not consider appropriate. Especially in Japan, where the elderly are expected to outnumber younger people in the future, when creating public policy it is worth considering a variety of possibilities available to the older generations that can facilitate social networking outside of families, and accommodate a system where old people help each other. Numerous studies have demonstrated that forcing one group's norms and expectations onto another does not yield positive outcomes. Pressing the norms and expectations of middle-aged or younger adults on the elderly would not be productive. In this sense, the issues addressed by an inquiry on aging are simultaneously universal and specific. I have no doubt that there are many more insights that readers can draw from the chapters presented here. Ideally, this volume will encourage greater attention to the latter part of the life span by illuminating the richness of the lives and interactions of the elderly and offering convincing evidence against the simple decrement-based "ageist" view.

References

Backhaus, Peter. 2009. Politeness in institutional elderly care in Japan: A cross-cultural comparison. *Journal of Politeness Research* 5 (1): 54–71.

Boden, Deirdre, and Denise Bielby. 1986. The way it was: Topical organization in elderly conversation. *Language and Communication* 6: 73–89.

Coulmas, Florian. 2007. *Population decline and aging in Japan: The social consequences.* New York: Routledge.

Counts, Dorothy Ayers, and David R. Counts. 1985. *Aging and its transformations: Moving toward death in Pacific societies.* Lanham, MD: University Press of America.

Coupland, Nikolas, Justine Coupland, and Howard Giles. 1989. Telling age in later life: Identity and face implications. *Text* 9: 129–151.

Eckert, Penelope. 1984. Age and linguistic change. In *Age and anthropological theory*, ed. D. I. Kertzer and J. Keith, 219–233. Ithaca, NY: Cornell University Press.

Goffman, Ervin. 1967. *Interaction ritual: Essays on face-to-face behavior.* New York: Pantheon.

Hamaguchi, Toshiko. 2001. *Co-construction of meaning in intergenerational family conversations: A case of the Japanese demonstrative pronoun "are."* PhD diss., Georgetown University.

Hamilton, Heidi E., ed. 1999. *Language and communication in old age: Multidisciplinary perspectives.* New York: Garland.

Hashimoto, Akiko. 1996. *The gift of generations: Japanese and American perspectives on aging and the social contract.* Cambridge, UK: Cambridge University Press.

Ikels, Charlotte, ed. 2004. *Filial piety: Practice and discourse in contemporary East Asia.* Stanford, CA: Stanford University Press.

Johnson, Malcolm L., ed. 2005. *The Cambridge handbook of age and ageing.* New York: Cambridge University Press.

Kendig, Hal, Akiko Hashimoto, and Larry C. Coppard, eds. 1992. *Family support for the elderly: The international experience.* Oxford Medical Publications. Oxford: Oxford University Press.

Long, Susan Orpett, ed. 2000. *Caring for the elderly in Japan and the U.S.: Practices and policies.* Routledge Advances in Asia-Pacific Studies. London: Routledge.

———. 2005. *Final days: Japanese culture and choice at the end of life.* Honolulu: University of Hawai'i Press.

Majeski, Robin, and Merrily Stover. 2005. Interdisciplinary problem-based learning in gerontology: A plan of action. *Educational Gerontology* 31: 733–743.

Matsumoto, Yoshiko. 2005. "We'll be dead by then!"—Comical self-disclosure by elderly Japanese women. In *Proceedings of the 30th annual meeting of the Berkeley Linguistics Society*, ed. Marc Ettlinger, Nicholas Fleischer, and Mischa Park-Doob, 268–279. Berkeley, CA: Berkeley Linguistics Society.

———. 2007. Dealing with changes: Discourse of elderly Japanese women. In *Japanese/ Korean Linguistics* 15, ed. Naomi H. McGloin and Junko Mori, 93–107. Stanford, CA: CSLI Publications.

Ministry of Health, Labor, and Welfare. 2008. *Abridged life tables for Japan 2007.* www .mhlw.go.jp/english/database/db-hw/lifetb07/1.html.

National Institute of Population and Social Security Research. 2002. *Population projections for Japan: 2001–2050.* www.ipss.go.jp/pp-newest/e/ppfj02/ppfj02.pdf.

National Research Council, Committee for Monitoring the Nation's Changing Needs for Biomedical, Behavioral, and Clinical Personnel, Board on Higher Education and Workforce. 2005. *Advancing the nation's health needs: NIH research training programs.* Washington, DC: National Academies Press.

Nussbaum, Jon F., and Justine Coupland, eds. 2004. *Handbook of communication and aging research.* 2nd ed. Mahwah, NJ: Lawrence Erlbaum.

Plath, David. 1980. *Long engagements: Maturity in modern Japan.* Stanford, CA: Stanford University Press.

Ryan, Ellen Bouchard, and Joan E. Norris. 2001. Epilogue—Communication, aging, and health: The interface between research and practice. In *Aging, communication, and health: Linking research and practice for successful aging,* ed. Mary Lee Hummert and John F. Nussbaum, 279–297. Mahwah, NJ: Lawrence Erlbaum.

Statistics Bureau of the Ministry of Internal Affairs and Communications. 2006. www .stat.go.jp/english/data/handbook/c02cont.htm.

Traphagan, John W. 2000. *Taming oblivion: Aging bodies and the fear of senility in Japan.* Albany: State University of New York Press.

———. 2004. *The practice of concern: Ritual, well-being, and aging in rural Japan.* Durham, NC: Carolina Academic Press.

Wu, Yongmei. 2004. *The care of the elderly in Japan.* London: Routledge Curzon.

Varied Lives and Experiences of the Elderly

1 Successful Aging through Participation in Social Activities among Senior Citizens

Becoming Photographers

Keiko Takahashi, Makiko Tokoro, and Giyoo Hatano

THIS CHAPTER EXAMINES how the Selection, Optimization, and Compensation model proposed by Paul and Margaret Baltes and their colleagues applies to elderly Japanese participating in the avocational activity of photography after retirement. Depending on how long they had studied photography, three groups of senior shutterbugs—Old-timers, Main-stayers, and Newcomers—were intensively interviewed and evaluated by several assessment measurements as to how they made progress in (a) acquisition of knowledge and skills; (b) improvement of life satisfaction and quality of life; and (c) expansion and enhancement of social relationships. Our findings indicated that their progress toward successful aging could indeed be described by the Selection, Optimization, and Compensation model. In addition, the data suggested that a model that describes successful aging should include socioemotional factors, such as subjective life satisfaction and socioemotional support from others, especially among the general population of the elderly.

A Model of Life-Span Development: The Selection, Optimization, and Compensation Model

A psychological model of life-span development, the Selection, Optimization, and Compensation model (hereafter the SOC model), proposed by Paul and Margaret Baltes and their colleagues, has provided a framework for the examination of success in aging (e.g., Baltes and Baltes 1990; M. Baltes and Carstensen 1996; Baltes, Lindenberger, and Staudinger 1998; Baltes, Lindenberger, and Staudinger 2006). The SOC model is based on the assumption that any process of development involves selection of and selective changes in adaptive capacity.

It assumes that individuals attempting to age successfully recognize that not all opportunities can be pursued. For this reason, they *select* appropriate goals or possible outcomes for living by choosing from alternative pathways to such goals (*elective selection*) and/or selecting in response to a decline in resources or loss (*loss-based selection*). They organize their lives around the achievement of these goals and outcomes through *optimization* or channeling of their efforts toward their goals, as well as through *compensation* for their deficiencies or losses pertaining to such goals by using available tools and resources, including the help of others. The researchers also assumed that the *orchestration* of these processes is central to achieving adaptive mastery and continued lifelong development (Baltes and Baltes 1990; Freund, Nikitin, and Ritter 2009).

By constructing a self-report-type SOC questionnaire and showing its predictability for successful aging, these researchers and others have given further operational clarification to the model (Baltes, Freund, and Lang 1999; Freund and Baltes 1998; 2002a). For example, as predicted by the model, some studies have indicated that SOC scores obtained by questionnaire positively correlate with subjective indicators of well-being among older people (Chou 2002; Freund 2008; Freund and Baltes 1998; 2002b; Wiese, Freund, and Baltes 2002), while others have suggested that dominance of the components of the SOC varies with aging and physical condition (Carstensen, Isaacowitz, and Charles 1999; Bourgeois 2003; Freund and Baltes 2002a; Jopp and Smith 2006). However, at present, we would need more detailed qualitative examinations of the SOC model itself to ascertain whether it is generally applicable to successful aging among ordinary people who are not endowed with exceptional talent like the great pianist Arthur Rubinstein, a favorite example used by P. Baltes and his colleagues to describe the SOC model (Baltes and Baltes 1990; Baltes, Lindenberger, and Staudinger 1998).

A Longitudinal Study of Senior Shutterbugs

Our challenge in this study was to examine how well the SOC model could describe aging among Japanese people participating in avocational activities after retirement. In societies such as Japan, retirement begins at a relatively early age. Most employed people retire upon reaching the mandatory retirement age (usually 55–60), and full-time housewives, having reared an average of two children, are released from parental obligations in their fifties. However, both groups of people are likely to live past age 80. Accordingly, many people are eagerly looking for self-actualizing activities after retirement. Senior citizens over 65 in Japan enjoy a variety of activities, one of the most popular of which is practicing some form of art, such as photography, painting, ceramics, calligraphy, poetry (*haiku*) composition, or flower arrangement. Most of these aesthetic practices in modern Japan are essentially social learning activities that have developed and become widespread since the late seventeenth century. Individuals, regardless of gender or social status, usually belong to a group or a class where they can meet other participants as well as a tutor (Ikegami 2005).

The goals and expected outcomes of the vast majority of elderly people who have already retired from their careers do not involve success in a profession or generating income. In this vein, the definition of successful aging should be broader than the mere "overall maximization of gains while minimizing losses" posited by Baltes and others (e.g., Baltes and Baltes 1990; Baltes, Lindenberger, and Staudinger 1998), or simply "the ability to maintain three key behaviors and characteristics: low risk of disease or disability, high mental and physical function, and active engagement with life" defined by Rowe and Kahn (1998, 38). Rather, first, successful post-retirement aging, especially among ordinary seniors, should include not only acquisition of domain-specific knowledge but also a maximization of life satisfaction and the expectation of an active life against the physical, cognitive, social, and financial losses associated with retirement and aging. Second, although Baltes and his colleagues have not explicitly conceptualized this, the successful aging of ordinary elderly people requires social feedback, such as acknowledgment and appreciation of their efforts and warm concern and emotional support from significant others.

In this study, we examined to what extent the original SOC model aids in describing the development of ordinary elderly citizens who are successfully aging through participating as amateurs in the learning and practice of photography. More precisely, we examined the importance of social and emotional factors in the SOC model for successful aging after retirement (Takahashi and Tokoro 2002; 2010). Using the expert-vs.-novice paradigm, we attempted to explore the specifics of how the seniors we studied actualized the SOC in their practice of photography. We assumed that our "experts," those who had been actively involved in photography for longer periods, would show a more advanced level of SOC than people with fewer years of participation identified as novices or early learners (e.g., Goodnow, Miller, and Kessel 1995).

Participants and Procedure

Thirty-two senior amateur photographers who were studying photography in a photography group with an instructor (Mr. Hanazato, hereinafter Mr. H) in

Ueda, a medium-sized city in Nagano Prefecture in central Japan, agreed to participate in our four-year longitudinal study. The city of Ueda is located in a basin surrounded by scenic mountains, and local residents have opportunities to take different photos virtually each day of the year, according to seasonal changes.

The entire photography group consisted of 69 elderly persons (44 males and 25 females, ages 59–89) who had started to learn photographic techniques in a public seminar for senior citizens offered by a local governmental office in the 1980s. Most of the members started when they were over the age of 60, that is, after their retirement and completion of parental responsibilities. Since then, most of them have continued to learn in a monthly seminar given by Mr. H, with new members joining the group each year. Thus, there were differences in how long each member had been in the group. Some of them had participated for more than ten years, whereas others had joined quite recently.

As shown in Table 1.1, rather than employ a strict expert-vs.-novice paradigm, we divided the 32 amateur senior citizen photographers according to seniority determined by how many years they had belonged to the photography group. All of them began learning photography after joining the group. This four-year longitudinal study contained: 15 Old-timers, who had participated in the seminar for more than ten years ($M = 11.1$ years); 12 so-called Main-stayers, who had participated for more than two years but less than six years ($M = 4.3$ years); and five Newcomers, who had participated for 23 months or less ($M = 1.0$ year). The Old-timers were significantly older than their Main-stayer and Newcomer counterparts. Aside from the chronological age differences, all three groups had similar cultural backgrounds. All of them were fully literate (years of education: $M = 12.9$, $SD = 2.76$). Most of the males had had careers in companies or civil service, and all the females were full-time homemakers. With one exception, the participants were living with their spouses and/or children and grandchildren. Only 20 percent had some kind of job with income, and, as far as could be determined, all others lived on their pensions.

Table 1.1. Participants at Time 1

	n (female in parentheses)	Age (SD in parentheses)	Years of membership (SD in parentheses)
Old-timers	15 (5)	75.47 (6.51)	11.20 (1.93)
Main-stayers	12 (2)	66.56 (5.11)	4.25 (1.06)
Newcomers	5 (1)	65.52 (5.68)	1.00 (0.71)

Photography Practices of the Participants

The participants were each attending one of four classes that consisted of 8 to 23 students, according to the districts in which they lived. Most of them attended each month. They were encouraged to take as many photographs as they could and to pick out as many as they wished to bring to class. In every class, following a lecture on the theories and techniques of photography, each of the students' photos taken during the previous month was reviewed and commented upon by the instructor, Mr. H, in front of the entire class. In addition to attending the class, the students drove together to scenic spots to take pictures almost every week and sometimes had photo picnics.

They were afforded three different opportunities to ascertain their progress and the quality of their photos: through comments given by Mr. H at the monthly seminar; through submissions to various contests for amateur photographers supported by public institutions such as newspaper publishers, photography magazines, and photo-film companies; and through evaluation for awards by a world-famous photographer, Eikoh Hosoe, who chose the best 18 photos out of 500 to 600 anonymously submitted photos each year over a 15-year period. Through these evaluative procedures, the amateur participants were able to gain an appreciation of the aesthetic standards of photography, a key goal of their practice. Interestingly, such evaluative procedures as these are not at all novel; since the seventeenth century, Japanese who have actively enjoyed aesthetic pursuits have invariably expected and requested qualitative judgment (Ikegami 2005).

As predicted, over the 15 years, the Old-timers' photos were most often selected among the best 18 by Hosoe (4.5 awards for the Old-timers, more than twice as many as their juniors). However, if we focus on the recent four years covered by our study, the number of awards won by the Main-stayers increased in the last two years. The number of award-winning photos among the Old-timers decreased during this period, probably because of their aging.

Interviews and Assessments

Each year, the participants in our study were individually interviewed for 60–120 minutes regarding their current photographic activities, acquired knowledge of photography, and practice-related interactions with others. A semistructured questionnaire was used. All narratives were transcribed verbatim and the contents of their replies and remarks were analyzed. In addition, they were assessed as to (1) their psychological well-being based on five different scales consisting of (a) a subjective evaluation of their health, (b) the subjective life-satisfaction scale, (c) the Center for Epidemiologic Studies–Depressed Mood Scale (Radloff 1977), (d) the Self-Esteem Scale (Rosenberg 1965), and (e) the Loneliness Scale (Russell, Peplau, and Cutrona 1980); and (2) their social relationships by (a) the Affective Relationships Scale (Takahashi and Sakamoto 2000) and (b) the hierarchical mapping method (Antonucci 1986). Moreover, we regularly observed their seminars and interviewed Mr. H in order to gain an understanding of the participants and his teaching aims and policies.

In this study, we examined how well the SOC model could be applied to the data at hand, with specific focus on (1) how and why these seniors had selected this activity and committed themselves to it; (2) how they optimized their efforts and means to achieve their goals; and (3) how they compensated for insufficient resources of knowledge and technique.

Selection, Optimization, and Compensation among the Photographers

Selections of Goals and Outcomes

Nearly half of the participants reported having artistic interest in other domains, such as painting, flower arrangement, calligraphy, or woodcarving. Some others reported having long been interested in photography but not having had enough time to learn about it before retirement. All participants from all three groups told us that they had started to attend the seminar by chance either through public information, a visit to a photo exhibition, a recommendation by their spouse or some other family member, or by invitation from friends. However, once they had started, they were very much involved in *only* or *selectively* doing photography. Thus, the *selection* of one pursuit, while giving up others, is substantially important in the process of the SOC.

Elective Selection

Everyday practices of doing photography   As shown in Table 1.2, most of the participants in the three groups regularly attended each monthly seminar. Encouraged by Mr. H to take photographs every day, they took an average of 205.6 shots per month ($SD = 233.81$) and brought to each class an average of 10.1 photos ($SD = 8.84$). Compared with the Newcomers, those in the two experienced groups, especially the Main-stayers, claimed to be very much involved: "I'm always thinking about photography." The Old-timers and Main-stayers brought four to five times as many photos to class as the Newcomers.

In addition to attending the monthly seminar, the participants were highly motivated to seek helpful hints from several resources: camera magazines, books, appreciation of others' photos, discussions with peers, and comments from Mr. H. There were some differences among the three groups. As Table 1.2 indicates, the Main-stayers reported that they had significantly more resources for acquiring knowledge than the Old-timers or the Newcomers. In brief, the Main-stayers were more active "learners" and "practitioners," whereas the New-comers were least active in everyday photographic activities and the Old-timers appeared more inclined to build upon accumulated experience.

Selection of photographic themes   When asked which aspects were important for their own progress in photography, our participants had plenty to say. A majority of the Old-timers pointed out that it was very important to have a clear theme for photography in addition to technique and effort. In contrast, the Newcomers insisted that suggestions given by their instructor were use-ful, while placing an emphasis on effort. However, at Time 4, after three years' learning and experience, the erstwhile Newcomers were now citing the impor-tance of technique, whereas the Main-stayers referred mainly to the impor-tance of having a theme for one's photography. Thus, in the beginning stages of learning, the participants did not seem to be clearly aware of the important factors in photography—they insisted that effort and a sincere attitude toward photography were essential. As they learned and acquired concrete techniques and methods for the selection of scenes and subjects and the manipulation of the camera and other equipment, they later came to realize that they needed a consistent theme to express through their photos.

In fact, as Table 1.2 indicates, at Time 1, 87 percent of the Old-timers already had a particular thematic preference for their photography, such as nature, human beings, or flowers, whereas only 25 to 40 percent of the Main-stayers and Newcomers showed the same tendency. However, at Time 4, 75 to 91 percent of the participants had settled on their own themes.

At Time 4, the Old-timers seemed to continuously improve their technique and to be on the lookout for new, advanced equipment, and all in all to be independent, expert shutterbugs. Although the Old-timers often voiced great respect for their instructor, Mr. H, they indicated that they would like to be independent of him. They would often tell us something like, "Mr. H would prefer to cut this tree out of this picture, but I like this framing." While these students would clearly take into account Mr. H's comments, they felt free to have their own opinions and to express these differences in their photography as well as in their oral reports to us. Thus, our senior shutterbugs developed in the direction of being independent and having their own themes for photography; that is, they autonomously broadened or narrowed down their themes and set their own goals.

Loss-Based Selection as Coping with or Adjusting to Aging

With regard to the physicality of aging, our participants were not exceptional. Many of them were suffering as a result of their own and/or their partner's physical problems, such as high blood pressure, arthritis, and rheumatism. We

Table 1.2. Summary of findings among Old-timers, Main-stayers, and Newcomers

Domain	Old-timers (O)	Main-stayers (M)	Newcomers (N)	Differences
Everyday practices				
Percentage of attendance at seminar	80%	100%	100%	ns.
N of shots in a month (mean, SD)	166.3 (119.8)	263.0 (346.5)	130.8 (138.4)	M > O, N*
N of photos for a seminar (mean, SD)	10.80 (8.2)	9.92 (9.2)	2.20 (4.4)	O, M > N*
N of resources for acquiring knowledge (mean, SD)	4.7 (.96)	5.6 (.67)	4.4 (2.51)	M > O, N*
Awards				
Awards (Time 1) (mean, SD)	4.53 (3.11)	1.58 (1.13)	.60 (.55)	O > M, N *
Awards (Times 1–4) (mean, SD)	.91 (.83)	1.50 (1.20)	.75 (.50)	M > O, N (*)
Theme for photography				
N of Ss who referred to theme for progress	10 (15)	3 (12)	0 (5)	O > M, N*
N of Ss who had thematic preference (at Time 1)	13 (15)	3 (9)	2 (5)	O > M, N**
Acquisition of knowledge				
N of Ss who gave concrete knowledge to beginners	6 (15)	2 (12)	0 (5)	O > M, N*
N of techniques suggested to beginners (mean, SD)	2.13 (1.19)	1.50 (1.51)	1.00 (1.00)	O > M, N*
N of Ss who referred to importance of instructor	2 (15)	3 (12)	4 (5)	N > O, M*
Awareness of technical progress (mean, SD)	1.47 (.83)	1.50 (.80)	.80 (.45)	O, M > N (*)
Evaluation of others' photos (Time 1) (mean, SD)	3.40 (1.18)	2.08 (1.38)	3.20 (2.05)	O, N > M***

would like to point out that they had a flexible attitude toward coping with aging. For example, although we mentioned that these senior shutterbugs gradually found their own themes, this does not necessarily mean that they stuck to the same themes forever. Even though they continuously pursued and deepened their themes, we observed that some of the participants were compelled to change their themes because of physical and/or social constraints. For instance, one participant changed her theme from nature to flowers because the progressive weakening of her legs had forced her to give up walking in the mountains. Another woman chose her cat as a photo subject instead of mountains when her husband's serious illness kept her at home. Although this was not an easy

Domain	Old-timers (O)	Main-stayers (M)	Newcomers (N)	Differences
Evaluation of nontraditional photo (Time 4) (mean, SD)	1.90 (.94)	1.13 (.35)	1.25 (.50)	O, N > M**
Positive aspects of nontraditional photo (mean, SD)	1.09 (1.14)	.25 (.46)	.25 (.50)	O > M, N (*)
Negative aspects of nontraditional photo (mean, SD)	1.55 (.82)	3.63 (1.60)	1.00 (.82)	O, N < M***
Social relationships				
Reasons for belonging to the group: Being motivated	72%	89%	100%	ns.
N of social figures nominated in three circles	12.09 (8.92)	14.11 (8.25)	7.25 (2.36)	ns.
N of family members nominated in the 1st circle	1.18 (1.33)	1.78 (1.72)	1.25 (1.50)	ns.
N of peers nominated in the 1st circle	3.45 (7.63)	.56 (1.33)	.75 (1.50)	ns.
Subjective evaluation as to cognitive and socioemotional competence				
Awareness of changes: Cognitive awareness	11 (15)	11 (12)	4 (5)	ns.
Awareness of changes: Life satisfaction	8 (15)	10 (12)	1 (5)	M > O > N (*)
N of awareness of changes (mean, SD)	1.67 (1.05)	2.75 (1.14)	2.00 (1.22)	M > N > O*
Psychological assessment: Self-esteem	29.32 (4.53)	30.50 (5.16)	30.20 (3.70)	ns.
Psychological assessment: Life satisfaction	16.40 (1.72)	16.25 (2.22)	16.80 (1.30)	ns.
Psychological assessment: Depression	8.48 (3.87)	9.83 (6.21)	7.38 (4.54)	ns.

(*) $p < .10$,   * $p < .05$,   ** $p < .01$,   *** $p < .001$

decision for this student because she had been enthusiastic about her previous theme, we observed Mr. H giving her valid suggestions to find an alternative theme, and in the seminars her peers encouraged her in her new challenges.

Optimization of Everyday Practices for Goals and Outcomes

Everyday Practices for Goals

Respondents in all three groups stated that taking many exposures was critical for becoming a good photographer, because Mr. H had always taught that taking frequent exposures was the only way for them to progress. Interestingly, some of the Main-stayers tended to take photographs in enthusiastic bursts of activity, whereas each of the Old-timers had already worked out a steady pace, as shown in Table 1.2. Moreover, the Old-timers noted a significantly larger number of strategies for taking good photographs than the less experienced learners. First, they believed that photographers must have a clear theme when they take pictures. That is, they would keep this theme in mind while choosing a particular subject or detail to focus on. They also pointed out the importance of the timing of a shot, taking time to explore appropriate shots, paying careful attention to the light, and so on. Some experts who were taking photos of rugby games deliberately trained themselves to move their fingers quickly to be able to follow and capture the speedy movements of the sport (Ericsson, Krampe, and Tesch-Romer 1993). Furthermore, to try to prevent the weakening of their leg muscles, 63 percent of the participants reported performing daily physical activities, such as walking and weight lifting, to compensate for any diminished faculties.

Knowledge Acquisition

Data related to our participants' acquisition of knowledge indicated that the Old-timers had richer expertise as to technique and equipment. For example, we asked the participants what kinds of hints they would offer beginners. At Time 1, as shown in Table 1.2, the Old-timers made significantly more suggestions as to specific techniques (e.g., framing, lighting) than either the Main-stayers or the Newcomers. In contrast, the Main-stayers tended to discuss the general aspects of photography, and the Newcomers stressed the importance of effort (e.g., taking many photos) as well as asking the instructor for suggestions. However, three years later, at Time 4, these junior participants, who were no longer Newcomers by this time, were able to offer more specific technical suggestions.

Integration of Acquired Knowledge

Our subjects' progress toward integrating their acquired knowledge was observed in their evaluations of others' photos. In contrast to their less experienced counterparts, the Old-timers tended to evaluate others' photos in terms of the theme instead of focusing on more concrete technical aspects. We discovered this when giving the participants a photo evaluation task. In the task, they were asked to point out the strengths and weaknesses of several photos. Weaknesses could be pointed out either directly or indirectly, such as by suggesting an alternative approach or decision (e.g., "I would have taken the target in this way rather than that way") (see Table 1.2).

For example, at Time 1, we showed our subjects an amateur photo depicting a boy kicking a ball, which had been published in a magazine for photographers. First, their comments were scored in terms of how favorable they were toward this photo using a five-point scale (from 5: explicitly mentioning the photo as excellent/ideal, without pointing out any weakness; to 1: describing the photo as poor/unlikable, without pointing out any positive features). Compared with the Main-stayers, the Old-timers evaluated the photo more positively. Second, we found that 10 out of the 15 Old-timers evaluated the photo from a thematic perspective, saying, "This is a terrific picture that has caught the dynamic movements of the boy and ball," or "This is a very nice shot that successfully expresses a boy who was very much involved in kicking the ball." Meanwhile, 7 of the 12 Main-stayers pointed out deficiencies in the technique of the picture, saying such things as, "We need the boy's face in this photo," or "We don't need this chair in this picture." Moreover, at Time 4, when shown a nontraditional type of photo taken by a young female professional photographer, Rinko Kawauchi (2001), which violated traditional photo techniques (a photo taken against the sun, with a flare, faded color, and many apparently unstructured objects), all of the Main-stayers pointed out these violations as weak points of the photo. The Newcomers typically said, "It is very difficult for me to evaluate this photo." However, five of the Old-timers spoke highly of this photo, saying, "This is a nice shot," and pointed out the effective lighting (as Mr. H did when asked for his evaluation of this photo). Thus, of all our senior shutterbugs, only some of the Old-timers could appreciate underlying themes and were open to being drawn to new devices which surely violated established photographic principles and/or techniques.

Being Motivated by Awareness of Competence and Life Satisfaction through Photography

Our participants often claimed that there was a great depth to photography. They professed that the more they met its challenge, the more motivating it became. When we asked our participants about their subjective awareness of any changes they had undergone through practicing photography, we found that they clearly noticed that they were changing. First, as shown in Table 1.2, at Time 1, the participants, including the Newcomers, stated that they definitely had come to be aware of changes in nature and were now enjoying careful and precise observation of individual objects and points of interest through photography. Second, both the Old-timers and the Main-stayers said that they recognized that the practice and activity had enriched their lives. Many voiced keen enjoyment. Here is what some of them had to say: "The more [photography] I do, the more profoundly I'm attracted to doing photography"; "Through photography, I now feel how pleasant my life is"; "I can no longer imagine my life without photography"; and "I was pleased to recognize that through my photos I could express my preferences and ideas." Third, many reported that they had been able to establish and deepen social relationships because of photography. Many, especially the males, reported that their social relationships, including marital/family relationships, had changed thanks to participating in the photography group. Some of them reported that they definitely would have felt isolated after retirement if they had not used a camera.

Compensation for Insufficient Technique, Knowledge, and Motivation

Cognitive and Emotional Support from Peer Photographers and the Instructor

As already mentioned, the participants compensated for their limited knowledge and technique by getting information from various resources, such as photography magazines and exhibitions. In addition, they asked advice from and shared their photographs with peers during and after the monthly seminars. Main-stayers, in particular, said they appreciated receiving information from peers. The Newcomers referred to the instructor and reported that his comments and lectures were useful and encouraging. In contrast, the Old-timers did not explicitly refer to the instructor as often, and some of them even confessed that they sometimes differed from him in their evaluations of photographs. In this sense, the Old-timers were becoming autonomous: they acted independently of others and even of the evaluations they received from the instructor, although they mentioned that they received many "hints" from his comments and from viewing others' pictures in seminars and at public exhibitions.

Moreover, most of the photographers voiced appreciation for the emotional support and understanding shown by peers and Mr. H, who did things such as drive the participants to photography sites, provide encouragement, and share experiences. Thus, the photographers gained not only knowledge from others, but also "invisible" emotional support. They reported that they shared experiences not necessarily pertaining to photography, including emotionally laden ones, with their peers and the instructor.

Social Relationships among the Shutterbugs

Using the network mapping procedure developed by Antonucci (1986), we asked the participants who was important to them when doing photography at Time 3. They were shown a diagram depicting three concentric circles and were asked to think of persons important to them and to place each person's name in one of the three circles. In the innermost circle, they were instructed to place the names of persons who were the most important to them and their photography. In the next circle, they were asked to name persons who were less important; and for the outer circle, to select persons who mattered to them, but not so much in relation to their pursuit of photography. On the average, a total of five to eight persons were named in the three circles. Information about each person named was then collected, including age, gender, relationship, and psychological relevance to the respondent. As shown in Table 1.2, most of the participants showed that they appreciated having peer photographers in the innermost circle. Although the Old-timers named a greater number of peers, there were no significant differences among the groups. Interestingly, in the innermost circle, the participants often named their family members as important to them in doing photography. They voiced both emotional and instrumental reasons for choosing family members. For example, about 40 percent of people in all three groups reported that family members supported them financially and helped them instrumentally with such tasks as preparing lunch for photography group picnics and driving together to "shutter spots." They also reported that family members encouraged them by showing appreciation for their photos and celebrating their awards. The Main-stayers told us that their family members helped them choose some of the shots that they brought to monthly seminars and gave them advice, whether or not their family members happened to have any special knowledge of photography.

In the second circle, most participants nominated peer photographers. They mostly exchanged knowledge with peers, especially among the Main-stayers and the Old-timers. The exchanging of information about "shutter spots"—where to go to take good pictures—was very important for them, because the seasonal peaks of the natural world (blossoming flowers, new leaves, waterfalls, and sightings of animals) last only a short time. When we asked the participants why they practiced photography in a group rather than alone, they told us that their peers emotionally supported and motivated them in ways that went beyond the exchange of advice related to technique.

Successful Aging among Ordinary Elderly Citizens after Retirement

These findings indicate that the senior shutterbugs definitely learned, expanded their social relationships, and achieved life satisfaction through the cultural and aesthetic practice of photography. In addition to the cognitive aspects, the present findings indicate that the socioemotional aspects of the practice of photography, such as having one's work recognized and admired and sharing pleasant experiences with peers and family, highly motivate retired citizens to achieve their goals in a nonvocational yet serious leisure activity. We have summarized our findings as to each component of the SOC in Table 1.3.

Can we conclude that these photographers might be said to have achieved a state of successful aging? Our answer is yes. To ascertain the products of Selection, Optimization, and Compensation, we examined their psychological well-being. As shown in Table 1.2, there were no significant differences in psychological well-being between the groups. If we consider their significant age differences, however, it seems rather astonishing that the experts could keep pace in quality of life with the early learners, who were much younger. It is noteworthy that participants attributed their happiness and ability to evaluate how they were changing to photography.

Selection, Optimization, Compensation after Retirement

The present findings indicate that once senior citizens joined the photography group, they were very much involved in its practice. The longer they participated, the more competent they became—and perceived themselves to be. Their sense of life satisfaction also strengthened. Thus, they truly actualized the SOC. In addition, they stated that they were very much satisfied not only with having become competent shutterbugs but also with being important, ac-

Table 1.3. Selection, optimization, and compensation among the three groups

	Selection	*Optimization*	*Compensation*
Old-timers	Being selectively involved in photography. Having their own theme. Changed own theme, because of aging.	Taking many photos. Stressing importance of own theme and perseverance to catch good chances. Having clear knowledge to support others as well as themselves. Practicing techniques if they need them. Organizing knowledge to evaluate others' photos.	Acquiring knowledge from many sources. Exchanging techniques and knowledge with peers. Getting emotional support from peers. Getting instrumental support from family members. Sharing emotional experiences with peers.
Main-stayers	Being selectively involved in photography.	Taking many photos. Having clear knowledge to support themselves.	Acquiring knowledge from many sources. Exchanging techniques and knowledge with peers. Getting emotional and instrumental support from family members. Sharing emotional experiences with peers.
Newcomers	Being selectively involved in photography.	Taking many photos. Stressing importance of effort.	Acquiring knowledge from many sources. Exchanging techniques and knowledge with peers. Getting emotional support from family members. Depending on the instructor.

tive participants in their own families as well as in their voluntary horizontal social network. Furthermore, it is noteworthy that they quite often declared, "I'm an amateur." As professed amateurs, they insisted on keeping the expenses for supplies and equipment within limits in order to gain the understanding and support of their partners and family members. Thus, they recognized that their goals were very different from those of anyone attempting or continuing to practice a profession after retirement.

This suggests that successful aging among the elderly in an advanced, modern society should include not only acquisition of valued knowledge and expertise but also a maximization of life satisfaction, despite the fact that "successful aging" has traditionally been defined as the maximization of gains and minimization of losses (e.g., Baltes and Baltes 1990; Baltes, Lindenberger, and Staudinger 1998; 2006) or the ability to maintain key elements of mental and physical health (Rowe and Kahn 1998).

Coping Successfully with Aging

Our silver-haired photographers were not exceptional in having to cope with the health problems associated with aging. Many of them were suffering as a result of their own and/or their partner's physical problems. It is clear that many of the participants were intentionally walking every day in order to try to prevent or delay the weakening of their physical abilities. Moreover, it is noteworthy that they had a flexible attitude toward coping with aging. As we have noted, one woman successfully found another photo theme when her weakening legs forced her to give up walking in the mountains. In contrast, one man was almost devastated after developing a disabling physical problem because he could not bear to let go of his attachment to going out and taking photos of mountain scenes. These examples suggest that degeneration or disease itself was not necessarily a decisive factor in coping with aging. This stands in contrast to the common assertion among psychologists that disease and/or disability are fatal for successful aging (Montross et al. 2006; Strawbridge, Wallhagen, and Cohen 2002). The critical factor was whether the person could accept reality and/or whether she or he had others who could provide assistance and help in coping with aging.

Were These Shutterbugs Special?

We should emphasize that the elderly people in the above-mentioned study were typical retired persons, not people of any special renown or social status. All of them were ordinary Japanese citizens. Prior to age 60, they had worked and had no leisure time to seriously practice photography. After retirement, some of them chanced to visit a photo exhibition of this group, and others were told about this group by their spouses, who happened to learn about it through public announcements; this is what spurred them into photography. Although some of them were interested in artistic activities such as painting, flower arrangement, and calligraphy, none had any special experience in the arts. Our interviews with elderly citizens in the same city who were engaged in other kinds of activities indicated that they too were successfully aging through participation in such cultural practices as flower arrangement, learning to read old documents, and composing *haiku.*

.   .   .

The present qualitative analysis of a relatively small number of participants clearly reveals the possibilities of cognitive development and enhancement of life satisfaction among senior citizens through participation in cultural practices after retirement. The large amount of viable data our study has generated should contribute to a better understanding of the dynamics of successful aging.

Note

This research was funded by a research grant to Keiko Takahashi from the Univers Foundation. The authors would like to express their deep appreciation to Yoshimi Hanazato and his seminar participants. We are very grateful to our coauthor Giyoo Hatano for providing constructive input on this project. Sadly, his invaluable contribution to this study was curtailed by his death on January 13, 2006.

References

Antonucci, T. C. 1986. Social support network: A hierarchical mapping technique. *Generations* X (4): 10–12.

Baltes, M. M., and L. L. Carstensen. 1996. The process of successful aging. *Aging and Society* 16: 397–422.

Baltes, P. B., and M. M. Baltes. 1990. *Successful aging: Perspectives from the behavioral sciences.* New York: Cambridge University Press.

Baltes, P. B., M. M. Baltes, A. M. Freund, and F. Lang. 1999. *The measurement of selection, optimization, and compensation (SOC) by self report.* Berlin: Max Planck Institute for Human Development.

Baltes, P. B., U. Lindenberger, and U. M. Staudinger. 1998. Life-span theory in developmental psychology. In vol. 1 of *Handbook of child psychology*, 5th ed., ed. R. M. Lerner, 1029–1143. New York: Wiley.

———. 2006. Life-span theory in developmental psychology. In vol. 1 of *Handbook of child psychology*, 6th ed., ed. R. M. Lerner, 569–664. New York: Wiley.

Bourgeois, S. 2003. Strategies of adaptation to age-related losses in everyday activities of independent seniors. *Dissertation Abstracts International* 63 (10-B): 4890.

Carstensen, L. L., D. M. Isaacowitz, and S. T. Charles. 1999. Taking time seriously: A theory of socioemotional selectivity. *American Psychologist* 54: 165–181.

Chou, K. L. 2002. Financial strain and life satisfaction in Hong Kong elderly Chinese: Moderating effect of life management strategies including selection, optimization, and compensation. *Aging and Mental Health* 6: 172–177.

Ericsson, K. A., R. Th. Krampe, and C. Tesch-Romer. 1993. The role of deliberate practice in the acquisition of expert performance. *Psychological Review* 100: 363–406.

Freund, A. M. 2008. Successful aging as management of resources: The role of selection, optimization, and compensation. *Research in Human Development* 5: 94–106.

Freund, A. M., and P. B. Baltes. 1998. Selection, optimization, and compensation as strategies of life management: Correlations with subjective indicators of successful aging. *Psychology and Aging* 13: 531–543.

———. 2002a. Life-management strategies of selection, optimization, and compensation: Measurement by self-report and construct validity. *Journal of Personality and Social Psychology* 82: 642–662.

———. 2002b. The adaptiveness of selection, optimization, and compensation as strategies of life management: Evidence from a preference study on proverbs. *Journal of Gerontology* 57B: 426–434.

Freund, A. M., J. N. Nikitin, and J. O. Ritter. 2009. Psychological consequences of longevity: The increasing importance of self-regulation in old age. *Human Development* 52: 1–37.

Goodnow, J. J., P. J. Miller, and F. Kessel. 1995. Cultural practices as contexts for development. *New directions for child development* 67. San Francisco: Jossey-Bass.

Ikegami, E. 2005. *Bonds of civility: Aesthetic networks and the political origins of Japanese culture.* New York: Cambridge University Press.

Jopp, D., and J. Smith. 2006. Resources and life-management strategies as determinants of successful aging: On the protective effect of selection, optimization, and compensation. *Psychology and Aging* 21: 253–291.

Kawauchi, R. 2001. *Utatane* (A nap). Tokyo: Little More.

Montross, L. P., C. Depp, J. Daly, J. Reichstadt, S. Golshan, D. Moore, D. Sitzer, and D. V. Jeste. 2006. Correlates of self-rated successful aging among community-dwelling older adults. *American Journal of Geriatric Psychiatry* 14: 43–51.

Radloff, L. S. 1977. The Center for Epidemiologic Studies—Depressed Mood Scale: A self-report depression scale for research in the general population. *Applied Psychological Measurement* 1: 385–401.

Rosenberg, M. 1965. *Society and the adolescent self-image.* Princeton, NJ: Princeton University Press.

Rowe, J. W., and R. L. Kahn. 1998. *Successful aging.* New York: Dell.

Russell, D., L. A. Peplau, and C. E. Cutrona. 1980. The revised UCLA Loneliness Scale: Concurrent and discriminant validity evidence. *Journal of Personality and Social Psychology* 39: 472–480.

Strawbridge, W. J., M. I. Wallhagen, and R. D. Cohen. 2002. Successful aging and well-being: Self-rated compared with Rowe and Kahn. *Gerontologist* 42: 727–733.

Takahashi, K., and A. Sakamoto. 2000. Assessing social relationships in adolescents and adults: Constructing and validating the Affective Relationships Scale. *International Journal of Behavioral Development* 24: 451–463.

Takahashi, K., and M. Tokoro. 2002. Senior shutterbugs: Successful aging through participation in social activities. *International Society for the Study of Behavioural Development Newsletter* 41: 9–11.

————. 2011. *Teinen go no sakusesufuru eijingu—Shinia shashinka no shōgaihattatsu* (Successful aging after retirement: Life-span development of senior shutterbugs). Tokyo: Kaneko-shobō.

Wiese, B. S., A. M. Freund, and P. B. Baltes. 2002. Subjective career and emotional well-being: Longitudinal predictive power of selection, optimization and compensation. *Journal of Vocational Behavior* 60: 321–335.

2 The New Elder Citizen Movement in Japan

Nobutaka Doba and Shigeaki Hinohara
in association with Haruo Yanai, Keiichiro Saiki, Hirofumi Takagi,
Mari Tsuruwaka, Masumi Hirano, and Hiroyoshi Matsubara

ALMOST EVERY COUNTRY WORLDWIDE must now contend with the reality of an aging population that is increasing more rapidly than was ever expected. In Japan, the population of elderly citizens aged 65 years or older has been increasing even as the total population has been in decline, and is expected to account for 27.8 percent of the total population by 2025. This is the fastest increase in the percentage of the aged observed anywhere in the world.

The rapidly increasing number of elderly throughout the world might represent a biological success for humanity if major health problems can be prevented until just prior to death and if elders' health needs can be fulfilled to ensure total physical, mental, and social well-being. Throughout history, greater longevity has enabled the aged to educate younger generations and pass on their values. This role of the elderly has ensured human survival and progress and is reflected in the recommendations of the International Plan of Action on Ageing, proposed and published by the United Nations (United Nations 2003).

In this sense, all efforts to help the elderly must be directed toward satisfying their needs for personal fulfillment realized through the achievement of personal goals and aspirations; this represents the realization of the full potential of the elderly. It is important, therefore, for public policies and programs to be oriented toward promoting opportunities for self-expression that challenge the elderly and help them contribute positively to their families and communities. The principal ways in which the elderly might find personal satisfaction include: (1) continued participation in their immediate and extended family (see Traphagan, this volume, on possible problems with the family; Hamaguchi, this volume, on the positive effects of family participation), (2) voluntary service to the community, (3) continued growth through formal and informal learning, (4) self-expression in arts and crafts (see also Takahashi et al., this volume), (5) participation in community organizations for senior citizens, (6) religious activities, (7) recreation and travel, (8) part-time work, and (9) participation in the political process as informed citizens (United Nations 2003).

To actually achieve these goals, however, the health status of the elderly in the physical, psychological/psychiatric, and social domains must be maintained at acceptable levels, and health-related quality of life (QOL) should be equally assured to all elderly people through well-established strategies for health maintenance and promotion. Indeed, the pivotal role of such strategies has already been clearly demonstrated in three longitudinal studies with long-term follow-up periods of 40 to 50 years. These were performed on three diverse cohorts, namely, the Inner City cohort, the Terman Women cohort, and the Harvard Men cohort (Vaillant 2002). It is interesting to note that, at the time of the last study, all the Terman women were old-old (70 to 79) and a third of the Harvard men were oldest-old (80 plus), while only half of the Inner City men were beyond the age of young-old (60 to 69). The lower average age of the Inner City cohort at the time of the last study was thought to be due to lower education level, higher prevalence of obesity, and a high frequency of alcohol/nicotine abuse among the subjects. The most interesting findings were seen in the Harvard Men Cohort Study, which identified clearly defined risk factors at age 50 that were useful for predicting whether participants would successfully reach 75 to 80 years of age. The following six risk factors were identified: (1) heavy smoking, (2) alcohol abuse, (3) instability of marriage, (4) sedentary habits, (5) obesity, and (6) immature adaptive coping styles defined by inadequate emotional maturation without the development of increasingly adaptive coping mechanisms.

Another important concept seen in favorable aging is the notion of successful aging proposed by Rowe and Kahn based on the MacArthur Study (Rowe and Kahn 1999). If we believe that one of the goals of health policy should be to improve a lower rate of life prolongation in the face of impaired QOL, preventive strategies have to be effectively and aggressively implemented to eliminate general physical frailty, dementia requiring extensive support, unsociable lifestyles, and disabilities among the elderly. Avlund and others have defined successful aging as a life status characterized by both the physical ability to live independently and to socialize (Avlund et al. 1999). Rowe and Kahn also advocate a complete reversal of stereotypical views related to the elderly as being

(1) unhealthy, (2) too old to gain new knowledge or master new technologies, (3) too late in life to start learning, (4) too late in life to change anything because of inherited qualities, (5) too low in voltage to light up, and (6) a big social burden (1999). It is clear that images of the lifestyles of the elderly need to be drastically changed in the era of the aged society (see Hori, this volume, for a discussion of changing images of the elderly).

A Japanese experimental project relevant to our above discussion that is bringing an innovative approach to the lives of the elderly has been carried out by the Life Planning Center Foundation, a nonprofit organization in Japan. First, we will describe the center's activities, the center's contribution to the lives of elderly people, and some aspects of their characteristic lifestyles. Our project represents a positive step toward healthy aging despite the social difficulties presented by aging (see Traphagan, this volume, for a discussion of elder suicide in rural Japan).

The Concept of "New Elder Citizen" at the Life Planning Center (LPC) Foundation

Activities Sponsored by the LPC Foundation

The Life Planning Center (LPC) Foundation is a nonprofit foundation established in 1973 by coauthor Shigeaki Hinohara, MD, the chairperson of the board at the LPC Foundation and also the honorary director of St. Luke's International Hospital, Tokyo. The aim of the LPC Foundation is to promote a healthy QOL in adult populations through holistic and comprehensive strategies for facilitating lifestyle modifications, mainly based on health education. The principle behind all of the activities at the LPC Foundation is based on the maxim of Socrates: "It is not living, but living well which we ought to consider the most important." The objectives of this foundation are (1) to help individuals gain an improved awareness and understanding of health; (2) to promote strategies for maintaining and improving one's own mental and physical health by lifestyle changes; and (3) to assist people in maintaining a high quality of life throughout all of its stages. The foundation educates the public through five specialized divisions: (1) Center for Health Education, (2) Division of Psychological Counseling, (3) Life Planning Clinic, (4) Peace House Hospice and Institute of Hospice Research, and (5) Community Visiting Nurse Stations in Chiyoda (Tokyo) and Nakai (Kanagawa Prefecture).

The Center for Health Education is equipped with an audiovisual room, a small library, and classrooms that are used to promote health education among the general population and to provide professional medical and nursing education for medical and nursing students, physicians, nurses, and other allied health educators. The Home Care Associate Training Class that was started in 1976 is now government certified as a Home Helper Training Course, and many health volunteers who completed the Health Volunteer Training Course that began in 1982 have been actively assisting patients in hospitals, clinics, and other welfare agencies. Also, a Blood Pressure Self-Measurement Training Class was started in 1974 as part of a campaign aimed at helping people take responsibility for their health through blood pressure self-monitoring. In addition, the foundation offers special continuing education programs for physicians, nurses, and other allied health personnel. Finally, the LPC Foundation has offered a series of international workshops and forums to provide innovative information in the fields of medicine and nursing to physicians, nurses, and health science educators.

The Life Planning Clinic, a medical clinic that opened in 1973, undertakes comprehensive health management programs, including dietary guidance, exercise instruction, and psychological services with holistic counseling. Along with the usual outpatient medical services, the clinic also provides a half-day comprehensive health check-up centered on education for self-care that is in line with the main goal of the clinic to help patients manage their health continuously throughout their lives. Since most chronic diseases are now believed to result from unfavorable life habits, the function of the clinic is to motivate patients to mitigate risk factors in their lifestyles.

Along with the above-mentioned preventive educational activities, the LPC has also implemented unique disease management activities in the Peace House Hospice for cancer patients and Community Visiting Nurse Stations to help patients, especially elderly patients with chronic diseases, work together with their family doctors.

Roles of the New Elderly

With the start of the twenty-first century, Japan has been facing a declining birth rate and an aging society. Both have become serious social issues and the subjects of heated public discussions. Most arguments in Japan emphasize the negative aspects of aging and devalue the aged by contending that the increase in the aged population will compromise the productivity of society and break down the pension system. With regard to these societal circumstances, Hinohara, now in his late nineties, has noted that these views present an inaccurate picture of the elderly, since there are many people, including himself, who do not fit into this outmoded image of the aged. He has envisioned the creation of an entirely new image of the aged, naming them the "New Elderly" in order to counter the currently held conception of people over the biological age of 65 as aged and not contributing to society. Hinohara has argued that elderly people can play a pivotal role in communicating the value of peace and human life and in transmitting valuable traditions to the younger generation through their verbal and nonverbal behavior in daily life. The "New Elder Citizen Movement" supported by members of the Association of the New Elderly promotes these more positive aspects of aging, which tend to be overshadowed by the anticipation of problems such as elderly isolation, which often leads to suicide (Kōsei Rōdō Shō 2008) (see Traphagan, this volume, for discussions of elder suicide and the living conditions of the elderly in rural areas).

Establishment of the Association of the New Elderly

The Association of the New Elderly was launched in September 2000. It was initially a group of senior citizens aged 75 years or older. The group includes elderly people who may have chronic illnesses and/or age-related physical problems, but are mentally alert and living independently and vibrantly in their daily lives. As of September 2010, the association had a membership of 11,455 people from all around Japan, as well as several non-Japanese nationals living in the United States, Australia, Mexico, Brazil, Korea, Taiwan, and other countries. There are 35 local chapters, extending from Hokkaido in the north to Okinawa in the south, that have individually developed and created their own programs based on local needs in cooperation with central leadership.

The association espouses three themes: (1) to love, (2) to initiate, and (3) to endure; and advocates five goals for those elderly aspiring to be New Elder Citizens: (1) to acquire a favorable lifestyle, (2) to maintain an active role in society and close friendships regardless of gender, race, or generation, (3) to maintain hope and faith, cultivate the strength and power to endure any difficulty that one might encounter, maintain an indomitable spirit which should encompass a deep sympathy for others in difficult situations, and extend comfort to people who have lost hope in life, (4) to provide loving care for others and feel gratitude for daily life, and (5) to be aware that it is never too late to initiate or create something, regardless of age. These principal concepts, originally developed by Hinohara, are described in detail below in order to define the New Elder Citizen Movement.

Love and Tolerance

In encouraging the elderly to love, the association posits that the objects of love should be not only parents and children, brothers and sisters, but all life forms. Loving should not only express one's feelings of love, but should also be accompanied by a feeling of tolerance or willingness to take on a burden, to sympathize with others, and to sacrifice oneself for the sake of others. No difficulty, including small quarrels among children, disagreements between people, and political conflicts among races or nations, can be solved without a love and tolerance that can only be realized by words of forgiveness. To forgive is not to blame or find fault in others for mistakes or failures. To tolerate is to pardon others for their mistakes and/or failures and sympathize with them. This concept of love and tolerance is found in "Last Poems #10," written by Rabindranath Tagore (1865–1941), the first Nobel Prize winner in Asia, two months before his death (Tagore [1941] 1998). To end one's life wrapped in love and tolerance, with the satisfaction of having given all one could have, is the ideal expressed in Tagore's poem that encapsulates a critical theme of the New Elderly.

A Challenge: Get Started!

The New Elderly have sufficient time that they can freely use for themselves. The most important issue is not the length of time, but the quality of time that is left. The remaining time can be used not only for continued development of one's knowledge, skill set, and lifestyle, but also for new challenges. In the Association of the New Elderly, voluntary circles have been organized for members to enjoy various activities, including a Hula Dance Circle, Classical Music Appreciation Circle, Chorus Circle, English Conversation Class, Mathematics Class, History Research Class, Mountaineering Circle, Traveling Circle, and Class to Discuss World Affairs, along with more unusual circles, such as a class that teaches the elderly how to walk in a way that is charming or attractive and that allows them to fit in with the younger generation. Many other classes and circles have been successively developed, especially in local branches, according to the needs of the various localities. In each activity, members learn from one another and further develop themselves over time (see also Takahashi et al., this volume, for a similar example of group activities).

The Experience of Enduring Cultivates the Feeling of Sympathy for Others

Senior citizens who are at least 75 years old have lived through the hard and painful days during and after the Second World War. Their difficult experiences have instilled in them a strong wish to keep younger generations from repeating the same mistakes. To this end, they see themselves as performing a critical role by helping young people worldwide to understand the preciousness of peace and human life. A series of four books entitled *Handing Down Wartime Experiences to Later Generations*, told from the perspective of different members of the Association of the New Elderly, was published from 2002 to 2005.

Although World War II is long over, even now in the twenty-first century, war and conflict continue among many nations all over the world, and there are still numerous areas where people's safety is threatened by food shortages and potentially fatal communicable diseases. Just as Albert Schweitzer devoted his life to saving people from these kinds of suffering by acting according to his principle of respecting all life forms on earth, a strong desire for the renunciation of war and sympathy for people living in underdeveloped countries informs the basic principles of the Association of the New Elderly. The elderly who experienced the war must pass down their horrifying experiences to the younger generation in order to show that life is irreplaceable, and therefore must be cherished. With this in mind, some members of the association visit schools to talk to children about their war experiences.

A Close Resemblance between Health and Happiness

We have long been accustomed to living in a stressful society characterized by keen competition, where school children are rated based on their scholastic achievements and company employees are evaluated based on the number of tasks they accomplish. It seems clear, however, that although elderly people wholly devoted themselves to the rebuilding of society in their younger years, their efforts were not as successful as they had hoped, despite the fact that they effected a dramatic economic rehabilitation of the country in the immediate postwar period. At present, disputes over rapid, worldwide social and economic change and Japan's international role in this process are raging. Efforts at amending the constitution to bolster self-defense capabilities have intensified since the turn of the century. Against such a backdrop, the sanctity of peace and human life are being threatened.

The twentieth century saw extraordinary scientific and technological advances in material civilization, yet despite this, many people in the latter half of the century lamented a rampant and persistent disregard for humanity. Many in Japan and elsewhere thought that the coming twenty-first century would usher in a new era filled with hope and happiness, where humanity would reach a new level of existence (Gouaze 1996). However, their expectations were dashed early in the new century. Beginning with the 9/11 attacks, the world once again descended into chaos in the wake of successive catastrophes. Those who had thought that the era of ideological, ethnic, and religious conflicts had passed were left feeling betrayed.

The association advocates the ideal that the New Elderly have the responsibility to love, to initiate, to endure, and to teach successive generations about world peace while drawing upon their experiences. As the social status, wealth, and fame that we so eagerly seek are only superficial achievements that cannot be carried over into death, the association stresses health and happiness. Happiness may be found only within oneself and from the feeling of fulfilling one's wishes. People can feel happy if they feel healthy despite having physical difficulties. On the other hand, people may neither be happy nor feel healthy even if they do not have any physical difficulties. With this in mind, the New Elderly must be sufficiently sensitive to create an environment in which these most important yet unseen aspects of experience can thrive.

To Be a Model for the Succeeding Generation

Approximately 6.6 billion people currently live on earth (Sōmushō Tōkei Kyoku 2006). China, with a population of 1.288 billion, and India, with a population of 1.0068 billion, head the list, and 11 other countries have populations of over 100 million. Japan, with a population of 128 million, is the country with the largest percentage of people over age 65 (21.1 percent). The corresponding percentages for Russia, with a population of 145 million, and the United States, with a population of 295 million, are 12.9 percent and 12.3 percent, respectively. Among other countries with populations of less than 100 million, the percentages are high for the following major European countries: 19.7 percent for Italy (with a population of 58 million), 18.8 percent for Germany (with a population of 83 million), and 16.3 percent for France (with a population of 83 million). In China, too, the percentage is expected to exceed 15 percent by 2030, because of the single child policy adopted in the 1970s. The birth rate in Korea is also declining and the society is aging at a rate surpassing that of Japan and will soon exceed the percentage in Japan. Therefore, aging of the population is a common issue throughout the world. In light of such circumstances, Japan must take the lead in presenting some sort of model for dealing with the mass retirement of the baby boom generation along with a declining birth rate.

In this aged society, the elderly must play a pivotal role in leading the succeeding generation and serve as role models for aging by changing their lifestyles. As mentioned earlier, the Association of the New Elderly initially consisted exclusively of elderly citizens over the age of 75. Recently, the age limit for membership was eliminated so that the New Elder Citizen Movement could be extended to include all generations, in order to help younger people learn about what constitutes a valuable life. With any adult now eligible to join, those members over 75 years of age are designated as senior members, those ranging from 60 to 75 years old are designated as supporting members, and those ranging from 20 to 60 years old are designated as junior members. Although it may be difficult for those under age 60 to imagine successful aging for themselves in the future, younger members who join the Association of the New Elderly can find ideal role models in senior members who are 10, 20, or even 50 years older. Their lives illuminate the aged world that remains unknown to younger people still holding jobs and raising families.

There are approximately 2,400 members living in the Tokyo Metropolitan Area for whom we have been providing various kinds of social activity classes, based on their needs (see also Takahashi et al., this volume, for a study on social activity classes in Nagano Prefecture). Each activity class is organized and managed by the members themselves through a steering committee. The activities shown with a single asterisk in the following list are related to conversational activities, such as discussions on various topics in English; those shown with double asterisks, such as talking to younger generations about wartime experiences, include cross-generational activities with schoolchildren.

Calligraphy

Chorus

Computer skills (learning and teaching)

English conversation (discussing various topics in English)*

Enjoyable mathematics**

Flower arranging

Composing *haiku*

Healthy breathing (*qigong*)

Visiting historic sites

Hula dancing

Listening to classical music

Lively discussions (conversing on various topics)*

Mountaineering

Narration (talking to the younger generation, especially about wartime experiences)**

Talk about current worldwide affairs*

Positive thinking conversations*

Reciting Chinese poems

Conservations about life with schoolchildren**

Softball (slow pitch)

Tennis

Some members of the association are deeply interested in medical, psychological, and social research and hope to maintain and improve their health by participation as research subjects. As chairman, Hinohara devised an observational study to examine this cohort, known as the New Elder Citizens Health Research Volunteers (HRV), over time. The following sections describe their characteristic lifestyles with reference to the research results.

Studies on the Cohort of Health Research Volunteers (HRV)

The following paragraphs summarize the results of studies that were conducted between 2002 and 2005 (Doba, Sato, et al. 2004; Hinohara and Doba 2005).

Objectives and Design of the Study

The New Elder Citizens are a self-selected cohort, and thus they are likely to be different from the general population of the elderly in terms of both their physical health status and psychosocial behaviors. A number of them have professional backgrounds in a variety of specialized fields, including medicine, psychology, sociology, nutrition, education, and statistics, although the majority are company retirees and elder homemakers. It will be of great interest to investigate how this group of people will confront the physical and/or psychosocial problems that accompany end-of-life issues. Through observations and interventions, we can hopefully develop effective ways to support the physical, psychological, and social challenges faced by the coming generations as they age. This project started in November 2002, and 408 elders had been examined by the end of April 2006. We plan to follow this cohort for at least five years, and if possible, ten years. Written informed consent was obtained from all participants and the study was approved by the Ethics Committee of the Japan Society of Health Evaluation and Promotion.

The 408 subjects registered so far consist of 185 males (78 ± 5 y/o) and 224 females (77 ± 4 y/o). In addition to administering a comprehensive health questionnaire to obtain a detailed personal health history, we screened them for depression and assessed their mental states, and performed a number of examinations including a routine physical examination, morphometric and functional evaluations of the musculoskeletal system, functional tests for muscle force, metabolism, walking/balancing abilities and cardiovascular functions, blood tests (including hematologic and blood chemistry tests), evaluation of levels of selected hormones and cytokines, and genomic evaluations. This study is expected to be complete after a five-year follow-up period, and we plan to check the health of the subjects each intervening year and also at the end of the five-year period by administering structured questionnaires by telephone, mail, or in-person interviews as necessary. We will present below some of the results that have been obtained from our initial evaluations.

Demographic Background

In all, 47 percent had lost a spouse, and widows significantly outnumbered widowers. There was no gender difference with regard to hearing ability. Twelve percent suffered from urinary incontinence, which was observed more frequently in females than in males. No gender-related differences in memory were observed. Only 2.8 percent of all subjects were smokers, which is an extremely low rate compared to that of the ordinary Japanese elderly population; also, the prevalence of smoking was significantly lower in females than in males. About 80 percent of the total subjects did not have a propensity for falls, but overall more females were prone to falls than males. Ten percent had a history of fractures associated with falls, and the prevalence of fractures was significantly higher in females than males. Overall, 72 percent of the subjects reported no pain problems, but pain problems were encountered significantly more frequently in females than males. About 73 percent of the subjects had no insomnia problems, and there was no gender difference in the prevalence of insomnia (Table 2.1).

The personal interests of the subjects in their daily lives were varied and diverse, as shown in Table 2.2. Their interests were quite different from those of the general population of Japanese elderly, who exhibit less varied interests which are usually limited to a few items, such as TV watching, traveling, and gardening (Harada 2001). Harada's study compared 17 different interests as held by elderly people in Japan, Denmark, America, and Italy. When the present findings are compared to Harada's results, it is clear that the interests of the

Table 2.1. Demographic findings and gender differences in the cohort of health research volunteers

	Total (%)	Male (%)	Female (%)
No falls	79.9*	86.3	74.1
Good hearing	75.8	75.8	69.3
No insomnia	72.7	72.5	72.9
No pain problems	71.7*	85.6	72.3
Good memory	52.7	54.9	50.6
Widow/widower	46.8*	37.9	58.4
Urinary incontinence	11.9*	4.6	18.7
Fracture due to fall	10.0*	4.6	15.1
Smoking	2.8*	4.6	1.2

* $p < 0.001$

Table 2.2. Diversity of individual interests in the cohort of health research volunteers (%)

Males (n = 85)	Females (n = 104)
Sports (49.4)	Music (37.5)
Reading books (29.4)	Sports (26.9)
Music (27.1)	Painting (26.9)
Traveling (25.9)	Reading books (22.1)
Playing go (10.6)	Traveling (14.4)
Painting (10.6)	Handicrafts (13.5)
Calligraphy (9.4)	Dancing (10.6)
Photography (9.4)	Composing haiku (8.7)
Reciting Chinese poems (7.1)	Flower arranging (8.7)
Composing haiku (7.1)	Cooking (8.7)

New Elderly match those of their Western counterparts, while differing from those of traditional Japanese people. The main interests of the subjects of the present study are summarized here; these include attending lectures, visiting art exhibitions, domestic traveling, and attending concerts (see Figure 2.1).

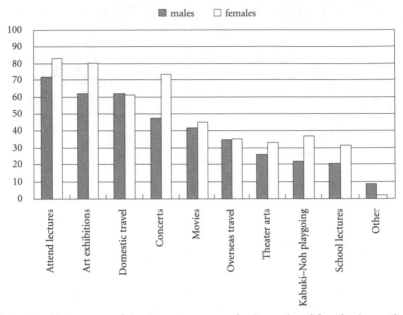

Figure 2.1. Main reasons for going out among males ($n = 133$) and females ($n = 156$) in the cohort of health research volunteers.

Behavioral Characteristics as Evaluated Using the LPC Life Habit Inventory

By the early 1990s, a multiple choice question (MCQ) inventory had been developed by the Life Planning Center Foundation, which included 132 questions for the assessment of lifestyle and 23 scales for the assessment of life habits, such as (1) dietary habits (6 scales), (2) smoking and drinking (2 scales), (3) life attitudes (7 scales), (4) health status (3 scales), (5) personality (3 scales), (6) exercise habits (1 scale), and (7) self-efficacy (1 scale) (Takagi et al. 1991).

Based on a principal component analysis (Spearman 1904) of these scales, the following five main representative factors were extracted: (1) a positive attitude characterized by extroverted behavior and taking the initiative, (2) health consciousness characterized by health-oriented lifestyles and an interest in cooking, (3) personal reliability characterized by tradition, duty, and empathy, (4) psychosomatic instability characterized by psychosomatic complaints and emotional instability, and (5) undesirable dietary habits characterized by high calorie, fat, salt, and sugar intake. A detailed description of the Life Habit Inventory is given in Takagi et al. (1991).

We performed a comparative study of life habits using this inventory of a general elderly cohort ($n = 5,206$) and an HRV cohort ($n = 163$); the results for females are shown in Figure 2.2 (Takagi and Yanai 1998; Doba et al. 2003). The Z-score method was chosen to compare the two data sets obtained from the two different cohorts. Scores between −0.5 and +0.5 were not considered to be statistically significant. Significant differences between the two cohorts were observed in the scores for several life habits; the characteristic findings may be summarized by saying that the HRV cohort exhibited a low-salt diet and a health-oriented lifestyle which included volunteer activities, habitual exercise, an extroverted and empathetic attitude, taking the initiative, and an absence of emotional instability. These tendencies were observed more clearly for all items in males rather than females, as shown in Figure 2.3.

The principal component analyses also revealed that the most noticeable differences in this cohort related to life habits in subjects of both genders, namely, high social motivation, health-oriented awareness, and emotional stability, as shown in Figure 2.4 for females and Figure 2.5 for males. The differences were more pronounced in females than males, especially with regard to health-oriented behavior.

Self-efficacy, proposed by Bandura (1997), is another interesting concept used in theories of behavioral change. This indicator is thought to present one's strong confidence that he or she can plan, practice for, and achieve goals. We developed an MCQ type of test consisting of six questions based on Bandura's original concept; full marks garnered 12 points. These are as follows: (1) proper competence of judgment in which one can exercise reasonable decision making in a variety of changing situations (2 points), (2) competence in which one can attain goals with planned practice (2 points) and cooperation with others (2 points), (3) effort in future life planning through which one can clearly make a future life plan (2 points) and always doing one's best to achieve one's goals (2 points), and (4) always fully applying one's abilities (2 points). The result of comparisons of self-efficacy between the control and the HRV cohorts revealed slightly but significantly higher scores for males in both cohorts, and higher scores for both genders in the HRV cohort (Table 2.3).

Physical Characteristics

Two aspects of physical characteristics were investigated, namely, (1) general health conditions related to diseases and/or disease-related risk factors or predictors (Doba, Sato, et al. 2004), and (2) morphometric and functional measurements related to physical, biochemical, and mental status (Doba, Shimada, et al. 2004).

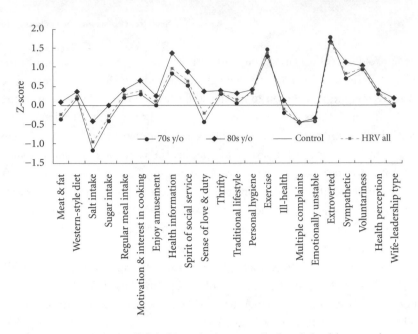

Figure 2.2. Comparison of life habit scales between the female health research volunteers (HRV) ($n = 77$) and the female control cohort ($n = 3{,}029$). Source: Doba et al. 2003.

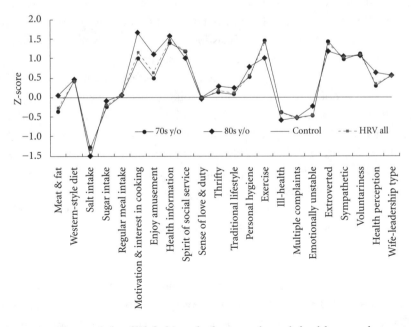

Figure 2.3. Comparison of life habit scales between the male health research volunteers (HRV) ($n = 86$) and the male control cohort ($n = 2{,}177$). Source: Doba et al. 2003.

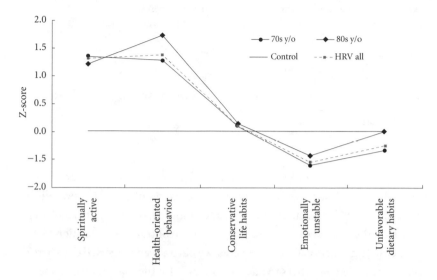

Figure 2.4. Comparison of principal life habit factors derived from 22 life habit scales between the female health research volunteers (HRV) ($n = 77$) and the female control cohort ($n = 3{,}029$). Source: Doba et al. 2003.

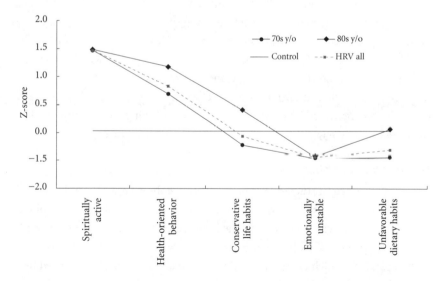

Figure 2.5. Comparison of principal life habit factors derived from 22 life habit scales between the male health research volunteers (HRV) ($n = 86$) and the male control cohort ($n = 2{,}177$). Source: Doba et al. 2003.

Table 2.3. Comparisons of the self-efficacy scale between the HRV cohort and the control cohort obtained from the Oita study (full marks garnered 12 points)

Control cohort (obtained from Oita Study)		HRV cohort	
Males ($n = 293, 70 \pm 9$ y/o)	$8.6 \pm 2.3^*$	Males ($n = 86, 78 \pm 5$ y/o)	$10.0 \pm 1.6^*{}^{**}$
Females ($n = 536, 68 \pm 10$ y/o)	7.7 ± 2.6	Females ($n = 77, 78 \pm 4$ y/o)	$9.4 \pm 2.0^{**}$

$^* p < 0.05$ (male vs. female), $^{**} p < 0.01$ (Control vs. HRV)

In relation to the former, in the National Cardiovascular Survey 2000, the HRV cohort exhibited a significantly lower prevalence of coronary heart disease, stroke, hypertension, diabetes mellitus, and smoking, but not hypercholesterolemia, than the general elderly cohort (Kōsei Rōdō Shō 2000). In relation to morphometric and functional measurements, we have already reported elsewhere the various measurements that serve as the standards for the evaluation of aging processes (Doba, Shimada, et al. 2004; Hinohara and Doba 2005). Normality can be defined variously in different circumstances. We have identified these measured values as standard following the notion of cultural health proposed by Sackett and others (Sackett et al. 1997). Their definition of normality is: (1) Gaussian (i.e., the mean ± 2 SD), (2) percentile within the range of 5 to 95 percent, (3) culturally desirable (preferred by society), (4) absence of risk factors (carrying no additional risk of disease), (5) diagnostic (range of results beyond which target disorders manifest), and (6) therapeutic (ranges of results beyond which treatment does more good than harm). Cultural health might be defined as a culturally desirable state preferred by society, like the successful aging concept proposed by Rowe and Kahn (1999).

Dietary Characteristics

We also compared the dietary habits in the HRV cohort ($n = 319$) and a general elderly cohort ($n = 133$) living in the western part of the Tokyo Metropolitan Area. The dietary characteristics of the latter cohort in relation to food selection were represented by frequent intake of rice with *miso* soup and *tsukemono* (salted pickles), which are typical traditional Japanese foods characterized by a high salt content, as shown in Figure 2.6. In contrast, the HRV cohort showed lower intakes of rice, oils, and meats, and greater intakes of seafood, brightly colored vegetables, eggs, milk, and fruits than the cohort of general elderly citizens.

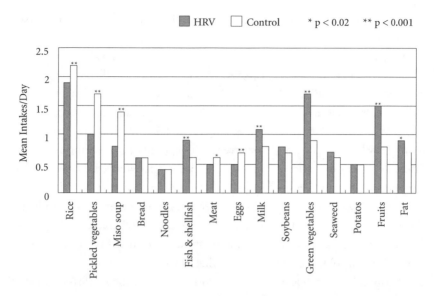

Figure 2.6. Comparison of mean intake of selected food items between the health research volunteers (HRV) ($n = 319$) and the control cohort ($n = 133$).

In another study performed on 272 subjects in this HRV cohort, the subjects were stratified into four groups based on their intake of brightly colored vegetables and seaweed and their average daily intake of each selected food item (17 items). The results were then compared among the four groups. Intake tendencies similar to those for brightly colored vegetables were observed for fish, meats, soybeans, seaweed, potatoes, and fats. Furthermore, seaweed intake was similar to observed intake of food items like rice, pickled vegetables, soybean paste, fish, eggs, milk products, soybeans, brightly colored vegetables, and potatoes. Therefore, a person who reports a high daily intake of brightly colored vegetables or seaweed may also be expected to show a high intake of other healthy foods (Matsubara et al. 2008).

What Keeps Them Thriving

Mrs. M was a 76-year-old widow when she joined the Association of the New Elderly in 2000. She had been interested in English literature and had been involved in the translation of several famous English novels. She had always been intellectually active and expressed new ideas in various media, especially animation, including her opinions concerning social, economic, and political issues. In short, she was one of the many socially active members of the Association of the New Elderly.

Mrs. M had already been diagnosed at age 40 with mitral valve disease (mitral regurgitation due to prolapse of the valve) with primary hypertension. For many years before joining the association, she had been treated uneventfully with loop diuretics until 2004, when she first developed shortness of breath on light physical exertion. After several diagnostic tests, she was diagnosed with pulmonary hypertension due to severe mitral regurgitation and coronary heart disease with multivessel lesions. In 2005, she had a successful percutaneous coronary intervention for stenosed coronary arteries; later that year, her mitral valve was replaced with an artificial valve. Her recovery from surgery was smooth and she was discharged from the hospital following cardiac rehabilitation.

Comprehensive geriatric assessments were performed first in 2003 when she was 76 years old, and again in 2008 when she was 81 years old. Although her hand grip did not change and no clear evidence of sarcopenia (loss of skeletal muscle) was found over this five-year period, she lost 6 kg, and her walking speed decreased from 3.8 sec/5m to 8.3 second/5m (less than the 15th percentile of the same age group). She also exhibited a reduced resting metabolic rate (less than the 15th percentile of the same age group) and showed a reduction in daily physical activities consistent with the frailty criteria of Fried et al. (2001).

Her physical frailty over the five-year follow-up period was obviously due to the burdens of serious illness. She has, however, remained psychosocially active as clearly demonstrated by her maintained self-efficacy (score 11 after Bandura), low depression scale (score 5 after Beck), and high score for MMSE (mini-mental state examination: 28/30). She still lives alone in spite of moderate physical disabilities and her continued psychosocial activities have kept her vivacious. She enjoys reading books, attending art exhibitions, listening to music, debating social and political issues, and publicizing her opinions.

Living with a positive state of mind helps many people live longer with a good QOL. There have been a number of studies concerning this issue that are informed by the approaches of social psychology, psychiatry, and geriatrics. For example, in the psychiatric approach, people who have lost their sense of purpose in life are often targeted for study, and therefore asserting oneself is identified as a main goal (Kamiya 1980; Kobayashi 1989). On the other hand, in the field of geriatrics, successful aging is defined by the capacity to live a life of fulfillment with a high QOL (Rowe and Kahn 1999).

In a departure from previous approaches, Tsuruwaka used a narrative-based approach in which elderly in several different living situations gave free-form descriptions of a "life worth living (*ikigai*)" (Tsuruwaka and Okayasu 2003). Tsuruwaka had been voluntarily assisting in the care of elderly living in several nursing homes and at daycare rehabilitation facilities, where she interviewed 50 subjects who agreed to participate in her study. She also applied this same approach to 51 members of the Association of the New Elderly. Through these nonstructural narrative-based interviews, Tsuruwaka identified several specific lifestyle features. According to her findings, the following five aspects might be used to characterize the lifestyles of her interviewees.

First, most of the elderly living in nursing homes expressed the importance of continuing intimate relationships with family members, neighbors, friends, and most interestingly, with their ancestors. For example, they reported that they obtained a sense of satisfaction from conversing with others, living with grand-children, and celebrating birthdays together. These kinds of cross-generational relationships among the elderly can be seen as reinforcing the sense of solidarity from which most people, especially the elderly, seem to derive peace, security, and comfort.

Second, although the elderly no longer aspired to the grand ambitions of their younger years, they found a sense of meaning in accomplishing what they could in the present moment. For instance, they pursued interests and took on new challenges even when faced with illness. Mrs. M, for example, has always been curious enough to be interested in almost everything and to discuss, write, and publicize her opinions, even though her cardiovascular condition, which has been serious enough to warrant multiple medications and frequent hospital visits, has resulted in moderately decreased instrumental activity in daily life.

Third, the elderly reported that they obtained a sense of satisfaction from day-to-day living as well as past successes. For example, many indicated that they enjoyed seasonal changes, facing each new day with a sense of vigor, pray-ing for the health and well-being of their families, and appreciating the present moment. They also reported that they drew strength from reflecting on how they had lived their lives up until this point, prior careers, educational and life experiences, experiences during the war, and people they had met. This sense of fulfillment also encourages Mrs. M's daily life activities and may be the basis for her self-confidence.

Fourth, many reported that they felt a sense of fulfillment from being needed by others. For example, senior citizens who still enjoyed good mobility were happy to help out friends who suffered from age-related leg problems, and those suffering from ailments such as hearing impairment were pleased to assist others with similar conditions and to provide emotional support for others in similar situations. In a larger, more cultural sense, the critical role played by the elderly is echoed in the aforementioned UN recommendation which stresses that the main role of the elderly in society should be the transmission of culture to the succeeding generation. Within a small family or a community, or even in a global situation, the influential force of the elderly is indispensable to human survival.

Fifth, many respondents said that they found meaning in affirming the value of their ways of living by wanting to show young people how pleasurable aging can be, by living in their own way despite institutionalization, and by living as independently as possible. Such affirmation is another important component in helping the elderly to thrive.

All five elements are critical to maintaining a sense of satisfaction for anyone, but the loss of any one of them presents particular dangers for the elderly. For example, loss of independence and autonomy, limited options and restricted freedom, and feelings of uselessness with regard to one's existence all inhibit QOL. According to Tsuruwaka's study (Tsuruwaka 2003), members of the Association of the New Elderly seem to be more strongly characterized by a sense of achievement, fulfillment, and affirmation of life throughout their whole lives.

From her analysis, the following characteristic factors were extracted in the HRV cohort: (1) high self-efficacy, (2) engaging in a broad range of activities, (3) a high degree of freedom, and (4) a sense of being useful to society. Tsuru-kawa also described their characteristic ways of living in relation to their daily activities (Tsuruwaka 2003):

1. Social networks: They cleverly used social networks established before their retirement, solved problems in innovative and skillful ways, and performed tasks more efficiently than others.
2. Health maintenance and promotion: They showed particular interest in their health, and practiced healthy exercise and dietary habits.
3. Progress and advancement: They always tried to be successful in their endeavors and sought advancement of their knowledge and skills.
4. Meaningful social contributions: They always tried to maximize their abilities through meaningful and widely recognized social contributions.
5. Plain living and high level of thinking: They always thought of issues clearly and from a global perspective. They exercised reasonable judgment and were efficacious in their thinking.

6. Goal-oriented lifestyle: They set clear goals to live by.
7. Continuation of their own lifestyle: They always tried to maintain their chosen ways of living.

Summary and Conclusions

As we face the aging of Japanese society, various plans are being proposed to overcome the special problems associated with this change in demographics. Among them, the movement of the New Elder Citizen led by Hinohara offers many reasonable and promising strategies to help senior citizens to live their lives with a sense of control and dignity. It is also true, however, that there is a dark side to aging. There are numerous senior citizens in both rural and urban areas who have been living with poor health or diminished economic resources and in isolated situations that will require extensive social support.

In this chapter, we have discussed the issues faced in the aging of society, which is emerging as a common global problem throughout the world. Several attempts to manage these problems have been mentioned, including those referenced in the UN recommendation. After discussing several challenges presented by aging, we introduced a new movement in Japan to improve the outlook for aged society, which emerged in the Association of the New Elderly at the Life Planning Center (LPC) Foundation in 2000 led by Shigeaki Hinohara. We described some details of the organization and activities at the LPC Foundation as well as the underlying concepts and activities that are carried out by the New Elder Citizen Movement.

We have also described some of the characteristic habits of these elderly, who adhere to the guiding principles of this association and serve as suitable lifestyle models for the next generation. Our future research will closely follow this cohort to see how they will continue their lives and face death, and we will try to support them and minimize their difficulties whenever they are in need of our knowledge and skills. Through these mutual interactions, we may be able to gain some insightful ideas about the continued health of the elderly and their end-of-life care.

Note

We are deeply indebted to Yoshiko Matsumoto and Molly Vallor for their constructive comments, and we would also like to express our appreciation to Sadako Fujino, a senior member of the Association of the New Elderly, for her contributions to the English descriptions of the way of living of the New Elderly.

References

Avlund, K., B. E. Holstein, E. L. Mortensen, and H. Schroll. 1999. Active life in old age: Combining measures of functional ability and social participation. *Danish Medical Bulletin* 46: 345–349.

Bandura, A. 1997. Self-efficacy: Toward a unifying theory of behavioral change. *Psychological Review* 84: 191–215.

Doba, N., M. Hirano, H. Matsubara, S. Hinohara, K. Saeki, E. Nishiyama, H. Takagi, and H. Yanai. 2003. LPC shiki seikatsu shūkan kensa ni yoru shin rōjin no kōdō tokusei ni kansuru kenkyū (A study of the specific behavioral pattern of the New Elderly by using the LPC Life Habit Inventory). *Iji Shinpō* 4149: 26–32.

Doba, N., J. Sato, M. Hirano, Y. Iwashimizu, M. Tsuruwaka, Y. Matsubara, T. Kushiro, and S. Hinohara. 2004. LPC ni okeru shinrōjin no shintaiteki kenkō tokusei ni kansuru kentō: Dai 5-ji junkanki shikkan kiso chōsa (2000) tono hikaku o moto ni shite (Comparative studies on the physical health characteristics of New Elder Citizens at the Life Planning Center and the elderly subjects recruited in the fifth national survey of cardiovascular diseases). *Sōgō Kenshin* 31: 469–474.

Doba N., M. Shimada, S. Saito, M. Nasu, A. Kuratsuji, I. Motoda, J. Sato, N. Kai, M. Miyazaki, T. Kushiro, and S. Hinohara. 2004. Kenjō kōreisha no sōgō hyōka ni okeru keitai, kinō, ketsueki shoshihyō no kijunchi, oyobi, seisa ni kansuru kentō (Studies on the standardization and gender differences of anthropometry, selected physical functions, and several blood parameters derived from the healthy elderly cohort in comprehensive health evaluation). *Sōgō Kenshin* 31: 609–616.

Fried, L. P., C. M. Tangen, J. Walston, A. B. Newman, C. Hirsch, J. Gottdiener, T. Seeman, R. Tracy, W. J. Kop, G. Burke, and M. A. McBurnie (Cardiovascular Health Study Collaborative Research Group). 2001. Frailty in older adults: Evidence for a phenotype. *Journal of Gerontology* 56: M146–M156.

Gouaze, A. 1996. *Demain la médecine*. Paris: Expansion Scientifique Publications.

Harada, Y. 2001. *Jinkō genshō no keizaigaku* (Economics of population reduction). Tokyo: PHP Institute.

Hinohara, S., and N. Doba. 2005. The future profile of health promotion and disease prevention in Japan. *Methods of Information in Medicine* 44: 342–347.

Kamiya, M. 1980. *Ikigai*. Tokyo: Misuzu Shobō.

Kobayashi, T. 1989. *Ikigai to wa nanika? Jiko jitsugen e no michi* (What does "ikigai" signify? The way to self-realization). Tokyo: NHK Books.

Kōsei Rōdō Shō (Ministry of Health, Labor, and Welfare). 2000. *Dai 5-ji junkanki shikkan kiso chōsa hōkoku* (Report of the fifth national survey of cardiovascular diseases). www.mhlw.go.jp/toukei/saikin/hw/kenkou/jyunkan/jyunkan00/gaiyo.html.

———. 2008. *Jisatsu shibō tōkei no gaikyō* (Statistics on suicide deaths). www.mhlw.go.jp/toukei/saikin/hw/jinkou/tokusyu/suicide04/index.html.

Matsubara, Y., M. Hirano, N. Doba, and S. Hinohara. 2008. Life habits and health status of active Japanese senior citizens: A structured self-check questionnaire study with a special reference to the progress of frailty. *Okinawa Wellness Longevity Journal* 1: 1–14.

Rowe, J. W., and R. L. Kahn. 1999. Active life in old age: Combining measures of functional ability and social participation. *Danish Medical Bulletin* 46: 345–349.

Sackett, D. L., W. S. Richardson, R. G. Rosenberg, and R. B. Haynes. 1997. *Evidence-based medicine: How to practice and teach EBM.* New York: Churchill Livingstone.

Sōmushō Tōkei Kyoku (Statistics Bureau of the Ministry of Internal Affairs and Communications). 2006. *Sekai no tōkei* (World census). www.stat.go.jp/data/sekai/index.htm.

Spearman, C. 1904. General intelligence objectively determined and measured. *Journal of Psychology* 31: 1–10.

Tagore, R. [1941] 1998. Last Poems #10. Trans. Wendy Barker and Saranindranath Tagore. *Mānoa: A Pacific Journal of International Writing* 10 (1): 24.

Takagi, H., K. Saiki, S. Hinohara, N. Doba, H. Yanai, and M. Mizuguchi. 1991. Construction of life habit inventory. In *Methods and applications in mental health surveys: The Todai Health Index,* ed. S. Suzuki and R. E. Roberts, 103–121. Tokyo: University of Tokyo Press.

Takagi, H., and H. Yanai. 1998. Seikatsu shūkan shakudo no shinraisei to inshi kōzō no kentō (Reliability and factor structure of lifestyle scales). *Tōkei Sūri* 46: 39–64.

Tsuruwaka, M. 2003. *Katari kara mita "ikigai"* (The "life worth living" [ikigai] of the elderly from a narrative perspective). PhD diss., Waseda University.

Tsuruwaka, M., and O. Okayasu. 2003. Katari (narrative) kara mita kōreiki "ikigai" no shosō (The "life worth living" [ikigai] of the elderly from a narrative perspective). *Seimei Rinri* 13: 159–157).

United Nations. 2003. *International plan of action on ageing of United Nations.* www.un.org/esa/socdev/ageing/madrid_intlplanaction.html.

Vaillant, G. E. 2002. *Aging well.* Boston: Little, Brown.

3 Tension, Dependency, and Sacrifice in the Relationship of an Elderly Couple

Susan Orpett Long

THIS CHAPTER EXPLORES how social change and interpersonal history affected a Japanese couple giving and receiving elder care. Despite, or because of their increasing preponderance in the population, the elderly are often viewed in negative and stereotypical terms, and the aging of society is seen as a "social problem" which requires the attention of policy makers. Less attention has been paid to the subjective experience of aging. This chapter utilizes a dramaturgical metaphor (Goffman 1959) to better understand the experience of aging during an era of rapid social change. Using the Japanese concepts of *soto-zura* (public mask) and *uchi-zura* (inward-facing representation), I suggest that older people remain active social agents in the social process of constructing new personas as they respond to external circumstances and to their understanding of the inner selves they have become.

How to conceptualize "self" in Japan has been the topic of significant discussion in the anthropological literature. Rosenberger (2001), drawing on Goffman, speaks of Japanese women as operating in multiple arenas: front stage where social performances occur, and backstage where there is space for spontaneity and personal expression. Contrasting terms in Japanese suggest that the distinction is appropriate to Japan, where in daily life as well as academic analysis, distinctions are made between inner (*uchi*) and outer (*soto*), between a "front" public orientation (*omote*) and private "back" orientation (*ura*), and between public expression (*tatemae*) and true feeling (*honne*). Bachnik (1994) has argued that Japanese selves should not be conceptualized as being at either of these poles, but as that which moves along a continuum of inner and outer relationships in response to specific social situations. Taken to the extreme, this approach assumes that there is in Japan no sense of an individual self aside from the specific social contexts in which it is manifest. In contrast, Lebra (1984; 1992) and Plath (1980) describe Japanese selves that while multidimensional, retain a historically situated inner core that continues to grow and change even in old age. In the Confucian idea of the life course, the *soto-zura* (public mask) and the *uchi-zura* (inward-facing representation) ideally come to converge in old age so that there is less distinction between the public presentation and inner experiences of self. But I would argue that achieving this convergence is challenged by rapid change in the front-stage arena, such as the dramatic shifts in gender expectations and the demographic trends of late twentieth- and early twenty-first-century Japan.

Demographic trends have focused Japan's attention on caregiving of the elderly; social changes have led to the inclusion of new expectations and skills in the definition of caregiver roles. An increasingly common scenario is that an elderly spouse serves as the main caregiver, with little to no support from additional family members. The incorporation of this new role for the spouse may lead to *soto-zura* (public masks) of acceptance or competency which are far from the reality of what the elderly couple feel, affecting their ability to communicate effectively and assist capably.

This chapter investigates how in the case of one Tokyo couple, rapid social changes combined with the history of their relationship to leave a wide gap between the experience of aging and its portrayal to outsiders. An analysis of multiple interviews with husband and wife reveals carefully constructed *soto-zura* masks and offers glimpses of the *uchi-zura* behind them. A reliance on their public faces alone to characterize their experiences of giving and receiving would miss the wrinkle lines, where the *soto-zura* and *uchi-zura* are not in accord.

I will begin with a brief introduction to the demographic and social changes regarding care for frail elderly in Japan and introduce a major Japanese policy response, a long-term care insurance system (*kaigo hoken seido*). I will then present an overview of the motivations of family caregiving found in a study of family caregiving in Tokyo and a small city in northern Japan. In the last section I will present and analyze a case of a husband caring for his wife in which these social changes collide dramatically with interpersonal tensions to widen the gap between *soto-zura* and the *uchi-zura*. On the surface, the husband seems highly motivated and has adjusted to his new role. He relies for assistance on paid service providers through the long-term care system. Yet below the surface are the husband's and wife's narratives of tension, dependency, and sense of sacrifice. These themes are not new to their relationship, but take on new significance when the *soto-zura* must be reconstructed. This in-depth look at a contemporary caregiving situation suggests that to understand the lives of older people, we must look behind the public face to the uncertainties and tensions, and to the meanings of personal adaptations to changing social realities.

Social and Demographic Change

The Aging of Society and the Decline in Caregiver Availability

It is well known that Japan has a rapidly growing proportion of elderly in its population, one of the highest in the world. In 2007, about 21.5 percent of the population was 65 years of age or older, a dramatic change from only 20 years earlier when only 10 percent was in that category (Kōsei Rōdō Shō 2009). Most of these older adults continue to be self-sufficient and active, but advanced age is correlated with increased need for assistance in daily living. It is useful to think about the aging of Japan from another statistic. In 2006, over 29,000 people were 100 years old or older, a number that nearly quadrupled from the mid-1990s. The government estimates that by 2055 there will be 273,000 centenarians in Japan (National Institute of Population and Social Security Research 2008).

Changes in caregiving are due to several factors: the demographic shifts of increased life expectancy, and even more dramatically, the decline in the birth rate. In 2007, life expectancy in Japan was 85.99 for women and 79.19 for men. The completed fertility rate was 1.37 (Kōsei Rōdō Shō 2009). The size of the Japanese population as a whole began to decline in 2005, and the proportion of that population under 16 is shrinking (17.5 percent in 2005; Kōsei Rōdō Shō 2009). Household size is declining as a result not only of the smaller number of children, but also of the increased likelihood of older people living independently or with only a spouse. These demographics are accompanied by social changes in the availability and attitudes of those who in the past were expected to take on family caregiving tasks.

In the early part of the twentieth century, life expectancy in Japan was only in the mid-forties. The official family system, created by the government and based on upper-class patterns of the previous Tokugawa period (1600–1868), was expected to provide support and care to household members who did reach old age. In that family system, the oldest son (or alternate heir) succeeded his father as household head and had responsibility for household continuity and the care of all of its members, including his elderly parents. However, the gendered division of labor within the household and in society more broadly allocated the day-to-day tasks of nurturing and bodily care to women, so that in reality, the wife of the head of household actually performed the work of caregiving. A minimal welfare system was the undesirable alternative for those with no family to provide such support.

Factors such as geographical mobility, the size of urban dwellings, and changes in the desirability of co-residence from the perspectives of both older and younger generations has led to an increase in older people living alone. In 1960, 86 percent of those 65 years and older lived with an adult child, but by 2000, only 48.2 percent did so. Instead, 8 percent of men and 17.8 percent of women in that age group lived alone, while another third were living with (only) a spouse. Even for those older adults living with a child, it can no longer be assumed that it will be the elder son and his wife who will be the caregivers when the need arises. Daughters are an increasingly popular choice. Moreover, having an adult woman living in the same household does not mean she is available for caregiving, since women have increasingly entered the paid labor force to work outside the home. In 2008, women made up 41.5 percent of the Japanese labor force (Statistics Bureau 2009b). Over 60 percent of women between the ages of 15 and 64 participated in paid employment, and of that group, the majority were married (Statistics Bureau 2009a).

The Policy Response: The Long-Term Care Insurance System

By the 1980s these changes led to serious concern in government circles about who was going to take care of the growing elderly population. Having one middle-aged couple needing to care for four elderly, frail, or ill parents is a difficult enough proposition in terms of American meanings of caregiving. By Japanese standards it is impossible. To try to do so is to compromise the quality of care. Interviews and observations of not only elder care but also care for children and the sick suggest that the ideal caregiver puts aside any other roles that compete for her time and attention. Nurturing means the continuous presence of the caregiver (Caudill and Weinstein 1969), who takes on a protective role (Craighill-Saiki 1997). Goals include not only the physical comfort of the care recipient but also the creation of an atmosphere in which conflict and confrontation are avoided (Long 1997). Such a style of caregiving is emotionally as well as physically exhausting, and as people came to live longer with chronic illnesses, the burden experienced by caregivers increased.

This common approach to caregiving is exemplified by a wife in the following excerpt from an interview about her caregiving experience:

> Interviewer: Do you sometimes go out and leave your husband home?
>
> Caregiver: Never. I don't go out alone leaving him. . . . So when he goes to daycare . . . I stay home and do laundry, cleaning . . . and cook meals. . . . He's back around three in the afternoon and dinner is at four, so I have to prepare for that while he's gone. . . . I scrub the bathtub . . . it's quite busy even when he's gone.
>
> Interviewer: You don't go out to see friends?
>
> Caregiver: No, no, no, no. Never once! Well, sometimes I feel like, why not do that? But I think it's more fun going out together than just me alone. So we go out together . . . always two of us together. So to go to the supermarket, I call for a ride, shop, and then I carry all the shopping bags. . . . I can't buy a lot though. . . .
>
> Interviewer: You carry all the bags?
>
> Caregiver: I go with my backpack on . . . so my hands are free to push the wheelchair.[1]

Another caregiver, a husband, explained that his wife, who was paralyzed from a stroke, followed him around the room with her eyes. "She feels secure to find that I am here. She is always looking for me."

Given the high expectations for the person in the caregiver role, it is not surprising that with the increased nuclearization of the family and a legal change away from single-child inheritance has come behavioral resistance on the part of daughters-in-law who were previously thought to be the "natural" caregiver for their husband's parents. That a daughter-in-law will take on that role is no longer a shared assumption. Caregiving arrangements have become the subject of negotiation before and during marriage, and the cause of divorce, relocation, and anger (Traphagan 2003; Jenike 2003). At the societal level, public awareness of the issue of elder care was raised by government surveys and predictions, media attention to the problem, and even the publication in 1972 of the popular novel *Kōkotsu no hito*, in which the central character is a woman caring for her senile father-in-law (Ariyoshi 1984). The aging of society and the problems of caring for elderly family members became common themes in public discourse.

In the 1980s, Japanese bureaucrats responded by creating the Gold Plan, and later a revised Gold Plan, which set out goals for the development of institutional and community-based care services. Recognizing that family care alone was no longer a feasible assumption, the Gold Plan vastly expanded local government services for frail older people that were paid with tax revenues. Whether simply because tax money could never sufficiently fund a program of the scale needed or because politicians were looking for votes from the increasingly large proportion of senior citizen voters, the national government continued to look for alternative approaches to the problem of elder care. After studying various European and American systems of elder care and years of political debate in the 1990s, it was decided to supplement the Gold Plan by creating an insurance-based long-term care program along the lines of Germany's, though it is a larger plan with more generous benefits than its model.

The Japanese long-term care system is a mandatory insurance program in which everyone over 40 years old pays insurance premiums, and everyone over 65 and/or suffering from a "disease of aging" is guaranteed certain services according only to their biological and social needs and *not* their ability to pay. The benefits are paid only in the form of services and equipment, and not in cash. The cost of the program is born equally by the insurance fund (that is, premiums) and a combination of national and local tax monies. The guarantee of services has created strong demand that encourages development of service-providing organizations. It has resulted in a tremendous expansion of day and residential programs and facilities for the elderly, which are owned by non-profit groups, entrepreneurs, and large corporations.

To utilize the services provided by the insurance system, an application is made at the local government office. This is followed by a medical examination by a physician and an assessment of problems in daily living by a welfare worker or care manager using a nationally standardized and computerized form. Based on this information, a committee consisting of medical, social service, and local government personnel determines eligibility and the level of care for which the person is qualified. The care level determines the yen-value of services which the person may receive, but decisions on which services will actually be used and which person or organization will provide them are made by the elderly person, family members, and if desired, a care manager. The great majority of those who use services rely on a professional care manager, who arranges schedules of home nurses, home helpers, daycare, equipment rentals, and applications for admission to nursing homes for short stays (respite care) or long-term residence.

Institutionalization is an option for those needing a great deal of assistance or nursing care, and demand for such services increased dramatically after the enactment of the long-term care system.[2] Although this may be a desirable situation for relieving family members of the burdens of caring for a severely frail or ill relative, it also violates traditional notions of who should be providing the care. It does not, however, challenge the cultural understanding that caregiving is one person's responsibility. The institution merely becomes a substitute for the normative daughter-in-law caregiver. This helps to explain the low rate of involvement of families in the lives of institutionalized elderly relatives that is frequently and unhappily noted by many nursing home directors (Wu 2004, 139–154). Nursing homes and similar facilities are used as temporary caregivers when the family caregiver is unavailable or to provide a break from full-time caregiving (respite care, or "short stay"). The concurrent use of family and professional caregivers in the home setting and the simultaneous use of multiple services inside and outside of the home significantly change the cultural meaning of caregiving. The long-term care system does not eliminate the need for family caregiving, but it changes the job description. If there are co-residing family members, generally someone will still assist with daily activities, supplemented if desired by visiting home health aides and nurses. On the other hand, new managerial duties for coordinating the services are an additional task for family caregivers. These changes impact the way people then shape their caregiver *soto-zura*. The faces of caregivers are no longer necessarily feminine, or of a younger generation, or of someone who must perform all the tasks themselves.

Transitions in Family Caregiving

Beginning in 2003, the Long-Term Care Insurance Study Group began to investigate how elder care was affected by the new system, which went into effect in 2000.[3] In addition to a large survey, teams of two researchers visited the homes of people eligible for services under the insurance system who were being cared for at home by a family member. In the first year of the project, 29 caregiver–care recipient pairs in Tokyo and in the Odate area of Akita Prefecture were interviewed. Those who were willing and available were interviewed again in subsequent years. Discussion topics included the nature of the care recipient's health and daily living problems, daily life for the care recipient and caregiver, use of medical and social services and the process of decision making regarding their use, family relationships, and the concerns and sources of pleasure for both caregiver and recipient. The case study of Mr. and Mrs. Yamaguchi presented in this chapter is based on these lengthy, open-ended interviews with each of them in 2003 and 2004.[4]

One change in family caregiving, with or without the long-term care services, is who is providing elder care. Even with social services, dealing with challenging demographics regarding elder care is leading to changes in roles and statuses within the family. The lines of gender, birth order, and residence by which care responsibilities have been, at least ideally, distributed have become increasingly blurred. Nationally, there had already been a shift away from the eldest daughter-in-law as sole caregiver. Data from a 2000 national survey on who was the primary caregiver of elderly people are shown in Table 3.1. Wives and daughters-in-law predominated, but together constituted only about 40 percent of caregivers. Men made up nearly 20 percent of those providing family elder care.

In our long-term care study, the 2003 survey of 1,500 families eligible for long-term care services found an even higher proportion of husbands, sons, and daughters than in the national survey, but there were large differences between the Tokyo and Akita samples. (See Table 3.1.) Wives were the most common caregivers in both locales, but more men and more daughters were primary caregivers in Tokyo. Daughters-in-law remained a significant source of family care for the elderly in Akita. The subsample of people was purposively chosen so that we could interview people in a variety of relationships to the elderly person needing care (Table 3.2).

Table 3.1. Relationship of family caregiver to care recipient in project survey and in national survey (%)

	National data[a]	Total for 2003 survey	Tokyo survey sample	Akita survey sample
Husband	9.1	14.2	17.6	8.2
Wife	20.8	27.7	26.7	29.5
Son	9.2	12.6	13.1	11.9
Daughter	19.0	20.8	24.2	14.9
Son-in-law	0.3	0.3	0.4	0.0
Daughter-in-law	27.7	19.8	14.3	29.5
Other male	[b]	1.0	1.0	1.0
Other female	[b]	3.6	2.8	5.0

[a]This column presents data from a 2000 national survey concerning the primary caregivers of elders who were eligible for long-term care insurance system services. From *Kaigo Sābisu Setai Chōsa* (Naikakufu 2004, 39).

[b]In this survey, "other" is not broken down by gender. The total for "other" was 6.1%.

Table 3.2. Interviewed caregiver characteristics

	Total ($n = 29$)	Tokyo ($n = 14$)	Akita ($n = 15$)
Gender			
Male	9	5	4
Female	20	9	11
Age			
30–39	1	0	1
40–49	1	1	0
50–59	7	4	3
60–69	9	5	4
70–79	8	2	6
80–89	3	2	1
Relationship to care recipient			
Husband	6	3	3
Wife	7	3	4
Daughter-in-law	9	5	4
Daughter	4	1	3
Son	3	2	1

They do not represent "typical" families but together portray a range of family caregiving decisions. For example, a daughter-in-law was the main caregiver for a 92-year-old woman, but she was not the wife of the eldest son but rather of the third son. Things had apparently not gone smoothly during a brief period of co-residence with the eldest daughter-in-law, the "traditional" choice; so from the time of marriage, this third daughter-in-law had lived with her mother-in-law. She felt that she was temperamentally better suited to that role than her elder sister-in-law, and although it was stressful, her employment outside of the home and the mother-in-law's continued work in the fields meant that they were too busy and tired to fight much. Now, with some dementia and loss of physical strength, the daughter-in-law told us, her mother-in-law was more docile, and with her own children grown and her retirement from her job, life was actually more relaxing now.

We also heard several interesting narratives of son caregivers. In an unusual case in Tokyo, a son in his fifties decided to close the family business and pursue his dream of being a writer. His wife, who had stayed home when their children were young and they lived as a nuclear family, was thus free to pursue her own career outside of the home. This was made possible by a decision to remodel the widowed mother's house and co-reside, with the son working from home and thus available to be the main caregiver for his mother, arrangements made several years in advance of her stroke that made such caregiving necessary. It is important to note that in these cases, the family members combined some "traditional" ideas about caregiving with demographic realities and new services.

In the interviews we asked about the motivations of caregivers to take on this role. Whether it was the old *soto-zura* mask of an expected caregiver of the past, worn by wife or daughter-in-law, or a newly constructed one worn by a son, daughter, or husband, motivations were multiple and complex. Over the course of an interview, many people expressed more than one of the ideas below, but it is useful to consider the variety of motivations.

Some caregivers took on the responsibility with the expectation that it would be temporary. They believed that they were managing a life crisis that was expected to pass. For example, a husband who owned his own business in Akita was taking care of his 74-year-old wife who was recovering from a serious fall which had required surgery and rehabilitation. This was the husband's second marriage; the new wife had worked in the company office and assisted with young employees in particular. Both expressed in separate interviews how much they looked forward to getting back to their jobs. They did not seem to even consider the possibility that there might be a need for ongoing care, or that one or the other might not be able to continue working.

Another common motivation for becoming a caregiver was the personal relationship with the person needing assistance. In particular, for those who had received assistance in the past from the family member, a sense of gratitude for that support was a great source of motivation. One man told of how his wife had packed his lunch every day of his work career, and how on rainy days she would meet him at the bus stop with an umbrella for him. He expressed that caring for her now was an opportunity to pay back (*okaeshi*) the care she had given him over the years. Another husband caregiver reflected back on the time he was hospitalized for an injury while he was in the air force. His wife had come to see him every day. "I will never forget her caring. I was really supported emotionally and mentally by her visiting. Now it is my turn."

Sometimes, as in the case of the third daughter-in-law mentioned above, things did not work out with the expected caregiver. Changing employment or financial circumstances or personalities sometimes got in the way of a success-ful co-residence and thus of providing assistance in daily living. Work-related transfers or frequent travel may serve as a reason or excuse for asking a sibling to take over at least some of the care responsibilities. In another case, a daughter observed arguments and resentments between her mother and sister-in-law, and requested that her mother move in with her. Or sometimes, the caregiver was determined by the fact there was no one else available. We interviewed several families in which husband caregivers clearly expressed their regret that despite expectations of Japanese society in their younger years, they now had to take on the role of caregiver. This was sometimes because there was no daugh-ter-in-law in the family, or because all children lived away or had problems of their own.

Some family caregivers were motivated by their belief that family care is im-portant and better than institutional care, such as this wife who explained why she did not want to use respite care services to which her husband was entitled under the long-term care insurance system.

> Wife: It's every other month. I cancelled in February. We called it off because my heart gets feeling uneasy as the short stay day gets closer. . . . I feel I'd rather bear with it and do it by myself. . . . Sometimes the nursing staff there have a hard time handling his fistula and I get worried and that's hard on him too. . . .
>
> Interviewer: Would you talk a bit more about your uneasy feeling?
>
> Wife: Well, it's like I'm abandoning caring for him. . . . I feel sorry for him. They try to do it at the short stay facility, but it doesn't go smoothly. . . . Like with his urine. They can't do it right, especially male caregivers.

Yet she recognized that when she tried to manage his care totally on her own, she became tired and irritated. So despite feeling that she could do a better job, she had allowed the doctors and nurses to talk her into continuing to use the service.

Many caregivers saw caring for an elderly relative as a "natural" extension of previous caregiving or nurturing roles. For some, the additional role was assumed gradually and matter-of-factly. Others recognized that the extension of their household tasks to include elder care was "natural," but saw it as an ad-ditional burden. For example, one daughter-in-law caregiver told us that it was not so much providing more assistance for her mother-in-law that was burden-some, but rather feeling the continual criticism of her sister-in-law that she was not doing enough. In other families, the caregiver did not see the extension of the family caregiver role to include elder care as "natural," but rather as a new task that required additional study to be done well. Thus, in anticipation of her mother needing more help, the co-residing daughter of a 93-year-old had taken classes at a local nursing home and had read books about how best to care for the elderly, for example, how to assist in walking or how to cook healthy, low-fat meals.

Assumptions about and motivations for caregiving are part of the cultural context in which the tasks are performed. The work is cultural practice, or habitus (Bourdieu 1977), in which culture influences but does not determine behavior. There is thus a great deal of variation in practice on the theme of how to provide care. The caregiver's and care recipient's experiences of that practice are also interpreted in light of the assumptions and motivations. Responses of the recipient vary from gratitude to anger. Caregivers may be frustrated or calm or proud. These responses are not only personal but also interpersonal, grounded in the history of the relationship between them. In the case of Mr. and Mrs. Yamaguchi described below, a history of tension related to normative gender roles of their younger years has led both to develop soto-zura of proper behavior while experiencing frustration, anger, and pain.

Soto-zura and Uchi-zura of the Elderly Couple

Although all of the stories we heard in the interviews helped us to better understand the experience of family caregiving, the adjustments of husbands to the role of caregiver were perhaps the most interesting, given their pre–World War II socialization to male gender roles. For some, nurturing was not difficult; for others, even preparing a meal was a challenge. Some local governments provide classes in household management, cooking, bodily care, and basic nursing skills for older men. In addition to their upbringing, it appeared that the relationship through the marriage prior to the wife's illness or disability was extremely important in the discrepancy between the changes required to the soto-zura and the persons they thought themselves to be, especially in how they dealt with the crossing of gender roles as caregivers.

Introducing Mrs. Yamaguchi

When we met Mrs. Yamaguchi, she was 70 years old. Ten years earlier, she had suffered a stroke, after which she had rehabilitation and was able to get around very slowly with a walker. About two years prior to the first interview, she fell and broke her hip. From that point she has been unable to walk. In a question-naire completed prior to the interview, she indicated that she could not use her left arm and leg. In the interview she explained that in addition to left side pa-ralysis, both legs had atrophied and she was now unable to walk at all. She used the term *netakiri* (bedridden) several times to describe her situation.

The Yamaguchis lived on the second floor in a three-story building in a middle- to working-class section of Tokyo. Her husband, 76 at the time of the first interview in 2003, was her main caregiver, although he himself had dia-betes, vision and hearing problems, and a pacemaker for his heart. However, he looked healthy, claimed to feel well, and said he could eat and drink what-ever he wished despite the diabetes. In our interviews with Mr. Yamaguchi, he claimed to be busy from morning to night with caregiving responsibili-ties, although he did take time to work on his calligraphy, a serious hobby he had cultivated after his retirement from the fire department. He prepared food and did laundry and shopping, but acknowledged that he did not like to clean and did not feel comfortable bathing his wife, "because she is a woman." Apparently for these reasons, he reluctantly agreed to have home helpers and other care personnel through the long-term care insurance come in to the home despite his reluctance to deal with strangers. Mrs. Yamaguchi has been receiving benefits under the insurance service since its inception in 2000, and Mr. Yamaguchi expressed appreciation for the program, commenting. "Those who oppose the system would change their minds if they needed it. I am grateful for it." In addition to home helpers who assisted with housework as well as the bodily care of Mrs. Yamaguchi, Mrs. Yamaguchi attended a daycare program twice a week, and had home helpers come to carry her down the narrow steps to the street where the van came to pick her up and carry her back up when she returned in the afternoon. At the day care center she re-ceived a bath twice a week and enjoyed socializing with others. She has also made use of short stay (respite care) admissions to elder care facilities for a week at a time. Under the medical insurance system, she visited her doctor once a month and had a masseur come four times a week for treatment on non-daycare days.

The Yamaguchis both grew up in the countryside, and had an arranged marriage. They have three children who are all married and living in the Tokyo area. Mr. Yamaguchi acknowledges that he does not have close ties with them or the grandchildren, thinking that the grandchildren only come around for *otoshidama* (monetary New Year's gifts) at New Year's. He has rigid ideas about gender roles and on several topics commented that he was "*mukashi no hito*," an "old fashioned guy." He also had strong feelings about getting old:

> Getting old is not good. There's not much that's enjoyable. You can't eat, there's no one to go out and have fun with. I think it's good to not live too long. . . . I don't like getting together with old people.

But aside from his ageist and sexist comments, Mr. Yamaguchi presented himself as a charming, intelligent respondent who liked order, was on top of the caregiving situation, took time for his own hobbies, and wanted to do his best for his wife.

Mrs. Yamaguchi did not see it that way. When the interview team went into the house the first time, we explained the study and talked with both husband and wife together for a time. Then we asked for individual interviews. The husband brought us into an adjoining room, the formal Japanese-style parlor (*ōsetsuma*), to talk with him. However, we were separated only by a sliding *shōji* wall and a few tatami mats' distance from where the wife was lying in a hospital bed. When we finished the interview and returned to her room to talk with Mrs. Yamaguchi, her husband was barely out of the room before she exclaimed, "That was just a bunch of lies!" She then proceeded with a long list of complaints about her situation before we could get a question out of our mouths.[5]

Allegations of Abuse

In talking about visits from her elementary-school-aged grandchildren (the daughter's children), Mrs. Yamaguchi directly brought up the issue of abuse.

> They are very nice to me. They are always concerned about how I'm doing and ask when I'm going to get better. They get into bed with me and play with me, even touch me. Even though they're boys. And even though they're young, they call what grandfather does *gyakutai* [abuse]. "Grandma, that's *gyakutai*!" they say.

Her complaints can be clearly placed in the various categories of abuse identified in the gerontology literature.[6] She stated unequivocally that there was no physical abuse, but there was a great deal of psychological/emotional mistreatment. She claimed that he often says things such as greeting her with, "Oh, you're still alive." Although she is not able to get up and do it for herself, he does not open and close the windows of her room to give her fresh air or a breeze in the summer. If she asks for something she is ignored or yelled at with words like *chikusho* (damn it!) or *urusai* (shut up!), and doors may be slammed for emphasis. He tells others in her presence that his wife is ill so he can't play golf or go on trips, making her feel guilty. He gives her food that in her physical condition she cannot easily eat by herself, and does not assist her in eating.

To this list she added complaints of financial abuse. He handled all of the money, which is unusual in urban middle-class families, where husbands generally bring home their pay envelopes and hand them to their wives, who manage the household budget. Mr. Yamaguchi, in contrast, even took care of things such as his wife's government pension, which comes in her name. She does not know how much she receives or the amount her account has in it. Unlike Japanese housewives who give their husbands cash for daily expenses, Mr. Yamaguchi does not give her any personal spending money. In response, some financial responsibilities have apparently been transferred recently to the daughter, who is more responsive to Mrs. Yamaguchi's material needs and desires than is Mr. Yamaguchi.

Mrs. Yamaguchi referred to her husband as *tsumetai* (cold). Neglect was also part of the picture. In the 2003 interview, she claimed that she gets yogurt, a banana, and juice for breakfast, and no lunch, although if someone is there with them, he will put on a good show of serving a snack and assisting his wife to eat it. Ordinarily she gets only one cooked meal a day at dinner, and the exceptions are not that she sometimes gets more than one cooked meal, but that on the nights he goes out drinking she does not get any. She claimed that her daughter and neighbors have commented on her weight loss, and indeed she was extremely thin, in contrast to a photo she showed us from the recent past in which she was an attractive, stylish (*oshare*) woman. She interprets this neglect as largely intentional, but also related to his drinking. Since they have been married (and undoubtedly before), he frequently goes out drinking, sometimes until three in the morning. He comes home drunk and yells. Not only is he not home to assist her for long periods, but he leaves the door unlocked, which adds to her sense of insecurity. The next morning he sleeps late, and then remembers nothing. She claims that he is unable to stop drinking and used the term "alcoholism" to explain to her grandchildren that he neglects her because "It can't be helped. It's alcoholism."

Interpreting Mrs. Yamaguchi's Accusations

The concept of abuse (*gyakutai*) is quite new to Japan, but has spread rapidly in recent years. The term "elder abuse" was first used officially in a 1994 report by the Ministry of Health and Welfare. In this context, it included abuse or neglect by family members and questions concerning the property of elderly people with dementia (Sugioka 1999). An opinion poll about spousal abuse in 1995 found that 42 percent of its respondents had not experienced or heard of spousal violence, and only 34 percent had heard of it as a social problem through the mass media (Kozu 1999). Half of the respondents to a 1999 survey had heard of elder abuse, and of those, 18 percent knew a victim (Tsukada et al. 2001). Certainly, behaviors that would be classified today as abuse existed in Japan long before the term was introduced. But cultural expectations about power differentials in human relationships, the ideal of avoiding conflict, and the sense of shame if family problems became public meant that abuse and neglect were kept from the public eye. Definitions of these actions as criminal rather than as merely unethical, based on the assumption of individual rights, have come to be rapidly understood in contemporary Japanese society. The Society for the Study of Elder Treatment was founded in 1992. By 1996, this group of social welfare educators and elder care counselors had established the Japanese Center for the Prevention of Elder Abuse (Nihon Kōreisha Gyakutai Bōshi Sentā), which runs a helpline to support victims, abusers, and professionals. More recently there has been a great deal of public discourse, especially in the mass media, concerning a variety of forms of abuse, and elder abuse in particular, as policy regarding elder care has taken center stage with the development of new programs and services. More situations are seen and labeled, since increased home services provided through the Gold Plan and long-term care insurance mean that more nurses, care managers, and aides are going into people's homes (Kasuga 2004). They bring with them skills and an education that trains them to recognize, define, and attempt to resolve problems within this framework.

The first national study that attempted to determine the extent of the newly recognized categories of abuse and neglect of the elderly was conducted in 2004 by the Institute for Health Economics and Policy and funded by the Ministry of Health, Labor, and Welfare. By surveying 16,800 hospitals and home health centers nationwide, it found 1,991 cases of identified abuse, a number generally assumed to represent a fraction of actual cases. The average age of victims was 81.5 years; 76 percent of them were women. Sons of the victims were the largest group of abusers (32 percent), followed by daughters-in-law (21 percent), daughters (16 percent), husbands (12 percent) and wives (9 percent). Classifying the types of abuse revealed that psychological abuse was most common, found in nearly two-thirds of the cases. Neglect occurred in over half, and physical abuse also occurred in half of the cases in the study. The report also noted the significant finding that 54 percent of perpetrators did not recognize that what they were doing constituted abuse of the relative (Iryō Keizai Kenkyū Kikō 2004; *Daily Yomiuri* 2004). This is not surprising given the relatively recent origin of the concept in Japan.[7]

Mrs. Yamaguchi's words were serious accusations of abuse. As we left, my co-interviewer and I were thinking about her situation, and about the distinction between Mr. Yamaguchi's *soto-zura* of strong, male competence and the *uchi-zura* of a possibly abusive husband. The second interview turned our attention to the *soto-zura* and *uchi-zura* of Mrs. Yamaguchi. Had she carved the mask of an abused old woman as her self-portrayal to the world? If so, why?

When we returned for the second interview, Mr. Yamaguchi greeted us at the door and took us into the parlor as before, but this time without taking us in to greet his wife, who undoubtedly knew we had arrived. Her husband told us that Mrs. Yamaguchi's condition had recently been reassessed for the long-term care program. She had been at Level 3, but they were hoping that she would now qualify as Level 4. That change, he stated, would speed her permanent admission into a nursing home, for which there are long waiting lists. Although the previous year she had occasionally tried short stay (respite care) arrangements, she now goes regularly one week per month to a short stay placement.

In our subsequent discussion with her, Mrs. Yamaguchi expressed that she likes the short stays as a break from her current situation, but it was unclear that she really wanted to be institutionalized permanently. "They are very nice there, but it is easy to become dependent." She noted that here at home she has to do everything for herself. But she did say, in response to my question, that this year her husband is feeding her. She goes to eat in the dining room. She doesn't feel that she can complain because she thinks he is tired from all the caregiving tasks, and even his drinking is probably to relieve that stress. But she added that even physical abuse wouldn't be as bad as the verbal and mental abuse he gives her.

It is difficult to know how to interpret the first interview in light of the second. Much of the content of the second interview was repeated complaints of emotional and psychological abuse. But the reported changes seemed significant—that she gets out of bed to have meals, that she has week-long breaks from her husband's caregiving, and that she is ready to make excuses for his neglect and his drinking as due to caregiver burden. Has his behavior changed? Has her attitude changed, perhaps toward greater acceptance of her condition? Is she getting a bit senile? Or was the first interview exaggerated or even made up as an act for visiting researchers? Reviewing literature on elder abuse made me wonder whether she had not read descriptions of abuse and had already analyzed her own situation according to the professionals' criteria. What was *uchi-zura* and what was *soto-zura*?

Theories of Abuse and Mrs. Yamaguchi's Situation

Robert M. Gordon and Deborah Brill (2001, 205–213) have identified four major hypotheses that attempt to explain the causes of elder abuse. Examining the Yamaguchis' situation from each of these perspectives provides insights into their behavior and words. Yet we cannot understand the *uchi-zura* or *soto-zura* without taking into account the historical and cultural context of their lives.

The first hypothesis is that of the stressed caregiver. This approach argues that stress from caring for a dependent without adequate assistance is the cause of the abuse. "If caregiving is perceived to be stressful and burdensome, this increases the possibility that abuse will occur as a method of controlling the [older] adult" (Gordon and Brill 2001, 210). Although an enviable amount of assistance is provided to the Yamaguchis through the long-term care insurance system, Mr. Yamaguchi expressed both gratitude for those services and his sense of being overwhelmed by the caregiving role. The normative Japanese gender roles of the twentieth century contribute to his attitude. He indicated that there had initially been plans for the eldest son and his wife to live with them, but that had not worked out. Caregiving is supposed to be a woman's role, one which he does not want to take on and which creates stress for him. Mr. Yamaguchi presents a public face of being in charge, yet he is in charge of things that belong in a female realm. This leads to an ambivalent situation. In order to both give care and be masculine by his definition, he must let strangers into the home to help, which contradicts his notion of what a household is supposed to be. This adds to his stress and frustration. Moreover, ideal caregiving in Japan has incorporated the assumption that the caregiver be continuously present and available. Thus as he turns down invitations for golf outings with male friends, he has a strong sense of sacrifice. In particular, he pointed out that caregiving has meant that he cannot fully participate in the world of calligraphy which he loves, because "you can't have students coming in and out when you've got someone like this around." Whether alcoholic or not, going out drinking is not just a way to relieve stress, but a way to recover the traditional masculinity and youth that mean so much to his definition of self.

Another hypothesis found in the gerontology literature is the learned violence hypothesis. This violence may be due to a history of spousal violence where spouses have grown old together, or may be "revenge violence" that comes because of the role reversal of dependency. Mrs. Yamaguchi did not claim that abuse had been part of their entire marriage, and denied that physical violence was part of her current situation. However, suggestions of a history of the emotional abuse she describes did come out in the interviews. Mrs. Yamaguchi expressed that her husband assumed that she was continuously available to respond to his wishes, and told a story about his bringing home his drinking buddies at 4 AM without warning, expecting her to get out of bed, get dressed, and feed them. Their narratives describe a highly gendered division of labor which Mr. Yamaguchi considered part of his "old-fashioned" upbringing. They seemed to agree that behavior such as excessive drinking and lack of consideration for others was to be expected of men, and that women were assumed to have to put up with it. The relationship through the course of their marriage described in their stories is one of the intersection of social roles rather than of intimacy between two people, and they suggest that such a relationship was typical and expected in the time and place of their lives. Indeed, other couples in the interview sample appeared to have similar spousal relationships, which were not defined by them as abuse. Such accusations would seem to have to come from a different time or place, perhaps twenty-first-century gender role expectations or notions of abuse from abroad introduced to the Japanese public by the media.

The psychopathology hypothesis is a third explanation for abusive behavior. It claims that illness or alcohol or drug dependency on the part of the caregiver leads to a decreased ability to tolerate frustration and to control his or her own behavior—the idea of the "impaired abuser." Mrs. Yamaguchi perceives alcohol to be a major factor in her husband's behavior. His going out drinking leaves her alone with an increased sense of vulnerability, although his return is also dreaded, as it is accompanied by verbal abuse. In the context of contemporary Japan, this could perhaps be considered not psychopathology so much as gendered culturopathology. Much has been written in a positive vein of group drinking behavior among Japanese men in the literature on Japanese society. Going out together for ritualized drinking of large amounts of alcohol is thought to contribute to improved communication among male co-workers in a hierarchically structured workplace. It helps to develop and maintain a sense of group solidarity, and it serves a stress release function in a high-pressure, competitive society (Allison 1994, 145–167; Linhart 1986; Nakane 1970, 124–126; Vogel 1963, 104). Stephen R. Smith, an anthropologist who has studied drinking and alcoholism in Japan, notes that alcohol is "positively valued" and that generally "[people] see drunkenness as benign and show immense tolerance for the shenanigans of drinkers. A cliché that acknowledges cultural indulgence holds that Japan is a paradise for children, foreigners, and drunks" (1998, 287).

In our interviews, however, we heard many stories like the Yamaguchis' of the negative effects of such cultural patterns on late life. The development of masculine identity and male relationships through alcohol consumption seems to occur at the expense of the development of relationships of companionship with wives and other women. Sometimes when men begin to spend much more time at home after retirement, they are, in a sense, strangers in their own home. The definition of drinking-based relationships as positive and masculine has meant a lack of personal relationships from which personal caring in late life might be derived. Cultural patterns of alcohol consumption thus help to create *soto-zura* rather than build relationships.

The fourth approach to elder abuse relies on a dependency hypothesis. It suggests that mental and physical incapacity lead to vulnerability and thus dependence upon a caregiver. However, the caregiver also becomes dependent on his or her caregiving behavior for rewards, sometimes including financial support from the victim, and power. The issues of dependency and reciprocity characterize Mr. and Mrs. Yamaguchi's relationship, but of course in Japanese culture, the meanings and patterns of behavior involved reflect some culturally specific ideas about these human relationships.

Discussions of psychological dependency are common in the Japanese studies literature owing to the contributions of the well-known psychoanalyst Takeo Doi (1973). Doi claims that in contrast to the emphasis in Western societies on psychological independence and individualism, the Japanese seek relationships of dependency on others, with the mother-infant relationship serving as the prototype. Doi's interest is in the psychopathology of those who cannot overcome attempting to rediscover such a dependency in their adult relationships and are thus unable to function with the necessary psychological independence. Nonetheless, even for "normal" Japanese, relationships of uneven dependency are accepted and valued. Thus it is not considered unusual or pathological when an adult relationship is not mutual, but rather one party takes on a dependent role while the other takes a position of being depended upon. In many marriages, the wife assumes the role of substitute mother in being depended upon emotionally. However, this does not lead to a position of power in the relationship, since the dependency takes place within a nonegalitarian power structure and the wife's reliance on the husband's income.

The descriptions of their relationship by Mr. and Mrs. Yamaguchi imply the husband's *soto-zura* had been characterized by the sort of dependent machismo described for many mid-twentieth-century Japanese marriages (Salamon 1975). Mrs. Yamaguchi's vulnerability in her role as wife has increased because of her physical disability. Perhaps this is why there are no beatings, since there is no need for such behavior to control her. Yet in terms of dependency, there has been a dramatic role reversal with retirement and aging, and especially with Mrs. Yamaguchi's illness. She had depended on her husband for income; he now freely uses her pension as he wishes, according to Mrs. Yamaguchi. On the other hand, he depended on her for maintaining a secure and smoothly functioning home environment and for meeting all of his needs, things that he is now expected to provide for her. It is possible that his verbal abuse stems from his frustration with his current situation, while his continued desire for emotional dependence keeps him from abusing her physically (Takahashi, personal communication).

Part of the underlying basis for Mrs. Yamaguchi's assessment of her situation is her disappointment that her husband cannot and/or will not adjust to this change graciously. She expressed a strong sense of sacrifice. She had done her best and worked very hard to support him in his work over the years. For example, when there was a large fire in the city and firemen came from many districts to help, she made *onigiri* (rice balls) for all of them, over a hundred. She had played the supportive wife role diligently, providing her a sense of later entitlement (Borovoy 2005, xi). She expected reciprocity (*mikaeri*) when she became bedridden. But neither this attitude nor this behavior was forthcoming.[8]

Mrs. Yamaguchi's response to the lack of reciprocity seems emblematic of her perception of vulnerability and dependency. In numerous contexts in both interviews she spoke of how she asks as little as possible. She "lays low" for fear of upsetting her husband and inviting backlash from him such that he would do even less for her. They apparently talk very little, but every night before she goes to sleep, she says, "Thank you. Good night." There is nothing to do, from her perspective, but to bear with it (*gaman*). There's nothing that can be done about it (*shikata ga nai*), she said, over and over. Is this more sacrifice, or fear, or the *soto-zura* again?

As I have written in the past, I am not sure that *shikata ga nai* means that the person has given up (Long 1999). Her comments about her husband suggest that she wishes she could be more dependent, but she also spoke of her concern that institutional care makes it too easy to become dependent. There seemed almost a touch of pride in how she manages. Indeed, she has developed a social and psychological support network beginning with her daughter and grandchildren, but expanded to include home helpers who go beyond the requirements of their job by bringing her snacks and even stopping to pick up a new blouse for her at the market. Perhaps the care manager has intervened with arrangements for the short stays at nursing homes with awareness of Mrs. Yamaguchi's situation. What Wolf (1972) refers to as a "uterine family," a mother-children circle within the patrilineal household, probably began much earlier in her marriage, perhaps functioning in opposition to the husband/father. The tension is high. Mrs. Yamaguchi was clearly recruiting us, the interviewers, for her side of the perceived battle, prepared with a bedside table of supportive evidence such as newspapers, crossword puzzles, and family photographs. Mrs. Yamaguchi manages to obtain some degree of physical comfort from the touch of grandchildren and from the manipulations of the massage therapist who comes four times a week. She has not given up on life or on people, and her capacity for dramatically presenting her narrative to visiting researchers demonstrates that commitment.

Conclusion

On the surface, Mr. Yamaguchi has adjusted to his new role. He manages his wife's care and does some direct care, much more than he would have expected of himself given his age and gender. He relies for assistance on paid service providers to which his wife is entitled through the long-term care and medical insurance systems. He represents a new model of family caregiving, in which spouses care for each other in their old age rather than relying on children and daughters-in-law as in times past. Yet just below the surface are the husband's and wife's narratives of tension, dependency, and sense of sacrifice. Both wife and husband presented *soto-zura* masks, that of the abused victim and that of the caring and competent household manager. Yet even a brief look behind the masks reveals a backstage arena of self, a woman and a man who thought they were fulfilling expected social roles through the years, only to find in old age that these resulted in tension and a lack of ways to resolve it without an interpersonal history of working things out together. When they could no longer perform expected gender roles, dependency relationships were also reversed. Both had a strong sense of sacrifice for actions in the past and the present, and a sense of loss as those dependencies turned their world on its head. These provide us with hints of the *uchi-zura* behind the public faces.

The circumstances of Mr. and Mrs. Yamaguchi and the other nontraditional caregiving situations we have seen in our research are in part the result of policies designed to transition family caregiving into the uncharted terrain of twenty-first-century demographic and social realities. Home helper services that bring strangers into the home and cooking classes for elderly men challenge long-held assumptions and attempt to change behaviors to fit the new circumstances. They address the masks of gendered social roles, but do not question the additional adjustments required in getting the altered *soto-zura* to fit the inner selves sculpted by a lifetime of experiences in Japanese society. Today, elderly people are economically and politically viewed as consumers of societal resources; they are seen only by their public performance. To borrow Hendry's metaphor, the complexity of selfhood is often socially invisible as the inner experience of aging is wrapped in an outward-facing surface (Hendry 1993). Thus stories such as that of the Yamaguchis are a reminder of the need to keep both in mind to understand the meaning of aging and the nature of the aging society.

Notes

I am grateful to have had the opportunity to present a preliminary version of this chapter at the conference "Faces and Masks of Aging: Implications from the Lives of Japanese Elderly," at Stanford University, May 20–22, 2005. In writing this chapter, I am grateful for the efforts of Suda Yūko, Takahashi Ryūtarō, Nishimura Chie, and Ruth Campbell. I especially appreciate the skills and knowledge of my co-interviewers with the Yamaguchis, Muraoka Kōko and Yamada Yoshiko. Errors of interpretation are my own.

1. In subsequent conversations with this woman it became evident that the continual "togetherness" is not truly her idea of "fun," but rather an obligation based on her role as caregiver.

2. Many nursing homes maintain long waiting lists for admission. In the early years of the long-term care insurance system, this demand surprised policy makers and practitioners, who had expected that the stigma of institutionalization would encourage the choice of in-home services.

3. The project is entitled "Care for the Elderly since the Enactment of Public Long-Term Care Insurance in Japan." It received funding from the Japanese Ministry of Education, Culture, Sports, Science, and Technology and the Ministry of Health, Labor, and Welfare. The project leaders were Suda Yūko, a social gerontologist at Tōyō University, and Takahashi Ryūtarō, a geriatrician at the Tokyo Metropolitan Institute of Gerontology. Other researchers involved in the interviewing portion of the project came from fields such as sociology, nursing, and social work: Asakawa Noriko, Asano Yuko, Ruth Campbell, Izumo Yuji, Kodama Hiroko, Muraoka Kōko, Nishimura Chie, Nishida Masumi, and Yamada Yoshiko.

The study was designed as a ten-year longitudinal project with both quantitative and qualitative components. The first stage was a large-scale survey of family care-givers and care recipients, approximately 1,500 pairs (total), in a largely working class ward of Tokyo and in a small city and surrounding area in Akita. Several months after the survey, my colleagues and I conducted semistructured interviews with a subset of respondents, 29 care recipient–family caregiver pairs in both locations from whom we obtained informed consent for the interviews. They were selected to include both men and women as care recipients, and a range of insurance system care levels and relationships to the primary family caregiver (see Table 3.2).

In both locations, the majority of care recipients were female. Their age ranged from 65 to 92 years old, with an average age of 81. Their problems ranged from light to severe. We conducted a second round of interviews in the summer of 2004 and will continue to follow these families as long as they are willing and able to be interviewed. The Yamaguchis could not be interviewed in 2005 because of the temporary hospital-ization of Mr. Yamaguchi and subsequent placement of Mrs. Yamaguchi in respite care.

This chapter also draws on interviews about aging and elder care in the Kansai area in the 1990s with Phyllis Braudy Harris and Fujii Miwa, and from ethnographic work on end-of-life decisions in 1996 during an Abe fellowship.

4. The family name Yamaguchi is a pseudonym.

5. Because Mr. Yamaguchi is hard of hearing and because he turned on the televi-sion in the other room during our discussion with his wife, we do not believe that he heard what his wife said to us.

6. These are: physical abuse, psychological abuse, financial abuse, and neglect (Wolf 1996, 129; Brownell and Abelman 1999, 314).

7. A new law, "The Prevention of Elderly Abuse and Support for Caregivers," was put into effect in April 2006 and applies to both institutional and home caregiving situations. According to the law, suspected cases of elder abuse or neglect must be reported to local authorities, who are required to investigate each case. The law also requires local jurisdictions to improve their care of the elderly to ease the burden on family caregivers by providing respite care facilities (Osako 2006; Joyce 2005).

8. Van der Geest (2002) reflects on the importance of reciprocity in the experi-ence of aging among a formerly matrilineal population in rural Ghana. He found that respect must be reciprocal; it must be earned through caring for others earlier in one's life. The kind of respect and care given to elderly people was not a matter of status, but depended on the "silent book keeping" of give-and-take that characterized the social life of the community. Gender is not irrelevant in this calculus, since women are more likely than men to care for their children and others in their younger years. Japa-nese expectations for reciprocity are strong as well, though historically strong gender stratification might in some families counter the sense of obligation that a husband return his wife's nurturance.

References

Allison, Anne. 1994. *Nightwork: Sexuality, pleasure, and corporate masculinity in a Tokyo hostess club.* Chicago: University of Chicago Press.

Ariyoshi, Sawako. 1984. *The twilight years.* Trans. Mildred Tahara. New York: Kodansha International.

Bachnik, Jane. 1994. *Uchi/Soto:* Challenging our conceptualizations of self, social order, and language. In *Situated meaning: Inside and outside in Japanese self, society, and language,* ed. Jane M. Bachnik and Charles J. Quinn, Jr., 3–37. Princeton, NJ: Princeton University Press.

Borovoy, Amy. 2005. *The too-good wife: Alcohol, codependency, and the politics of nurturance in postwar Japan.* Berkeley: University of California Press.

Bourdieu, Pierre. 1977. *Outline of a theory of practice.* Trans. Richard Nice. Cambridge, UK: Cambridge University Press.

Brownell, Patricia, and Irvin Abelman. 1999. Elder abuse: Protective and empowerment strategies for crisis intervention. In *Battered women and their families: Intervention strategies and treatment programs,* 2nd ed., ed. Albert R. Roberts, 314–344. New York: Springer.

Caudill, William, and Helen Weinstein. 1969. Maternal care and infant behavior in Japan and America. *Psychiatry* 32: 12–43.

Craighill-Saiki, Shigeko. 1997. The children's sentinels: Mothers and their relationship with health professionals in the context of Japanese health care. *Social Science and Medicine* 44 (3): 291–300.

Daily Yomiuri. 2004. Poll: Sons responsible for 32% of abuse of old, April 19.

Doi, Takeo. 1973. *The anatomy of dependence.* Tokyo: Kodansha.

Goffman, Erving. 1959. *The presentation of self in everyday life.* Garden City, NY: Doubleday.

Gordon, Robert M., and Deborah Brill. 2001. The abuse and neglect of the elderly. In *Aging: Caring for our elders,* ed. David N. Weisstub, David C. Thomasma, Serge Gauthier, and George F. Tomossy, 203–218. Dordrecht: Kluwer Academic Publishers.

Hendry, Joy. 1993. Wrapping culture: Politeness, presentation, and power in Japan and other societies. Oxford: Clarendon Press.

Iryō Keizai Kenkyū Kikō (Institute for Health Economics and Policy). 2004. Kateinai ni okeru kōreisha gyakutai ni kansuru chōsa gaiyō (Summary of results of the survey on elder abuse in the home). *Gekkan Fukushi* (August): 48–51.

Jenike, Brenda Robb. 2003. Parent care and shifting family obligations in urban Japan. In *Demographic change and the family in Japan's aging society,* ed. John W. Traphagan and John Knight, 177–202. Albany: State University of New York Press.

Joyce, Colin. 2005. Japan moves to protect the elderly. *Daily Telegraph* (November 2): 18.

Kasuga, Kisuyo. 2004. Changing family structure and elder abuse issues in Japan. *Geriatrics and Gerontology International* 4: S226–S228.

Kōsei Rōdō Shō (Ministry of Health, Labor, and Welfare). 2006. *Summary of vital statistics.* www.mhlw.go.jp/english/database/db-hw/populate/pop4.html (accessed December 28, 2009).

——. 2009. *Kōsei tōkei yōran* (Health and welfare statistics). www.mhlw.go.jp/toukei /youran/indexyk_1_1.html (accessed December 28, 2009).

Kozu, Junko. 1999. Domestic violence in Japan. *American Psychologist* 54 (1): 50–54.

Lebra, Takie S. 1984. *Japanese women: Constraint and fulfillment.* Honolulu: University of Hawaii Press.

——. 1992. Self in Japanese culture. In *Japanese sense of self,* ed. Nancy Rosenberger, 105–120. Cambridge, UK: Cambridge University Press.

Linhart, Sepp. 1986. *Sakariba*: Zone of "evaporation" between work and home? In *Interpreting Japanese society: Anthropological approaches,* ed. Joy Hendry and Jonathan Webber, 231–242. Oxford: JASO.

Long, Susan Orpett. 1997. *Risōteki na kaigo to wa? Amerika kara mita Nihon no rinen to genjitsu* (What is ideal caregiving? Japanese ideals and reality from an American's perspective). *Hosupisu to Zaitaku Kea* 5 (1): 37–43.

——. 1999. *Shikata ga nai*: Resignation, control, and self-identity. In *Lives in motion: Composing circles of self and community in Japan,* ed. Susan Orpett Long, 11–26. Ithaca, NY: East Asian Program, Cornell University.

Naikakufu (Cabinet Office), ed. 2004. *Kōrei shakai hakusho* (White Paper on the aging society). Tokyo: Gyōsei.

Nakane, Chie. 1970. *Japanese society.* Berkeley: University of California Press.

National Institute of Population and Social Security Research. 2008. *Population by age.* www.ipss.go.jp/index-e.html (accessed December 28, 2009).

Nihon Kōreisha Gyakutai Bōshi Sentā (Japanese Center for the Prevention of Elder Abuse). n.d. www.jcpea.net.

Osako, Masako. 2006. The Japanese Diet has passed a new law, "The Prevention of Elderly Abuse and Support for Caregivers." International Longevity Center Japan. www .ilcjapan.org/English%20ver./CTAJ/CTAJ06-1.html.

Plath, David. 1980. *Long engagements: Maturity in modern Japan.* Stanford, CA: Stanford University Press.

Rosenberger, Nancy. 2001. *Gambling with virtue.* Honolulu: University of Hawaii Press.

Salamon, Sonya. 1975. "Male chauvinism" as a manifestation of love in marriage. In *Adult episodes in Japan,* ed. David W. Plath, 20–31. Leiden: E. J. Brill.

Smith, Stephen R. 1998. Good old boy into alcoholic: *Danshūkai* and learning a new drinking role in Japan. In *Learning in likely places: Varieties of apprenticeship in Japan,* ed. John Singleton, 286–303. Cambridge, UK: Cambridge University Press.

Statistics Bureau. 2009a. *Percentage of persons engaged in work by sex and age group / 2002, 2007.* Ministry of Internal Affairs and Communication. www.stat.go.jp/english/data /shugyou/pdf/sum2007.pdf (accessed December 28, 2009).

————. 2009b. *Population of 15 years old or more by labour force status, employed person by industry, and unemployed person.* Ministry of Internal Affairs and Communication. www.stat.go.jp/english/data/roudou/nen/sokuhou/ft/zuhyou/e054bh01.xls (accessed December 28, 2009).

Sugioka, Naoto. 1999. Current issues of elder abuse in Japan. *Education and Ageing* 14 (1): 61–73.

Traphagan, John. 2003. Contesting coresidence: Women, in-laws, and health care in rural Japan. In *Demographic change and the family in Japan's aging society*, ed. John W. Traphagan and John Knight, 203–228. Albany: State University of New York Press.

Tsukada, Noriko, Yasuhiko Saito, and Toshio Tatara. 2001. Japanese older people's perceptions of "elder abuse." *Journal of Elder Abuse and Neglect* 13 (1): 71–89.

Van der Geest, Sjaak. 2002. Respect and reciprocity: Care of elderly people in rural Ghana. *Journal of Cross-Cultural Gerontology* 17: 3–31.

Vogel, Ezra. 1963. *Japan's new middle class.* 2nd ed. Berkeley: University of California Press.

Wolf, Margery. 1972. *Women and the family in rural Taiwan.* Stanford, CA: Stanford University Press.

Wolf, Rosalie S. 1996. Understanding elder abuse and neglect. *Aging* 367: 4–13.

Wu, Yongmei. 2004. *The care of the elderly in Japan.* London: Routledge Curzon.

4 Generations Apart

Burdens, Bad Families, and Elder Suicide in Rural Japan

John W. Traphagan

Elderly who are living alone do not commit suicide all that often, but those who are living with children and grandchildren often commit suicide.

Satoh Keiko

ON A HOT JULY DAY, Mrs. Nakamura was outside stomping around her garden to try to scare away the snakes before she started weeding when she heard an ambulance. She didn't think much about this until a neighbor came by later in the afternoon to discuss what had happened. At lunchtime, Mrs. Sakamoto had come home from work to make lunch for her mother-in-law, as was her daily custom. When she arrived, her mother-in-law was nowhere in the house. After looking around the garden, Mrs. Sakamoto entered the barn, where she found her mother-in-law hanging from the rafters. This suicide shocked people in the neighborhood and led to a variety of explanations as to what had happened.

One explanation was based upon Mrs. Sakamoto's (senior) physical condition. She had been diagnosed with anemia earlier in the year and had lost interest in participating in community activities she had enjoyed prior to the diagnosis, such as weeding around the local temple.

"I heard this directly from her," said Mr. Nakamura, "that she was having physical problems. This was probably the reason that she did it."

"Well," said Mrs. Nakamura, "she wasn't able to do much work around the house and needed a lot of rest. . . . She wasn't energetic (*genki*) and seemed like she wanted to rest all of the time."

Mr. Nakamura thought the reason she had killed herself was related to a desire not to become a burden on her family should her physical and mental conditions continue to decline (Traphagan 2000, 2). But Mrs. Nakamura suggested that there may have been another reason, as well.

"Mrs. Sakamoto's son was deeply in debt," said Mrs. Nakamura. "He played pachinko all of the time and did other types of gambling. There were a lot of problems with the family. Maybe she killed herself to send him a message to get his life, and family, straightened out."[1]

Although the actual reason for Mrs. Sakamoto's suicide will never be known beyond the confines of her family (there were rumors of a suicide note), the interpretations of her suicide among those who knew her revolve around a single issue: family. In the interpretations given above, Mrs. Sakamoto's suicide is understood as a consequence of either: (1) a bad family, or (2) a desire to avoid burdening her family with care. The emphasis on family is a common theme when exploring the manner in which Japanese interpret the suicides of elders. On the one hand, elders may end their lives as a result of the loneliness associated with living apart from family members, or more often, the loneliness associated with living in close proximity to family members. In some cases, suicide may represent a form of sanction against younger family members, as in the phenomenon noted by Wolf involving women living in Taiwan in the mid-twentieth century (1972; 1975). The actual or assumed threat of suicide can become a strategy or weapon that elders use to manipulate their children (Ikels 2004b, 7; Wolf 1972, 159–160). For Japanese, self-aggression, even going as far as self-destruction, can be interpreted as a "sign of resentment against a source of frustration" in interpersonal conflicts (Lebra 1984, 48). Self-destruction is one possible strategy for a person attempting to cope with a wide range of conflicts, particularly where direct confrontation is not valued in interpersonal relationships. In this chapter, I will explore interpretations of elder suicide given by rural Japanese. In each case, perceptions about the causes of elder suicide revolve around the issue of family, even while the specifics of these interpretations can vary significantly.

As of the early twenty-first century, Japan has become a society with one of the higher suicide rates in the industrial world and ranks particularly high in elder suicide rates in rural areas (Pritchard and Baldwin 2002). Although for most of the second half of the twentieth century the suicide rate in Japan declined, and in the early 1990s the rate for Japan was similar to rates found in some European countries (Takahashi 1997, 137), there is cause for concern over recent suicide trends in Japan, because rates started rising in the 1990s.[2] And as Ozawa-de Silva (2008) has shown, disturbing trends, such as Internet suicide pacts among young Japanese, are closely related to issues of suffering, ideas about the afterlife, personal identity, and one's relationship to others.

For the year 2000, the suicide rate in Japan stood at 24.1 per 100,000 in the population, with a total of 30,251 deaths attributed to suicide.[3] By comparison, the United States had less than half the suicide rate of Japan at 10.7 per 100,000, with a total of 29,350 deaths attributed to suicide.[4] Elder suicide in rural Japan, where the proportion of elderly in the population is generally higher than in cities, has come to be interpreted as a particularly serious social problem. In 2000, according to Ministry of Health, Labor, and Welfare statistics, the national suicide rate for people over 90 was 47.8 per 100,000. For those between 85 and 89, the rate was 47.1, and for those between 80 and 84, it was 40.7. By contrast, the rate for people in their twenties and thirties was approximately 20 per 100,000 for the same year (Nakata 2002). Satomi Kurosu notes that sociological studies of suicide among the elderly outside Japan have repeatedly shown that urban, industrialized areas in which there has been some degree of breakdown in social integration, which can largely be understood in terms of changes in living arrangements and family connections, generally have higher elder suicide rates than rural areas (Kurosu 1991, 604). Japan is one of the few industrialized contexts (others are Greece and California) in which suicide rates tend to be lower in urban areas; this is particularly problematic in relation to males in Japan, as rural residence has been shown to be "the major factor in age-adjusted male suicide mortality" (Otsu et al. 2004, 1138; Matsumoto 1995).[5]

In Iwate Prefecture (where research for this chapter was conducted), suicide data show that the prevalence of suicide increases consistently from age 70 (Traphagan 2004b; 2005). Furthermore, Iwate and Akita prefectures both had considerably higher than national rates for the year 2000 and are higher than urban areas such as Tokyo and Miyagi Prefecture, the latter being the location of the regional urban center of Sendai, which has a population of about 1 million people. In Akita, 457 people committed suicide in 2000, representing 3.80 percent of the total deaths; in Iwate there were 454 suicides at 3.63 percent. By contrast, in large urban areas the proportion of deaths attributed to suicide was generally lower. In Tokyo, 3.32 percent of deaths were attributed to suicide, compared to 3.16 percent in Miyagi Prefecture, and only 2.68 percent in Fukushima.[6] It is important to avoid drawing too broad a conclusion from these numbers—some largely rural prefectures, such as Yamagata, also located in the Tōhoku region (where Iwate and Akita are located), show lower proportions. It is clear, however, that there is a general tendency for suicide rates to be higher in rural areas, particularly among the elderly.[7]

Not only are there higher rates of suicide among rural elders, but research by Otsu et al. shows that there was an increasingly strong correlation between the number of persons per household and suicide mortality between 1980 and 1990 (Otsu et al. 2004, 1141), suggesting that co-residence may be a contributing factor to elder suicide.[8]

When Is Suicide Suicide?

The general tendency in literature that deals with suicide in Japan, particularly since the publication of Ruth Benedict's *The Chrysanthemum and the Sword* (Benedict 1946), has been to emphasize cultural explanations for Japan's apparently high suicide rates and to argue that Japan is a country that permits suicidal behavior to some extent (Takahashi 1997, 138). Several scholars, including some Japanese, have argued for the particular proneness of Japanese toward suicide on cultural grounds, indicating, for example, that when faced with difficulties "Japanese people . . . are generally susceptible to a suicidal wish" (Iga 1986, 149). These types of assumptions are based upon stereotypes of Japanese culture and normally ignore the fact that it is not unusual for suicidal Japanese to show many of the same "risk factors" for suicide as people in other countries, "including psychiatric disorders, prior suicide attempts, lack of social support systems, male preponderance, older age, various kinds of loss, [and] family history of suicide" (Takahashi 1997, 138).

Defining "suicide" is difficult, particularly when cross-cultural attitudes and behaviors are taken into account. In social science literature on suicide, it is surprising how little attention is given to the manner in which self-killing is conceptualized in different cultures, even when there is a tendency to explain suicide on cultural grounds. Durkheim (1951) noted the complexities of defining suicide in terms of intention, as is often the case in Western philosophical literature, because this forces us to identify acts of self-sacrifice as suicides (Jones 1986, 82). For Durkheim, the emphasis was not on intentionality, but on whether or not the person knows that a specific action will result in his or her death: "The term *suicide is applied to all cases of death resulting directly or indirectly from a positive or negative act of the victim himself, which he knows will produce this result*" (Durkheim 1951, 44; italics in original). Durkheim is careful to distinguish voluntary from involuntary acts of self-killing, noting that this classification is inappropriate for the death of a person who, through hallucination, kills himself by, for example, throwing himself in front of a train while thinking that he is walking through a doorway (43). However, Durkheim also removes intent from his definition of suicide, arguing that it is too subjective and too difficult to observe in others to be useful analytically. Indeed, as Durkheim notes, a person is not necessarily entirely aware of the precise intent of any action, suicidal or otherwise (43).

Durkheim goes on to specify different forms of suicide, including "egoistic suicide" (which is tied to social integration and concepts of individualism and community), "altruistic suicide" (self-killing as a result of duty or a response to beliefs about the moral or virtuous), and "anomic suicide" (suicide that is associated with times of social crises and a failure of institutions to regulate social conditions). Durkheim's interests are directed toward the relationship of suicide to social structure; thus his definition and subsets of suicide are based upon notions of the relationship of the individual to society. There is relatively little attention given to the role of culture in defining what constitutes "suicide"; indeed, Durkheim is focused upon the analytical usage of the term rather than the cultural.

Here, my interest lies in the cultural. In Western biomedicine, for example, suicide, though often not defined with the precision provided by Durkheim, is typically viewed as a disease, requiring treatment; in some cases suicide is equated with self-destructive, aggressive, or even criminal behavior (Lester 2001, 7). Although biomedical definitions are influential beyond the medical world, it takes little effort to see that no definitions of suicide, be it Durkheim's biomedical, sociological, or otherwise, are applied uniformly throughout even Western society. For example, during the Vietnam War, U.S. Army Private Milton Olive III was awarded the Congressional Medal of Honor:

> For conspicuous gallantry and intrepidity at the risk of his life above and beyond the call of duty . . . [when he] saved the lives of his fellow soldiers at the sacrifice of his by grabbing [a live grenade that had been thrown into the midst of his company] in his hands and falling on it to absorb the blast with his body.[9]

If we contemplate Private Olive's action, it is obvious that he killed himself. Although from an analytical perspective we might define his action using Durkheim's notion of altruistic suicide, it is unlikely that the term "suicide" would be employed in a more general attempt to situate his behavior, perhaps in part because of the tendency in contemporary American society to associate suicidal behavior with mental disease. Rather than suicide, it is likely that Private Olive's action would be seen as an act of gallantry and sacrifice; indeed, he was posthumously honored with the highest recognition given to an American soldier. In general, it is reasonable to argue that in the United States we identify intention as being at the root of whether or not an act of self-killing is suicide. Private Olive did not commit suicide because he did not intend to kill himself; he intended to save the lives of others and his own death was a predictable, but unfortunate and undesired, byproduct of his action.

The appeal to intent draws upon a set of cultural presuppositions that emphasize autonomy and independence in decision making, assumptions that have routinely been viewed as universal by philosophers and others working from the Euro-American philosophical traditions.[10] Following this line of thought, for example, *seppuku* or *harakiri* (ritualized self-disembowelment that was practiced among the upper classes in premodern Japan) is regarded as suicide because the individual willfully killed himself. From a Durkheimian perspective, we might choose to classify the act as altruistic suicide because there was an element of duty associated with the act, but in either case, we would be associating this particular form of self-killing with suicide. The problem with this approach, of course, is that it ignores local conceptualizations of autonomy, independence, and the relative importance of these ideas in a particular cultural setting.[11] It also ignores local categorizations of death and self-killing that structure the ways people in that setting conceptualize a particular act. Indeed, precisely because there are different sets of assumptions about the nature of self-killing, direct translation of acts of self-killing as "suicide" from Japanese into English is problematic.

As I have noted elsewhere, Japanese identify various forms of self-killing using different terms (Traphagan 2005). The generic term for suicide is *jisatsu.* However, this term is not necessarily used for actions that are translated as suicide in English. For example, Japanese differentiate family suicide or *ikkashinjū* from *jisatsu* as do they a double suicide or love suicide, a theme frequently occurring in literature, which can be either *shinjū* or *jōshi*, neither of which employ the characters used in the term *jisatsu*.[12] Moreover, although the term *jisatsu* is used to represent the act of self-killing in some contexts, it does not necessarily imply actual success.[13] In one case, a Buddhist priest explained to me that one of his parishioners had attempted to hang herself, stating that "she did *suicide*," but that because she was found quickly she did not die (*jisatsu shita kedo, hay-aku mitsukatta kara nakunarimasen deshita*). Conceptually, this suggests that the term *jisatsu* does not necessarily imply death, but instead refers to a specific autonomous act that is intended to result in death, although I think the implication in most cases is that the person succeeded in killing him or herself.

In Western stereotyping of Japanese behavior, forms of self-killing that have been routinely imagined as "suicide" are the above-mentioned *harakiri* or *seppuku* and the acts of *tokkōtai* or the *kamikaze* pilots and torpedo bombers that Japan employed during World War II. As Takie Lebra notes, *harakiri* or *seppuku* refers to a form of ritual self-killing that was a "privilege reserved for the samurai class that saved the offender from the disgrace of being put to death by an executioner" (Lebra 1976, 190–191). Perhaps one of the most noted examples of *seppuku* comes in the based-on-fact story *Chūshingura* or the *Treasury of Loyal Retainers* (Keene 1997). In this case, the samurai Enya is ordered to commit *seppuku* as a result of a breach of acceptable behavior when he makes an attempt on the insufferable and insulting samurai Moronō's life. The order to commit *seppuku* in this instance is not an order to commit suicide, but is an offer of an honorable way to die as opposed to being executed. In short, *seppuku* is not suicide in any sense that resonates with Japanese concepts of suicide because it is not *jisatsu*, and thus the terming of the act as ritual suicide is incorrect.

Lebra argues that "institutionalized suicide"—I would prefer to term this institutionalized self-killing—reached a high point during World War II, when troops committed mass self-killing known as *gyokusai*, which refers to dying without surrendering by a group (Lebra 1976, 191). The term literally means "a beautiful collapse" or "destruction or end of life." An example of this would be the explosion of fireworks, which is at once destructive and beautiful, and there is a strong sense that this sort of death is both beautiful and honorable.

While one can debate the meanings of particular terms, it is important to point out that when asked if these practices (*harakiri*, the *kamikaze*, etc.) represent *jisatsu*, my informants without hesitation indicated that they do not. Instead, they represented honorable forms of death; in the case of the *tokkōtai*, there was a sense that these individuals had sacrificed themselves for their country, rather than having committed suicide. Emiko Ohnuki-Tierney's detailed discussion of the *tokkōtai* offers a good example of the complexities in understanding the motivations behind the attacks. She notes that, because of the atmosphere of the military at the time, it is difficult to consider the actions of these officers as voluntary—it was rare that they actually volunteered without hesitation or misgivings, and in some cases they were "volunteered" for the assignments. However, they did go off to die, often motivated less by a desire to kill themselves for the emperor than because "they could not bear seeing their comrades and friends offering their lives while protecting their own" (Ohnuki-Tierney 2002, 169). Others gave their lives in order to protect loved ones, such as wives or mothers, from the barbarians (Americans) who would arrive if Japan lost the war. What is clear from Ohnuki-Tierney's study is that there was a widespread sense of sacrifice among the *tokkōtai* and among those who witnessed their actions; the idea that they were committing suicide for the emperor was not a significant interpretation of their behavior.

Indeed, when I asked one couple about how they would interpret the act of the novelist Yukio Mishima, who killed himself via *seppuku* in 1970 in protest of what he perceived to be a decline in Japanese culture, they were uncertain about how to interpret this. The husband indicated that on the one hand Mishima probably viewed his demise as an honorable death, and thus not a suicide in the sense that *jisatsu* represents self-killing. However, they were uncertain as to whether or not it should actually be interpreted in this way by others, because it was unclear where the honor actually lies in Mishima's action. The salient points here are that *jisatsu* is generally not a form of self-killing that involves honor or bravery, and practices often viewed as suicide in the West, such as *seppuku*, are not necessarily defined that way from the perspective of the Japanese. Nonetheless, it is necessary to keep in mind that the term *jisatsu* itself can be modified to carry nuanced meanings that cannot necessarily be viewed as entirely negative; the term *inseki jisatsu*,[14] for example, refers to an individual who kills himself in order to take responsibility for an action by either himself or another (Takahashi 1997, 143; see also Fuse 1984). In discussing this form of self-killing, however, several of my informants displayed very mixed feelings, arguing that it represents an escape from a difficult situation and thus is an act of cowardice.

When discussing *jisatsu*, most informants indicated that it is associated with a range of negative concepts such as embarrassment or cowardice. If one kills oneself as a way of taking responsibility for the action of another, or out of loyalty or bravery, then it is not *jisatsu*. One man, in his sixties, whom I asked to discuss the meaning of *jisatsu* as opposed to *harakiri*, gave the following description:

> It is something I need to think about, but basically they seem different to me. There is a difference in relation to the motive (*dōki*) or purpose (*mokuteki*) of the act. I think it is really different. It is related to one's life (*inochi*) and one's

own way of thinking. In the sense of one's life they are the same, but there is a difference in relation to the motive behind it.

Adding further nuance to the distinction, this informant discussed the idea of *sekinin jisatsu* or "responsibility suicide," in which an individual kills him or herself as a means of taking responsibility for an action that is deemed improper or wrong (an example would be *inseki jisatsu* discussed above).

A Buddhist priest with whom I spoke responded to a question I asked in which I suggested that there is a conceptual linkage between *pokkuridera* (temples where people pray for a sudden death) and elder suicide in that both are predicated on a wish to die. To this he disagreed:

> In Japan, the desire for a sudden death is related to not wanting to be a burden on others. In the case of Japan, suicide creates a burden for others. For example, there was a person who hanged himself; the typical *sōshiki kuyō* [funeral ceremony] is done but after the place [temple] has to be purified by the priest with *oharai* [purification wand]. This adds to the burden on the living.

I add this comment because it helps us understand the distinctions that may be made in people's minds when it comes to suicide and other forms of self-killing in Japan. For this priest, the desire to die suddenly is different from suicide because it is motivated out of selflessness; by contrast, suicide is self-centered and creates additional burdens for the living simply by the fact that the death was a suicide and requires special ritual treatment. This is suggestive of a different conceptualization of suicide that relies less on the notion of autonomy and more on the notion of linkages to others. What makes an act of self-killing in Japan a "suicide" (*jisatsu*), while including the notion of autonomy, is more based upon the idea of the influence on others that the act causes. To burden others through the act of self-killing is a key element in defining the action as *jisatsu*; to kill oneself in a way that is not motivated by selfish actions—such as the action of a *kamikaze* pilot—is not easily equated with *jisatsu* for many Japanese.

Suicide, Family, and the Elderly

At the beginning of this chapter, I discussed the example of Mrs. Sakamoto, who hanged herself, and whose suicide was interpreted by neighbors in terms of her relationship to her family. On the one hand, it may have been a strategic message aimed at her gambling son, or, on the other, it may have been a way to avoid becoming a burden on family members if her health continued to decline. As noted above, in other conversations with my informants concerning elder suicide, family was the central theme in interpreting the motivations behind the actions.

Conversation 1: Women in the Old Persons Club

On a pleasant autumn afternoon, I joined a meeting of the women's section of the Old Persons Club (OPC) in Yamada, where I had been living for five months. The ages of the women in the group ranged from about 70 to the late eighties. They are a close-knit group, and many of the women have known each other as friends or neighbors for most of their adult lives. The meeting actually started an hour before the time I was invited to come and, given the tenor of the conversation while I was there, it seemed as though this provided a private time for these women to talk in a relaxed atmosphere outside the confines of their homes, where most of them live with their adult children and grandchildren. When I arrived, there was lively chatter about the spectacular house in which the meeting was being held. It had just been finished and incorporated a range of traditional Japanese building techniques and materials in a very modern environment to create an elegant effect.

Altogether, there were 15 women participating in the meeting. To some extent, open conversation was difficult because of the presence of Matsumoto-san, an 88-year-old woman whom I had met in other contexts and who tended to monopolize conversations in which she was involved. After some polite chit-chat, I was about to turn the topic to suicide when Matsumoto-san raised the issue (she and I had discussed this in the past, so she was aware that this was an interest of mine), stating that suicide is related to the lonely (*sabishii*) quality of some people's lives. Matsumoto-san continued, but because of a combination of her very strong dialect and lack of teeth, it was difficult to understand all that she said.[15] When she finished, the head of the local Women's Association, Ihara-san, who was also in attendance, offered her summary of what Matsumoto-san had said:[16]

> Ihara-san: Japanese are a people who mimic others (*mane suru hito*). After the war, we mimicked the family pattern of the U.S., but in doing so there were good things (plus) and bad things (minus). [The words "plus" and "minus" were spoken in English.] The bad thing is that the notion of *oya kōkō* (filial piety) has weakened.[17] Although in rural areas (*inaka*) there are more

people living in multigeneration families [than in cities], even if there is an image of the household as vibrant (*nigiyaka*), there are many who live in solitude (*kodoku*). This kind of solitude or isolation is part of the reason that suicide is common among the elderly. Even if the children and grandchildren are around, there are various things that interfere with the connection between the elderly and others—even things such as hearing loss. So even if there is a lively atmosphere, the old person may enter into a sense of loneliness.

JWT: Do you think that if a person has various physical problems they may feel that they cannot participate in the family and that might be why they commit suicide?

Ihara-san: No, that's not what I mean. . . .

Matsumoto-san: As for young people, the way of talking of old people does not come into their heads well, it doesn't make sense. A person who lives in a multigeneration family and who is living very quietly may end up committing suicide. Keeping one's feelings inside and enduring through one's interactions with younger people can be a source of suicidal feelings. Groups like the Old Persons Club provide a place in which one can relieve stress. It provides a context of friendship in which people can chat about things.

JWT: Do you view the people in this group [the Old Persons Club] as friends?

Ihara-san (and others): We do. It is different from being around our families. We can say things to each other that we cannot say around our families.

The discussion with these women provides an interesting interpretation of the causes associated with elder suicide. Matsumoto-san and others in the room attribute much of the phenomenon to changes in the family structure and values associated with that structure that occurred following World War II. This is a common theme in the narratives of older people in rural Japan when they discuss the problems that they face in contemporary society. Perceived changes in attitudes of the young toward the old, particularly in terms of an increasing resistance to following the expectations associated with filial piety, are typically viewed as being the root cause behind intergenerational misunderstanding and conflict. The values of younger and older people are viewed as being sufficiently different to prevent mutual understanding (Traphagan 2004).

The OPC provides a context in which older people can talk with aged peers, and thus avoid the difficulties that arise in intergenerational interactions. I think it is worth pointing out that from the perspective of my informants, this does not mean that the OPC is a context for talking about personal problems; in other words, the meetings are not group sessions for airing personal problems along the pattern typically seen in American ideas about counseling and psychology. All of my informants indicated that they do not talk about their stressful situations in these groups, but the fact of being in a context where there is a basic common understanding—perhaps something akin to *communitas* in the sense described by Turner (1977)—allows people to relieve stress. As one woman put it, "The stress leaves when we are together and we feel better after these gatherings." These are the people with whom, as Matsumoto-san explained it, one can "open up one's heart (*kokoro*)" to allow for a release from the loneliness and associated stress of living in a multigenerational family.

Conversation 2: Suzuki-san

From the example of a group discussion about elder suicide, I want to turn now to a conversation I had with a woman who was living with her husband in an apartment in the same neighborhood as the women described in the above conversation. Suzuki-san, who was 65 when we talked, had been devoting much of her time to caring for her husband, who had been ill with colon cancer and, although he appeared to be in remission, still tended to tire easily. Suzuki-san and I spoke on several occasions and I often noted that she looked quite a bit younger than her age, appearing as though she could be in her mid-fifties, and had a very energetic and optimistic air about her.

The Suzukis have no children, but very much wanted to have children when they were younger; during one of our conversations, Suzuki-san explained that she had been pregnant once but miscarried and was unable to conceive another child after that. Even with her past desire to have a child, one can see that as she has grown older, she has come to view children as something of a mixed blessing.

> JWT: Why do you think there are so many suicides among the elderly?
> Suzuki: For those who are living alone, they become tired, they do not have
> any reason for living (*ikigai*), and they are pitiful (*kawaisō*). . . . Also
> there are those who are sick and decide to commit suicide, but I really
> can't imagine it (*kangaerarenai*). Suicide is scary (*kowai*). I don't really
> have words to express it. Why would someone feel that he has to commit
> suicide? I can't understand it. I can't imagine it and I think it is something
> that one should not do (*suru beki ja nai*). People become tired [of life]

and then commit suicide. If there is no one to talk to, there is nothing to really stop one.

   People have their own problems (*nayami*) and that can cause one to come to feel that one's own feelings need to be dealt with. Japanese people, you know when they have some sort of problem, they keep it to themselves. They see it as something they have to deal with independently. People have a problem in their inner self (*kokoro*), but keep it to themselves and don't seek outside help to take care of it. This may contribute a great deal to suicide. People need to talk to family if they have a problem, but they can't really speak of their own problems to others. This causes stress to build up, and then the person comes to feel that suicide is the only way out.

JWT: And some elderly don't want to be a burden on family.

Suzuki: Yes, some people see that if they die it will be convenient (*raku*) for their family, but if they actually ask their family, it is not such a burden for them to be cared for, and the children want to care for them. For those who are living only as a couple, as compared to those who live in a family, they become much stronger because they do not have family members to lean on. They have to take care of things themselves. If you are living alone, you cannot depend upon or be indulged by another (*amaeru*), but if you are in the context of your family, you can depend upon others. Older people in families sometimes come to depend as children do. But I don't like this because if one is an adult, one should not be dependent upon others. If you feel that you can be dependent in your family, even though you can you may not want to and that may lead to suicide. But there is a sense that as people get older, they stop being able to persevere (*gaman*) and they return to childhood. For example, elderly people begin eating the foods children eat, and eat just what they want. They can't persevere at anything. But if a person in his forties or fifties looks at someone in his sixties, he doesn't see a child, he sees an adult. I think the dependence of a small child and that of an elder are not the same. And there are people who wonder what Grandma or Grandpa is saying when they are talking about their own problems all the time. Everyone around here is always worrying about what they will do, what they will do should they become ill. But for us it really isn't a problem. Since we don't have children, we do not have to worry about becoming a burden on them. Our situation is already decided; we will go to a nursing home, and since we do not have children, we don't have to worry about [becoming a burden].

In this conversation, the themes of loneliness and becoming a burden arise, but as with the conversations in the OPC, the focus of the interpretation comes back to the family. Indeed, Suzuki-san views elder suicide as a product of family relationships and a perceived loss of independence that comes with growing old within the confines of a multigenerational household. Lacking children, she believes that she is in a better position to avoid becoming a burden on others—she and her husband know that they will make use of institutionalized services that provide care if needed. What is interesting is that she frames the discussion about children (or lack thereof) in terms of the potential for stress and becoming a burden that she sees as an almost inherent part of close proximity. As one grows older, children become a focal point of tension—particularly if one needs care, although she recognizes that children may want to provide care for their parents. At the same time, the elderly become like children in that they can no longer persevere; they begin to act in a self-centered manner, concerned about their own problems, thus in some ways insulating themselves from the world of their children.

Proximity, Stress, and the Family

Throughout our conversations, the above informants and many others emphasized themes related to loneliness in old age, employing the word commonly used to describe elders who commit suicide—*sabishii*, a term that implies both loneliness and sadness. What is interesting in these conversations is that loneliness and stress are conceptualized as being stimulated through interaction with younger generations, particularly when the generations are of the same family and are placed into close proximity through co-residence. The idea that intergenerational co-residence breeds conflict is not an unusual one in Japanese society, even while there is a general assumption that older people are better off living with and being cared for by family members and that they are, to some extent, entitled to a living situation in which care is family-centered (Hashimoto 1996, 84).

As Akiko Hashimoto points out, filial co-residence is a central concept in terms of how Japanese conceptualize security in old age. For Japanese, security is derived from behaviors that emphasize protection and predictability, rather than those that emphasize autonomy and independence, which are usually associated with Euro-American societies (Hashimoto 2000, 20). The security associated with filial co-residence is seen as maximizing predictability and certainty, because expectations related to care are structured around the emotional and moral ties that connect family members. In this sense, co-residence is not merely a matter of ensuring security through proximity, but also symbolically represents a family in which those moral and emotional ties are in order and symbolically represent elders as living in a morally and emotionally healthy environment.

However, as we can see in these conversations, even while there may be benefits in terms of ensuring security by providing social support to elders, co-residence with younger generations also has the potential to generate significant personal cost. This is particularly clear in the comments by Suzuki-san, who frames her interpretation in terms of ideas quite opposite from the ideal of living in a multigenerational family. By emphasizing the concept of dependence, she argues that one is weaker precisely because one is living in a context in which one can depend upon family members: "If you live in a family, you have no need to get stronger. You become stronger if you are living as a couple." From her perspective, the fact that she herself lacks children makes suicide less likely because only the weak are likely to commit suicide—one is inherently strengthened by living as a couple and may be weakened by living in contexts in which one can depend upon others.

The idea that increasing dependence is a negative aspect of co-residence was a common theme among elder informants who lived alone. Many individuals commented that contrary to the popular idea that living alone is sad and lonely in old age, living apart from children may be a source of strength or provide, particularly for women, an environment of freedom from the necessity of caring for others. Such an environment was viewed in a very positive light. Indeed, one woman, who had been widowed several years earlier, commented that the time following the death of her husband had been the best of her life: "I have freedom now that I don't have to take care of children or my husband. I can do what I want." This freedom represented not only release from the necessity of caring for other family members, but also a release from the stress associated with living in an environment where divergent values between generations lead to conflict. For the women discussed here, the mere fact of living with one's children was a direct source of frequent and ongoing stress.[18]

Self-sufficiency, and along with this, burden avoidance, are central themes that older Japanese express when talking about the problems they face related to physical and cognitive decline as they grow older. Becoming a burden is not simply interpreted as a matter of requiring extensive care by family members, although this is sometimes given as a reason behind elder suicide (see Traphagan 2000). Among many elders, the simple fact of proximity without direct involvement with household duties is viewed as a potential burden on other family members. This perspective was conveyed very clearly by Tanaka-san, who repeatedly indicated throughout our conversations that she wanted to die soon:

> I want to die soon to go to be with my mother. Every night I think I want to die. I don't want to become a burden to my family. My physical condition is okay now, but I want to die before I become bedridden. I can't move to my natal household, even though they've said it's okay. It's a farm family and there is a lot of farming work going on. Because my legs are weak, I don't think I can help with any of the work there. My family has asked me to return, but I won't do it. They often tell me that I can just relax and enjoy myself and don't need to worry about doing any farm work, but if I move home and am not doing anything I'll feel like I'm in the way.

Although in the perceptions of many older Japanese, the ideal multigenerational family remains a desirable living situation in later life, the reality of potentially becoming a burden on family members mitigates the desire to co-reside. Surveys have shown a general decline in the desire of people to co-reside with their children in old age. A 1993 *Asahi Shimbun* survey showed that 58 percent of respondents wanted to live with a child, a number that had dropped to 46 percent in a 1999 NHK survey. While nearly half of the elderly population still desire co-residence, there has been a clear decline in the proportion of those wishing to live with children, while the proportion of those wishing to live alone has risen.[19]

Filial co-residence presents a variety of problems for old and young alike, and for many elderly, regular interactions with younger generations can be a source of social and psychological stress that results in part from perceived differences in values (see Traphagan 2003 for interview data from younger people concerning value conflicts). Inconsistencies in values across different generations lead to conflict, thereby generating stress in the elderly, particularly when they feel unable to express their opinions openly to younger generations. One woman in her mid-seventies expressed her opinion, with which another woman, also in her mid-seventies, agreed:

> Young people have too much freedom. In our day, life was really hard, so it was just seen as normal that you'd meet your fate. If you had a thought or an opinion, you didn't let it out. That's the way the people were around here. Maybe the thoughts of young people today are the same as those of our day, but in our day,

we didn't let out our opinions. For young people nowadays, life is really easy. I can give my opinions because it is my daughter. But if she were my daughter-in-law (*yome*), I would probably not say anything. If it is one's daughter-in-law, it's best to hold it in (*gaman*) rather than let out your opinion. In the old days, the mother-in-law had all of the power, but now it is the reverse.

Indeed, for both Matsumoto and Suzuki, filial co-residence in the context of the three-generation family is problematic—there are desirable elements, but there are also associated problems that generate loneliness. The multigenerational family is seen as having the potential to generate types of stress that could cause an elder to commit suicide. For these and other informants with whom I have discussed the topic, there is the sense that the context of the multigenerational family may actually intensify stress and promote elder suicide. It is clear that for these informants, the multigenerational family is neither positive nor neutral with respect to elder well-being; it is a potential source of negativity—stress, weakness, and dependence.[20]

Conceptions of suicide among my informants are framed by ambiguities in ways similar to what Hong Zhang finds among rural elders in China, where there is considerable ambiguity in relation to co-residence with adult children among elders. According to Zhang, among rural Chinese there is a sense that although spending one's elder years with children is normative and thus desirable, there also are feelings among many that as a lifestyle, co-residence is highly constraining (Zhang 2004, 79). Among rural Japanese, too, while there remains a sense, although weakening, that co-residence for the elderly is normative and desirable, it also can be a source of constraint and a continuous reminder that in contemporary rural Japan, the values of the elder generation are, in a sense, out of place (Douglas 2002). Co-residence becomes a constant reminder that one does not fit in the modern world, the world in which one's children and grandchildren live, and from which one can feel isolated, alienated, and lonely when confronted on a daily basis with the fact that one's generation—as so many elders in Japan describe themselves—is interpreted as being *furui* or obsolete.

This discontinuity between elders and the worlds of their children and grandchildren echoes a similar phenomenon that Macpherson and Macpherson (1987) note in relation to suicide trends in Samoa. The authors argue that in Samoan society, which is dominated by the elderly, there is resistance on the part of the elderly to accepting the expectations of young, untitled persons for education and alternate lifestyles. As younger people become "alienated from central values but . . . forced to continue to live by them," they sense their powerlessness to change the surrounding social conditions and opt to remove themselves from those social conditions through suicide (Macpherson and Macpherson 1987, 326). In Japan, we see something of the opposite situation; the elderly, living in a society dominated by the values of the young, are disaffected and thus may decide to remove themselves from the contexts of frustration and conflict that are associated with those values.

The Japanese elders discussed here, in ways similar to younger people in Samoa, are caught in a situation in which multiple and conflicting cultures occupy the same social (and often physical) spaces. In Japan, this is due in part to the rapid processes of social change that have occurred since the end of World War II, in which an older generation educated and socialized into expectations about elder lifestyles and interpersonal relations within the family have found themselves in radically different situations that emerged during the postwar era. It is this juxtaposition of different and conflicting cultures that contributes to the generation of stress, particularly for those elders who co-reside with their children and grandchildren—an arrangement that has the potential to generate responses such as suicide. Suicide becomes a way out, but not necessarily from a specific life that is too difficult to face; rather it is a way out from a social context that has become distantly removed from that to which one was socialized and which one anticipated earlier in life. In their minds, the elderly are disempowered by their position within Japanese society, rather than empowered by their status as elders. Thus, they come to feel that death is a reasonable alternative to the social situation characterized by values that seem remote from those which they acquired early in life and which shaped their expectations about old age.

Notes

This chapter draws on data from and is an expansion of an earlier publication that deals with elder suicide in rural Japan (Traphagan 2005).

1. This case is also discussed in Traphagan 2000, 1–3.

2. One of the more disturbing recent trends in Japan has been the development of suicide Internet sites where young people, in particular, can meet to find others interested in committing suicide or to make suicide pacts (NPR, June 24, 2003).

3. www.stat.go.jp/english/data/nenkan/zuhyou/b1917000.xls.

4. www.cdc.gov/nchs/fastats/suicide.htm.

5. As of 2000, 21.32 percent of the Japanese population lived in communities classified as towns or villages (*mura* or *machi*), while 78.68 percent lived in communities classified as cities (*shi*) and 21.61 percent of the total population lived in large cities

of one million or more. Although there are exceptions, cities are usually defined as having a population of 30,000 or above. Statistical Survey Department, Statistics Bureau, Ministry of Public Management, Home Affairs, Posts and Telecommunications (www.stat.go.jp/english/data/nenkan/zuhyou/y0204000.xls).

6. Japan Statistical Yearbook, Statistics Bureau, Ministry of Public Management, Home Affairs, Posts and Telecommunications (www.stat.go.jp/english/data/nenkan /zuhyou/b1919000.xls).

7. Overall suicide rates in many rural areas have been on the rise for some time. For example, in 1955, Akita ranked 39th among the 48 prefectures in Japan in terms of suicide rates. By 1970, Akita's ranking had risen to 7th, and since the mid-1980s the prefecture has consistently ranked in the top three nationally for suicide rates and has ranked number one in the nation since 1996 (Nakata 2002; Asahi Shimbun Akita Shikyoku 2000, 17).

8. Although methods of suicide common in Japan include gas asphyxiation, drowning, poison or drug ingestion, and jumping, by far the most common method is hanging. In 1996, for example, slightly under 60 percent of all suicides were hangings, followed by jumping from buildings (10.5 percent) (Takahashi et al. 1998, 275).

9. www.mishalov.com/Olive.html.

10. The meaning of suicide, and the moral implications, have long been discussed by philosophers, but the general definition has assumed that suicide is a form of self-killing devoid of force from outside. Plato's perspective is clear in the Laws (9.873c): "I mean the man whose violence frustrates the decree of destiny by *self-slaughter* though no sentence of the state has required this of him, no stress of cruel and inevitable calamity driven him to the act, and he has been involved in no desperate and intolerable disgrace" (Hamilton and Cairns 1961, 1432; italics in original). It is interesting that in this definition, the range of potential outside forces includes psychological stresses that would seem to indicate that self-killing in this case may not be defined as suicide for Plato. A fairly typical contemporary definition can be found on the website for Internet Encyclopedia of Philosophy: "Suicide is defined as an intentional and uncoerced self-killing in which the conditions causing death are self-arranged" (www.iep.utm.edu/s /suicide.htm).

11. Even from a Western perspective, there are questions about whether or not *seppuku* represents suicide, because one was typically given the option of committing *seppuku* as an alternative to being executed.

12. Japanese characters: *jisatsu* (自殺), *ikkashinjū* (一家心中), *shinjū* (心中), *jōshi* (情死).

13. Japanese do have a term for attempted suicide, *jisatsu misui* (自殺未遂); however, according to my informants it is possible to simply use *jisatsu* even when the person does not succeed.

14. Japanese characters: *inseki jisatsu* (引責自殺).

15. The local dialect in the region where I have conducted fieldwork is considerably different from standard (Tokyo) Japanese. Indeed, it is sufficiently distinct that native Japanese speakers often have considerable difficulty in understanding older people in the region, who tend to have a strong dialect. As an example, the standard word for "yes" in Japanese is *hai*; in the dialect used in and around Mizusawa by many older people, the word for "yes" is *nda nda*.

16. Although this was clearly for my benefit, some of the women in the group also indicated that they had difficulties understanding Matsumoto-san at times because her dialect was very strong.

17. See Ikels 2004a for a discussion of changing ideas about filial piety in East Asia.

18. Although men also respond that co-residence with younger generations can be a source of stress, it should be noted that I have run across very few men who would prefer to live alone. In part this is a result of the fact that most older (and many younger) Japanese men lack domestic skills such as cooking, cleaning, and laundry. Thus, living alone can present a major challenge.

19. JPOLL Japanese Data Archive, Roper Center for Public Opinion Research, University of Connecticut (www.ropercenter.uconn.edu/jpoll/home.html).

20. These data should not be taken as a representative sample indicative of the general opinions of the elderly concerning filial co-residence. Many, as noted above, prefer filial co-residence. And there are certainly many multigenerational families in which elders are happy and enjoy the warmth and closeness that is often associated with co-residing with children and grandchildren. Nonetheless, these data suggest that in the minds of some elders, the stresses associated with filial co-residence are sufficient to drive a person to suicide.

References

Asahi Shimbun Akita Shikyoku (Asahi Newspaper Akita Branch Office), ed. 2000. *Jisatsu: jisatsuritsu zenkoku—Akita kara no hōkoku* (Suicide: National suicide rates—Report from Akita). Akita: Mumyōsha shuppan.

Benedict, Ruth. 1946. *The chrysanthemum and the sword.* Boston: Houghton Mifflin.

Douglas, Mary. 2002 (1966). *Purity and danger: An analysis of the concept of pollution and taboo.* London: Routledge.

Durkheim, Emile. 1951. *Suicide.* New York: Free Press.

Fuse, Toyomasa. 1984. *Jisatsu to bunka* (Suicide and culture). Tokyo: Shinchōsha.

Hajime, Nakae, Ya Juan Zheng, Hiroshi Wada, Kimitaka Tajimi, and Shigetsu Endo. 2003. Characteristics of self-immolation attempts in Akita Prefecture, Japan. *Burns* 29 (7): 691–697.

Hamilton, Edith, and Huntington Cairns, eds. 1961. *The collected dialogues of Plato.* Princeton, NJ: Princeton University Press.

Hashimoto, Akiko. 1996. *The gift of generations: Japanese and American perspectives on aging and the social contract.* New York: Cambridge University Press.

———. 2000. Cultural meanings of "security" in aging policies. In *Caring for the elderly in Japan and the U.S.*, ed. Susan Orpett Long, 19–27. New York: Routledge.

Iga, Mamoru. 1986. *The thorn in the chrysanthemum: Suicide and economic success in modern Japan.* Berkeley: University of California Press.

Ikels, Charlotte, ed. 2004a. *Filial piety: Practice and discourse in East Asia.* Stanford, CA: Stanford University Press.

———. 2004b. Introduction. In *Filial piety: Practice and discourse in contemporary East Asia*, ed. C. Ikels, 1–15. Stanford, CA: Stanford University Press.

Jones, Robert Alun. 1986. *Emile Durkheim: An introduction to four major works.* Beverly Hills, CA: Sage.

Keene, Donald, trans. 1997. *Chūshingura.* New York: Columbia University Press.

Kurosu, Satomi. 1991. Suicide in rural areas: The case of Japan, 1960–1980. *Rural Sociology* 56 (4): 603–618.

Lebra, Takie Sugiyama. 1976. *Japanese patterns of social behavior.* Honolulu: University of Hawaii Press.

———. 1984. Nonconfrontational strategies for management of interpersonal conflicts. In *Conflict in Japan*, ed. Ellis S. Krauss, Thomas P. Rohlen, and Patricia G. Steinhoff, 41–60. Honolulu: University of Hawaii Press.

Lester, David. 2001. Suicide among the elderly in the world: Covariation with psychological and socio-economic factors. In *Suicide and euthanasia in older adults: A transcultural journey*, ed. Diego De Leo, 1–20. Seattle: Hogrefe & Huber.

Macpherson, Cluny, and La'Avasa Macpherson. 1987. Towards an explanation of recent trends in suicide in Western Samoa. *Man*, New Series, 22 (2): 305–330.

Matsumoto, Toshiaki. 1995. *Rōnenki no jisatsu ni kansuru jisshōteki kenkyū* (Research providing conclusive evidence for suicide in old age). Tokyo: Taga shuppan kabushiki kaisha.

Nakae, H., and H. Wada. 2002. Characteristics of burn patients transported by ambulance to treatment facilities in Akita Prefecture, Japan. *Annals of Burns and Fire Disasters* 28: 73–79.

Nakata, Hiroko. 2002. Rural regions struggle to stem elderly suicides. *Japan Times.* March 8.

Ohnuki-Tierney, Emiko. 2002. *Kamikaze, cherry blossoms, and nationalisms: The militarization of aesthetics in Japanese history.* Chicago: University of Chicago Press.

Ono, Yutaka, Eriko Tanaka, Hiroshi Oyama, Keiko Toyokawa, Takeshi Koizumi, Kiku Shinohe, Kyoko Satoh, Emiko Nishizuka, Harue Kominato, Kenji Nakmura, and Kimio Yoshimura. 2001. Epidemiology of suicidal ideation and help-seeking behaviors among the elderly in Japan. *Psychiatry and Clinical Neurosciences* 55: 605–610.

Otsu, Akiko, Shunichi Araki, Ryoji Sakaia, Kazuhito Yokoyama, and A. Scott Voorheesa. 2004. Effects of urbanization, economic development, and migration of workers on suicide mortality in Japan. *Social Science and Medicine* 58: 1137–1146.

Ozawa-de Silva, Chikako. 2008. Too lonely to die alone: Internet suicide pacts and existential suffering in Japan. *Culture, Medicine, and Psychiatry* 32: 516–551.

Phillips, M. R., X. Y. Li, and Y. P. Zhang. 2002. Suicide rates in China, 1995–99. *Lancet* 359: 835–840.

Pritchard, C., and D. S. Baldwin. 2002. Elderly suicide rates in Asian and English-speaking countries. *Acta Psychiatrica Scandinavica* 105: 271–275.

Takahashi, Yoshitomo. 1997. Culture and suicide: From a Japanese psychiatrist's perspective. *Suicide and Life-Threatening Behavior* 27 (1): 137–145.

Takahashi, Yoshitomo, Hideto Hirasawa, Akira Senzaki, and Kyoko Senzaki. 1998. Suicide in Japan: Present state and future directions for prevention. *Transcultural Psychiatry* 35 (2): 271–289.

Tester, Frank James, and Paule McNicoll. 2004. *Isumagijaksaq*: Mindful of the state: Social constructions of Inuit suicide. *Social Science and Medicine* 58: 2625–2636.

Traphagan, John W. 2000. *Taming oblivion: Aging bodies and the fear of senility in Japan*. Albany: State University of New York Press.

———. 2003. Contesting co-residence: Women, in-laws, and health care in rural Japan. In *Demographic change and the family in Japan's aging society*, ed. J. W. Traphagan and J. Knight, 203–226. Albany: State University of New York Press.

———. 2004a. Curse of the successor: Filial piety vs. marriage among rural Japanese. In *Filial piety: Practice and discourse in contemporary East Asia*, ed. C. Ikels, 198–216. Stanford, CA: Stanford University Press.

———. 2004b. *The practice of concern: Ritual, well-being, and aging in rural Japan*. Durham, NC: Carolina Academic Press.

———. 2005. Interpretations of elder suicide, stress and dependency among rural Japanese. *Ethnology* 43 (4): 315–329.

Turner, Victor. 1977. *The ritual process*. Ithaca, NY: Cornell University Press.

Wolf, Margery. 1972. *Women and the family in rural Taiwan*. Stanford, CA: Stanford University Press.

———. 1975. Women and suicide in China. In *Women in Chinese society*, ed. Margery Wolf and Roxanne Witke, 3–41. Stanford, CA: Stanford University Press.

Zhang, Hong. 2004. "Living alone" and the rural elderly: Strategy and agency in post-Mao rural China. In *Filial piety: Practice and discourse in contemporary East Asia*, ed. C. Ikels, 63–87. Stanford, CA: Stanford University Press.

Aging, Gender, and Sexuality in Japanese Popular Cultural Discourse

Pornographer Sachi Hamano and Her Rebellious Film *Lily Festival* (*Yurisai*)

Hikari Hori

THIS CHAPTER DISCUSSES aging and the aged from the perspective of gender and sexuality as represented in the feature-length dramatic independent film *Lily Festival* (*Yurisai*, 2001), directed by the female film director Sachi Hamano (b. 1948). The film, which Hamano says is about "elderly women's sex and love" (Hamano 2005, 83–85), narrates episodes revolving around the lives of seven women and one man who range in age from 69 to 91 years old. It is a comedy largely based on an award-winning contemporary novel of the same title, written by Hōko Momotani (b. 1955). The outline of the story is reminiscent of the eleventh-century Japanese classic *The Tale of Genji*, written by the female writer Murasaki Shikibu, describing the life of the attractive protagonist Genji and his numerous lovers. If any analogy is to be drawn between the movie and the classic novel, the film's narrative might be seen as a subversive version of the literary work.

The film is distinctive in its departure from the stereotypical characterization of the aged as recipients of caregiving, as often seen in contemporary Japanese media and films. This unusual portrayal was made possible by the career experience of Sachi Hamano, who has worked for over 30 years in the film industry as a producer and director of porn films. Hamano's directorship, with contribution from her longstanding collaborator, scriptwriter Kuninori Yamazaki, created a provocative cinematic narrative that undoes the centrality of the male hero of the modern novel from which the film is adapted.[1]

This chapter explores the politics of representation—in other words, it examines the problem of stereotypical images of aging and the aged in contemporary Japan. The representation of aging and the aged is a set of images created,

Figure 5.1. Themes of gender and sexuality in the independent feature-length film *Lily Festival* represent a departure from stereotypical depictions of the elderly. Still photograph from *Yurisai* (2001). © Tantansha

circulated, and reconstructed in society. It is constructed from multilayered discourses associated with political, educational, and cultural institutions, including the popular media. In turn, it shapes the views of members of society.[2] There are no definite ages, backgrounds, inherent physical characteristics, or specific financial situations that determine the category of "elderly people." In fact, health conditions, work-related productivity, personal experience, appearance, and many other elements socially attributed to aging and the aged vary according to the individual and her or his class, ethnicity, gender, sexuality, and other factors. Nevertheless, in media portrayals, the category is very often treated as existing a priori and is associated with social "problems," revolving around the issues of pensions and retirement, taxation, public assistance, long-term care insurance (*kaigo hoken*), multigenerational family housing, co-residence, introduction of foreign caregivers, changing family values, and even low birth rates. This problem-oriented category of "elderly people" is socially and culturally constructed; it is similar to notions of gender and ethnicity (for instance, women are normatively associated with domesticity, biological reproduction, and a gentle and caring "nature," while ethnic minority communities are often seen as volatile, traditional, or improperly socialized). In particular, I would stress that the image of aging is gendered. As Gee and Kimball (1987, 99) point out, for example, there is a double standard for aging, in that women are viewed as aging sooner and being less attractive than men at older ages. On the other hand, a positive image of the elderly—as sacred, possessing wisdom, solemnity, and serenity—is often associated with old men in Japanese classics (Wada 1995, 56).

Aging is a transitional process that proceeds day by day, and one that everyone faces at some point. Like the notions of gender, ethnicity, and other social identities, the aged are not a fixed, stable category. The lives of "elderly people" vary according to their individual situations and depend on their social positions, including gender, health conditions, and financial circumstances. Nevertheless, the term "elderly people" is often taken to indicate a fixed category of people who have inherent bodily and mental characteristics that make them different from "us." It is not only public policymaking, the welfare system, and circulating statistics, but also popular cultural stereotypes that operate in concert to create and re-create social views on aging and the aged. There is an urgent need to examine representations of aging and the aged from the perspective of gender and sexuality. Thus, the task in this chapter is twofold: first, to show examples of well-known conceptions associated with aging and the aged in contemporary Japanese culture in order to identify problematic representations of gender relations and the sexualized body. Second, to search for subversive images—in this case, those presented in the film *Lily Festival*—that, conversely, reveal the problems of mainstream images.

Therefore, instead of examining the more commonly discussed aspects of aging and the aged in society and media coverage, such as issues of insurance, pensions, the welfare system, and an unbalanced demography, this chapter centers on recent representations in Japanese popular media discourse and film to explore how aging and the aged are portrayed. As a point of departure for my analysis of such cultural representations, the central questions are: In the process of the construction, circulation, and reconstruction of images of aging and the aged, who creates and distributes such images? Which kinds of images are beneficial to which groups? What are deviant images and how do they challenge the norms?

I begin by locating widely distributed stereotypical characterizations from the past two decades in Japan, and examine how they are gendered and mobilized in contemporary popular cultural discourse. Second, I provide an overview of recent Japanese films on aging and the aged. Such films are mostly made by women, predominantly consumed by women, and discussed in light of women's issues, which empowers Japanese women. They have, however, highly effeminized and ghettoized the image of women's aging. Third, I discuss the film *Lily Festival* to see how it challenges popular discourse, as well as these recent films. I also examine the film from the perspective of the unusual career of Sachi Hamano, a director of both commercial porn films and independent feminist films, an aspect I believe to be essential to the film's representations of gender and sexuality.

Politics of Representation: "Elderly People" and Gendered Popular Discourse in Japan

Three compelling examples characterize the dominant gender stereotypes of elderly people that circulated widely in Japanese society from the 1990s up until 2001—right around the time that *Lily Festival* was produced—thereby providing a context for the subversive film. These examples from popular cultural discourse are: "grandpa" (*jitchan*), a term for elderly men used repeatedly by the comic (*manga*) artist Yoshinori Kobayashi (b. 1953) in the late 1990s; "wet fallen leaves" (*nure ochiba*), a popular figurative expression referring to retired men, which has been common in colloquial Japanese since the 1990s; and "old bats" (*babā*) and related derogatory remarks about postmenopausal elderly women made by Tokyo Metropolitan Governor Shintarō Ishihara (b. 1932) in the fall of 2001.

A series of socially critical comics by Yoshinori Kobayashi attracted a huge audience among young adults, especially in the early 1990s. His works have addressed controversial topics, including AIDS activism by hemophiliac patients infected by blood transfusions. Kobayashi was already an established comic artist who had been regularly published in boys' comic magazines (*shōnen manga*) when he began to explore social criticism in comics printed in magazines targeted at older readers during the 1990s.[3] After concentrating on the topic of AIDS cases caused by the negligence of governmental bodies and pharmaceutical companies, he shifted his interest to Japanese war responsibility. In the comic *New Manifesto of Arrogance* (*Shin Gōmanizumu sengen*), serialized in the bi-weekly magazine *SAPIO*, he insisted that the state of Japan is not accountable for aggression during the Asia Pacific War (1931–1945); he denied the existence of "comfort women" and belittled their suffering; and he emphasized that Japanese people should be patriotic instead of having a "masochistic" perspective on their own history.[4] A key term here, used by him repeatedly, was "grandpas." For him, it was "our grandpas" who served the country during the war and offered their lives to protect "us." To criticize Japan's past is, according to Kobayashi, to criticize and disgrace ordinary, good, innocent "grandpas"— Japanese males who experienced many hardships. In this rhetoric, elderly men are seen as having laid the cornerstone of the nation by enduring much suffering, and their criminal acts, including colonialism, invasion, and rape (though Kobayashi does not recognize these as crimes) are justified or ignored and displaced by attention to their hard work and national achievements. The term "grandpa" conveys a masculinized image of nation building and related ordeals, while also suggesting a strong sense of the common people, filial emotion, intimacy, and ordinariness. In Kobayashi's work, this image of elderly men is deployed to transform the historical conflicts perpetrated in Asia by the state of Japan into sweet and patriotic sentiments.

A second, contrasting example offers another interesting image of elderly men: the figurative term "wet fallen leaves," which has been used to refer to retired men since the 1990s. It is said that a housewife came up with the term, which was publicized by a feminist intellectual and soon became a popular new coinage.[5] It joined a similar, preexisting expression that referred to retired husbands as bulky garbage (*sodai gomi*), suggesting that they are useless and annoying, unable to do any household chores, and get in the way of housewives who are enjoying their later lives by meeting friends, going on trips, or taking continuing education classes. The new coinage refers to these men wanting to follow their wives wherever they go, sticking to them as if they were wet fallen leaves on the street, which are difficult to scrape off the pavement.

The third example comes from highly problematic remarks made by Tokyo Metropolitan Governor Shintarō Ishihara and known as the so-called "old bat comments" (*babā hatsugen*). Ishihara debuted as a novelist in 1956 and has been involved in politics since he was first elected to the House of Representatives in 1968. He has long been infamous among Japanese feminist and human rights activists for his numerous and varied racist and ultranationalist remarks. He said in a November 6, 2001, interview in the women's magazine *Weekly Women* (*Shūkan josei*), "I've heard that old bats are the worst, most harmful creation of civilization. . . . Men are reproductively active even at the age of 80 or 90, but women are not able to bear children after menopause. If such non-reproductive beings live as long as Kin and Gin,[6] they are a great bane of the earth. . . . Such a civilization [that allows such people to live long] will destroy the planet." Even after these remarks were denounced as sexist and ageist by feminist and human rights activists, Ishihara further insisted that he understood the legendary practice of abandoning old mothers in the wilderness because, in his view, the existence of elderly women is oppressive compared to the lives of other organisms (Regular Meeting at Tokyo Metropolitan Assembly, December 11, 2001). In this context, the role of women is limited to reproducing the next generation, and elderly women are seen as a serious threat to society because they are "useless." In addition to this image of harmful and useless elderly women, two other gendered connotations are implicit in these remarks: the meaning of one's life is found in one's reproductive ability, and women's longer life span is widely recognized as an important social phenomenon that somehow creates anxiety. Though Ishihara's remarks were reported in newspapers and other media, his political leadership as governor of Tokyo was not questioned by the general public.[7]

These three examples illustrate the range of gendered popular conceptions of the aged, which include gentle and ordinary elderly males who were former soldiers, dependent pathetic elderly men (who belong to a slightly younger generation than the former), and overemphasized nonreproductivity as a sin of elderly women. Notions of the "grandpa" and the useless "old bat" were popularized by public figures with considerable access to the media, and both cases went largely unchallenged by readers and voters. Interestingly, "wet fallen leaves" is the creation of an anonymous person, almost certainly a woman, and it is derived from the female view of men's later life by focusing on the male inability to contribute to the household and to a matrimonial partnership. In this sense, the coinage is clearly a projection of female critical views. However, "wet fallen leaves" has also a tone of women's resignation and tolerance rather than the note of condemnation and outright hatred of the other gender like that expressed by Ishihara. In addition, the superficial harmlessness of the term resonates with Kobayashi's "grandpas," which attempts to conceal the atrocities committed by ordinary individuals that were not limited to political leaders. (It should be sufficient to note that the historical narrative presented by Kobayashi and his advocates undermines the accountability of the wartime state of Japan, though further discussion is beyond the scope of this chapter.)

Male-related terms re-create a wide range of imagery, providing various imaginative narratives that locate elderly males individually and socially by emphasizing the wartime heroism of ordinary people, evaluating individual lives in the broader historical context, and lionizing the contributions of postwar hardworking corporate employees who were deprived of private pleasures. Their sexual or reproductive bodies are not the subject of debate but are implicitly interwoven into their individual life stories. The contrast is clear: the emphasis on female reproductive ability leads to a constructed notion of elderly females as entities that are useless to society and associates their bodies with norms of asexuality. How should women reclaim their life stories, bodies, social positions, and sexuality?

One answer to this question is provided by the film *Lily Festival*.[8] It ignores both reproductive lovemaking and the association of nationalist sentiments with the elderly male, while endorsing the view that overdependent men are no fun for women, even though there are fewer men as objects of love in an aging society. But before further discussing *Lily Festival* itself, I will turn to recent Japanese films on the theme of aging and the aged to locate *Lily Festival* not only in the context of Japanese popular discourse but also in terms of contemporary women's filmmaking.

Images of Aging and the Aged in Contemporary Films by Japanese Female Directors

Recent films focused on aging and the aged have been directed mostly by women, despite the very limited number of female film directors in Japan.[9] Since 1994, when the number of people over 65 reached 14 percent of the Japanese population (it is expected to reach 25 percent by 2015), aging has become a much-discussed topic in the media (Inoue et al. 1999). Accordingly, some Japanese films have begun to take up the topic not in the form of literary, allegorical drama, but through more urgent, commonplace depictions of daily life and struggles.[10] For the reasons discussed below, this seems to be a specialty of female directors. An overview of several contemporary documentary and dramatic films on this theme will further clarify representational issues of aging, gender, and sexuality.

Documentary filmmaker Sumiko Haneda (b. 1926) has directed both films and videos on the aged and elderly care, and is currently preparing a new film on this theme. She is the second female film director to emerge in the postwar period, her first film being *A Women's Class in a Village* (*Mura no fujin gakkyū*, Iwanami Productions, 1957).[11] Haneda's works on aging and the aged include *The World of Dementia* (*Chihōsei rōjin no sekai*, 1986), *How to Prepare for Your Aging* (*Anshin shite oiru tame ni*, 1990), *Welfare System Chosen by Residents in a Township* (*Jūmin ga sentaku shita machi no fukushi*, 1997), and its sequel *Welfare System Chosen by Residents in a Township 2: The Task Is What Lies Ahead* (*Mondai wa kore kara desu, jūmin ga sentaku shita machi no fukushi 2*, 1999). With the help of her husband, volunteers, and caregivers and services provided by the local government, Haneda herself looked after her elderly mother at home until she passed away around the time of the completion of the first *Welfare System Chosen by Residents in a Township*.

The World of Dementia was originally sponsored by a pharmaceutical company and commissioned by Iwanami Productions to educate caregivers and medical professionals, but it reached a much wider audience than expected. The film introduced the various conditions seen in elderly people with dementia, which had not been fully revealed in public at the time of the film's production in 1986, and screenings provided a chance for viewers to talk openly about the difficulty of caregiving at home and to share their experiences with others (Haneda 2002, 178–179). This groundbreaking documentary was screened nationwide at more than 1,200 sites and reached 300,000 viewers (Haneda 2005). Haneda explored issues related to the social welfare system for elderly people in her ensuing independent films, providing comparative perspectives from Sweden and Denmark, exploring local politics in Akita Prefecture related to the founding of a nursing home, and following up on the issue in Akita in the context of the newly implemented national long-term care insurance system. Her films report on the various conditions of dementia and provide perspectives on both Japanese and European nursing homes, as well as on the policy-making aspect of elder care, while stressing the importance of proactive involvement and intervention in the welfare system by taxpayers and local government officials.

In another example, Hisako Matsui (b. 1946), who was a TV producer for dramas and documentaries, has presented a different mode for narrating elder care. Her first fictional dramatic feature film, *Yukie* (1998), is about a Japanese woman who married an American military serviceman more than forty years ago. Having confronted racism, family problems, and other difficulties presented by interracial marriage, she now lives in the United States. The film portrays her marriage and her relationship with her children, her deteriorating health and memory problems caused by Alzheimer's, and her husband's caregiving. The film, set in the United States, is a utopian fantasy of Western culture seen from the point of view of a Japanese audience, as it shows a mutual partnership between a husband and wife that extends to the husband's caring for his wife.

Matsui's second dramatic feature film was the 2001 *Broken Plum* (*Oriume*). Based on an autobiographical essay by Motoko Kosuga, *Even If You Forget, You Can Be Still Happy* (*Wasurete mo, shiawase*, Nippon Hyōronsha, 1998), the film portrays housewife and part-time worker Tomoe as she struggles to care for her mother-in-law Masako, who lives with her family and has developed Alzheimer's. Tomoe had hoped to work full-time but gives up the idea when she decides to care for Masako at home rather than having her admitted to a nursing home. Through her care, Masako becomes more mentally stable and reveals a hidden artistic talent through painting, finally winning an award. For an independent production, the film was a great commercial success. It was first screened in Tokyo in a commercial theater for eleven weeks before being shown nationwide, ultimately reaching one million viewers. Local screenings were organized by area women's groups and attracted mostly women viewers (Matsui 2004). This sentimental film, which was enthusiastically received by Japanese housewives, shows positive prospects for an individual woman's dedication, which is presented as the solution to the problems of caregiving. This, I believe, is an idealized view of caregiving for the aged. The film emphasizes the woman's sacrifice of her career, the positive aspects of caregiving at home (as an initiative taken by a housewife), and its rewards, as in the discovery of her mother-in-law's artistic talent.

The melodramatic narratives of both of Matsui's films present family struggles and pivot around an old woman's confession or statement, made when she has temporarily come back to her senses, which becomes the point at which a family member decides to look after her at home. In both films, the families find the solution to their dilemma by wrestling with their own emotional and physical burdens. In other words, Matsui's fictional films present an idealized model in which the care of elderly parents depends on the ability of their children's—often daughters'—strong emotional commitment to overcome the insufficiency of familial and societal resources. For many Japanese women, in fact, caregiving very often becomes a personal struggle, and in the course of caregiving, they confront moral and financial choices about whether or not to look after aged parents or in-laws at home. This is precisely the reason the films found a large number of supporters among housewives in Japan. However, the central place in these films is occupied not by the aging persons themselves but by the caregivers. The voice of the aged accentuates the narrative or changes the course of the plot, but their lives themselves are curiously abstract compared to those of younger family members.

In contrast with Matsui's emphasis on family commitment to caregiving, Tazuko Makitsubo (b. 1940) provided different views in her two dramatic features. Makitsubo directed them from a wheelchair because of chronic rheumatoid arthritis while looking after her mother, who was suffering from worsening Alzheimer's.[12] Makitsubo worked as a continuity person for film and TV productions for eighteen years, and made her directorial debut in 1986 with a dramatic film about sex education in elementary school. Her recent dramatic features on caregiving are *Elderly Parents* (*Rōshin*, 2000), which is based on autobiographical essays by Haruko Kadono (b. 1937), and *The Place Where Mother Lives* (*Haha no iru basho*, 2003), which is based on a nonfiction book of the same title by the prominent writer Megumi Hisada (b. 1947). The director and the writers of the original works are all women who had personal experience with caregiving. The film *Elderly Parents* focuses on a housewife who provides care for her in-laws at home before getting a divorce to become a working woman. In *The Place Where Mother Lives*, the protagonist is a single working mother who struggles with caregiving at home. She has her elderly mother admitted to a nursing home, where her mother finds a peaceful, enjoyable, and dignified life. The film depicts a care system that benefits both the residents and their families, portraying a unique nursing home that provides not only medical care but also a liberated setting where residents can enjoy drinking, smoking, and courting. Both of Makitsubo's works address the emotional commitment and everyday struggle of elders' family members, as well as the welfare system that assists them.

Despite differences in the modes of presentation as well as in approaches to the theme of aging and the aged, these recent works have common features: the filmmakers and the writers of the original works are women; the films circulated widely but outside the commercialized distribution system and were well received among viewers, most of whom were women;[13] the films are independent low-budget productions (except Haneda's commissioned *The World of Dementia*), meaning there was more freedom to express views independent of sponsors such as pharmaceutical companies; and the elderly protagonists portrayed in the films are very often women. In other words, the theme is one that concerns women, both filmmakers and viewers. Likewise, issues related to aging and the aged in Japanese society are largely regarded as women's issues, as women have a longer life span and women are mostly responsible for caregiving. This explains why films on this theme tend to be about women, for women, and by women. On the one hand, the benefit is that these films open issues of later life to the general public, instead of treating them as personal and taboo. In fact, the screenings are often organized by local community activists, held at community centers, and accompanied by discussions with the film crews and producers, lectures by social workers, and/or question-and-answer sessions. Thus, unlike TV programs which provide a one-way flow of information, these film screenings create a space for gathering, education, outreach, and an exchange of experiences and information among viewers. This suggests that these films function as an interactive medium for discussing issues of both a private and a societal nature. On the other hand, these films and the issues they address are ghettoized and effeminized, as their themes are shared and discussed predominantly among women, who more urgently confront them in their everyday lives.

Lily Festival: Gender, Sexualized Aging, and Hamano's Directorship

The representation of gender difference and sexuality in *Lily Festival* contrasts with the centrality of caregiving in other contemporary Japanese films on aging and the aged. Other films focus on dementia and on the families' viewpoints rather than those of the elderly themselves, which reduces representations of aging to sickness and the related problems that younger family members must deal with. Contrastingly, *Lily Festival* is a lively and straightforward portrayal of the sexuality and desire of elderly people. It focuses on stories of individual elderly characters and directly addresses the positive aspects of their aging. The narrative could be criticized for paying little attention to social factors (the story is about more or less healthy, financially independent people), but this gives the film freedom to emphasize unconventional views of the gendered and the sexual experiences of its protagonists. In this section, I address the following questions: To what extent does *Lily Festival* challenge the societal treatment and stereotypes of elderly people in contemporary Japanese culture? How is the film different from other Japanese films about the aged and aging? What is the significance of Hamano's directorship in introducing and representing this theme?

The narrative first depicts the collective life of seven women in the Mariko Apartment. It then shifts to the female protagonists' competition to attract the sole male tenant Terujirō Miyoshi (75 years old). Finally, it closes with an exploration of an intimate relationship between two women, Rie Miyano (73 years old) and Renako Yokota (75 years old), that develops into a female-to-female sexual experience. Miyano had spent decades as an obedient housewife but is now enjoying life after the passing of her husband, who had committed infidelities.[14] Though she has health complaints and frequently goes to the doctor's office to receive treatment for high blood pressure and other ailments, she prefers living by herself to co-residing with her son's family. Yokota ran a bar until she retired at the age of 70, and she remains proud of her profession, which has connotations of sexual promiscuity and even prostitution. Her second husband, ten years her junior, died three years ago. She still wears makeup, fancy Western dresses, jewelry, and red nail polish, and her look conveys seductive charm toward men. The other protagonists are: Atsuko Namiki (76 years old), Teruko Satoyama (69 years old), Umeka Mariko (77 years old), Yoshi Kitayama (91 years old), and Nene Totsuka (81 years old).[15] Totsuka, a close friend of Miyano, is found dead in her room at the very beginning of the film, and her voice is occasionally heard as a narrator from beyond the grave. These women represent patterns of women's experience and of the life course of the older generation, such as marriage to an unfaithful husband, the confined life of a housewife, the problems of co-habitation with the younger generation, and living and dying alone in later life.

The story opens as Miyoshi moves into their building as the sole male tenant. Utterly unlike a typically reticent Japanese man, he charms the women with graceful gestures and eloquent rhetoric. All of them are flattered, become attracted to him, and dote on him, even the "man-hater" Namiki. Miyoshi's appearance, sporting leather pants, a stylish hat and jacket, and a ponytail, as well as his positive, entertaining, and cheerful conversation impress the women even more when they visit his room together. He states that he doesn't envy the young because he believes in being alive, and that, in his view, it is fun to live. Miyano had been the first of the tenants to meet him when she encountered his mover's truck lost on the road near the apartment and gave directions to the driver while Miyoshi sat next to him in the cab. After he has settled in, Miyoshi visits Miyano's room one afternoon and they make love in front of a Buddhist altar devoted to her late husband. Miyoshi then promises Miyano that she is the only person with whom he has such a relationship. Later, Satoyama finds out that Miyoshi is in fact married but was kicked out by his wife when she discovered that he had a long-standing relationship with another woman. Then, on the night that all of the women are throwing a formal welcome party for him, they find out that he has been simultaneously involved in relationships with four of them: Mariko, Namiki, Miyano, and Yokota.

In the final development of the story, Yokota and Miyano sit together one night, gazing at each other curiously, and talking about their experiences of Miyoshi and his "thing." The last sequence of the film portrays these two women enjoying a trip together, holding hands after spending an intimate night, and concludes with a serene shot of Miyano from a distance, with overlapped narration by the deceased Totsuka. In this final shot, Miyano reveals that she and Yokota did something "naughty" the previous night, and the film ends with Totsuka's voice, unheard by the living protagonists, announcing that she witnessed them together, and that she will continue to watch over all the women of the apartment building.

The party is the turning point of the narrative, as it redirects the narrative from hetero-normativity to possibilities of female-to-female relationship. The women angrily accuse Miyoshi of promiscuity and deception, but they also acknowledge that there are fewer available men as they age, because of the longer life span of women, while sexy, attractive, and fun men like him are even scarcer. The party scene is followed by several concluding sequences that celebrate women's sexual activity in a heterosexual community. They also introduce the spectrum of women's intimate relations from friendship to homosexuality: a notion suggested by Adrienne Rich (1986) in her use of the term "lesbian continuum." After the revelation of Miyoshi's promiscuity, the women in the apartment building accept it, and three of them continue to fuss over him. Mariko and Namiki continue to enjoy sexual relations with him and even seem to enjoy competing with each other—in a reversal of Sedgwick's model of homosociality, in which two men appear to be competing for a woman's love but are in fact reinforcing male bonding (Sedgwick 1985).

The film stresses that aging involves both transition and continuity by providing narration from the dead person's perspective, and by placing her death at the very beginning of the film and emphasizing her continued presence, rather than treating death as a form of resolution. It also embraces aging, independent thinking, sexual desire, female same-sex relationships, and transgression of gender identities, some of which are celebrated in Miyoshi's lines in the film. During the pivotal party scene he proclaims, "From the viewpoint of my younger self, this is the future. We can't return to yesterday, but we can live on into tomorrow." This reinforces earlier statements he had made in response to Namiki's pessimistic views on aging. She had decried sexism against elderly women in general, but he contradicted her by emphasizing diminished gender boundaries: "I think getting old is fantastic. . . . The older you get, the less distinctions between men and women matter. The important thing is what you think and feel as an individual." This perspective is further emphasized by the several significant ways the film departs from the original novel. Issues of gender and sexuality are raised by the following three components of the film narrative: a transgender fantasy enjoyed by Miyano, a female-to-female sexual relationship, and the cinematic style used to portray sexual relations.

A fantasy of reversed male-female roles occurs to Miyano when she first visits Miyoshi's apartment together with the other women, and all eye him admiringly. At this point, the image of Miyoshi as Snow White and the six women as dwarfs surrounding the princess is presented. Although this fantasy of reversed gender roles does appear in the novel, in the film its subversive quality is further stressed by the insertion of a color drawing in the style of a girl's comic (*shōjo manga*), as well as a live-action portrayal of Miyoshi as Snow White and the female characters as the dwarfs. Together with the effeminized drawing, this scene fully conveys a sense of lighthearted and comical gender reversal. The combination of one male princess and several female dwarf-admirers suggests the reality that there are more elderly women than men in Japan, as men's life expectancy is shorter, and that women might compete over scarce men in heterosexual communities.[16] However, this fantasy not only emphasizes imbalance in the gender ratio of one man to seven women; it also implies that aged men are socially de-masculinized in that they become bereft of status, physical strength, health, and often sexual potency. Therefore, the film's portrayal of Miyoshi as Snow White is a visualization of a de-masculinized man, reinforced by the evening gown, wig, and makeup that enable him to pass as the princess. But in fact, Miyoshi hereby escapes the very negative stereotype of retired men as wet fallen leaves, as this de-masculinization is part of his presentation as someone who is very attractive and deserving of the dwarfs' attention.

Second, the film treats Miyano, who is the subject of the gender-reversal dream, as the main protagonist. Its central story is her pursuit of sexual pleasure, which departs from the novel, in which the lily of the title represents Miyoshi, a strong stem that supports several flowers and provides the flowers with a source of energy and sexual pleasure. Following the revelation of Miyoshi's multiple affairs, the film's focus on Miyano creates a deviant and challenging narrative. The novel, conversely, ends with Miyoshi's confession about a woman he was once in love with. He deserted her in 1946 during the chaos of the immediate postwar era and later read in a newspaper article that she had starved to death. Since then, he has been compulsively having affairs with women. Yokota analyzes his behavior as a quest for redemption: he needs to feel in love, and the feeling alleviates his sense of guilt (Momotani 2000, 184). Thus, the novel takes the form of Miyoshi's journey: the women's past and present and their daily lives at the apartment converge with his past relationship, and are integrated into *his* story. The film, however, removes this confession and replaces it with his positive statements on aging and his upbeat, self-serving insistence that he likes everyone equally.

After the night of Miyoshi's party, Miyano and Yokota have a drink together in Yokota's apartment, begin spending time with each other, and eventually go off on an overnight trip together. Under more typical circumstances, these two women would not have ended up together, according to social norms of femininity which draw distinctions among women. Miyano, the virtuous domestic woman, stands in sharp contrast to Yokota, the bar owner, who is, in fact, the kind of a woman with whom Miyano's husband might have had an affair. The contrast between their roles echoes the dichotomy between monogamy and promiscuity, the housewife and the working woman. Their clothing symbolizes their opposing positions as well: Miyano wears a kimono, while Yokota pairs a Western dress with red nail polish.

In the apartment scene, Yokota makes a drink for Miyano, who carefully sips it, and they share fond reminiscences of the softness of Miyoshi's flaccid penis. This memory turns Miyano's attention to Yokota's soft earlobe.[17] This time a female-to-female bond is obvious, unlike the implicit rivalry between Mariko and Namiki. Later, when they set out on a trip and have a drink together on a tour boat, Miyano tells Yokota about her fantasy of Miyoshi as Snow White and the women as the Seven Dwarfs. They conclude this conversation by saying to each other, "At our age, the distinction between men and women doesn't matter"; "Anything goes!" This leads to a scene of the two women embracing each other in their hotel room. This same-sex relationship is foreshadowed by a pair of dolls, made by the late Totsuka, which stand close together and are gazed at adoringly by Miyano several times throughout the film. Although Miyoshi's affairs bring Miyano and Yokota together, they still maintain their own life-styles and accept each other's values, as suggested by scenes in which Miyano in kimono wears dark sunglasses like Yokota, while Yokota in her Western dress goes to a kimono exhibition with Miyano (Tsukamoto 2001, 16–17).

Third, the cinematic presentation of the sexual relations between Miyano and Miyoshi interestingly downplays the novel's cruel portrayal of his physical frailty. The novel describes him caressing Miyano's breasts and genitals, but at the same time it associates his kisses with his weak lungs: "He needed to breathe many times because of his deteriorated lung capacity" (Momotani 2000, 98). It also emphasizes his impotence: "It [his penis] was completely soft"; "There was no sign that it [his penis] would harden" (102–103).[18] The novel probes the male sexual body, relentlessly uncovering Miyoshi's physical frailness due to age-related deterioration, and foregrounding his desperate efforts to make love. However, the film takes a different tone in describing the lovemaking of Miyano and Miyoshi. It deploys a style of portrayal conventional in the genre of soft-core porn filmmaking: the camera focuses on Miyano's bare legs emerging from her kimono, her smiling face ecstatic with restrained pleasure, and her gasps. This stands in stark contrast to the novel's strong emphasis on depicting Miyoshi's age-related impotence and frail health, which disrupts its description of the intercourse itself. Though women's facial expressions, responses, and body are a visual site onto which men's sexual ability and libido are projected in typical commercial pornography, the major difference in *Lily Festival* is the film's quiet acknowledgment of Miyoshi's impotence, inability to achieve penetration, and earnestness. Miyoshi whispers to Miyano, "It's soft; is that all right?" but her pleasure is not affected by his dysfunction. Thus, the cinematic style of depicting intercourse appears conventional, but the narrative subverts the stylized male sexuality seen in pornographic genre conventions, which include aggressiveness, penetration, and pistonlike movement.

This subversion is further emphasized by the film's objectification of male sexuality in a different sequence, in which Kitagawa grabs Miyoshi's penis through his trousers. Ninety-one-year-old Kitagawa, the oldest tenant of the apartment, is clearly differentiated from the other women in the film. While she names her three cats after popular male figures in Japanese culture, she refers to male tenants as "master" regardless of their actual names.[19] Furthermore, her "hobby" is to put her hands onto the crotches of new male tenants to briefly fondle their genitals through their trousers. Her indifference to human male individuality, raw interest in male genitals, and habit of emitting sudden, apparently unmotivated shrieks symbolize unsocialized, deviant female sexuality. In one scene, Kitagawa, holding her cat, approaches Miyoshi in front of the building and summarily grabs his crotch. He appears mortified, while she tightly closes her eyes as if concentrating on her sense of touch. A second later, her cat meows loudly as if it spoke for her satisfied, triumphant sigh, or for Miyoshi's silent shock. Then she moves away from him, leaving him puzzled and motionless. The sequence highlights the way in which a man's body is tangible, vulnerable, and available to satisfy a woman's sexual curiosity. Kitagawa's "hobby" of grabbing men's genitals through their trousers is understood among the other tenants as an initiation rite for all new male tenants in the apartment building. Evaluating men's sexual organs in such a way seems to be allowed only for very old women, thus suggesting that aging might liberate women from normative feminine demeanor.

The unique and subversive qualities of *Lily Festival*, in contrast to other works of contemporary Japanese cinema, are made especially apparent when the film is viewed in the context of director Sachi Hamano's career as a female filmmaker.[20] The aforementioned directors—Haneda, Matsui, and Makitsubo—all started in the educational documentary film or TV industries, not as directors but as scenario writers, producers, or continuity people, which are not unusual career paths for aspiring women in those industries. In contrast, Hamano has had quite an unusual career for a female director in Japan. She entered the film industry in 1968 after graduating from high school, as an assistant director in low-budget 35mm pornographic filmmaking—a genre called pink film (*pinku eiga*) in Japan.[21] This is a subgenre of sexually explicit films that dramatically expanded in the mid-1960s, borne by numerous small independent film productions. These productions had low budgets, short shooting schedules, and small crews.[22] Since her debut as a director in 1971, Hamano has made more than 300 theatrical porn films, most of them commercially successful. She founded her own production company, Tantansha, in 1984 and has made films as both producer and director, teamed with screenwriter Kuninori Yamazaki, who shares her interest in presenting subversive female sexual practices.[23] After the advent of the VCR in the late 1980s, her films were often reformatted for video rentals after their distribution in theaters. Though there have been several women directors in porn filmmaking, no one else has managed to keep directing for long, and Hamano is the only woman who has regularly produced films with such commercial success.

Together with Yamazaki, Hamano has produced several adult films that celebrate women's sexuality, which can be interpreted as deviant in the context of the industry.[24] Such works include *Samejima Nao: Confinement* (*Samejima Nao: Kankin*, 1988), *Girls' High School Reunion: We Like It* (*Joshikō dōsōkai: Are ga suki*, 1991), and *Abe Sada in the Heisei Era: I Want You* (*Heiseiban Abe Sada: Anta ga hoshii*, 1999). In particular, her early 1990s series, *Reverse Massage Parlor* (*Gyaku sōpu*, 1992–1994), in which women receive superb services from good-looking young men, was said to be an underground hit among women (Kitahara 2000, 162–163). Her mid-1990s *Middle-Aged Woman* (*Obasan*) series, in which she employed a 54-year-old actress, also sold well, though it was taboo to use middle-aged actresses in the industry (Matsumoto 1996, 109). According to Hamano, the series attracted a middle-aged male audience. Though her films were mainly targeted at men and shown in adult film theaters,[25] a common feature of the aforementioned works is their emphasis on women gaining freedom from spatial and psychological confinement through sexual practices. While they contain nudity, caresses, and copulation in keeping with the conventions of pink films, the women in these films take revenge on men, make alliances with same-sex friends, and purchase men's sexual services. In this sense, Hamano's films succeed in "making a woman the hero-subject of the sexual narrative without . . . making her a victim-hero" (Williams 1999, 257),[26] which, in my view, means that her works display an interesting and deviant voice in the Japanese porn film industry.

In the past decade, while continuing her commercial porn filmmaking, Hamano has embarked on nonporn independent film productions. *Lily Festival* was preceded by *In Search of a Lost Writer* (*Dainana kankai hōkō: Ozaki Midori o sagashite*, 1998), the making of which mobilized more than 12,000 women supporters, fundraisers, and feminist activists and was widely endorsed by Japanese feminist communities. This film is an introduction to the forgotten female writer Midori Ozaki (1896–1971) as framed by a young lesbian couple's rediscovery of her life and work. Midori Ozaki was a writer whose works started to gain critics' attention in the 1920s and 1930s, but her literary career was disrupted after she went back to her hometown in Tottori Prefecture because of mental instability. The film reinterprets Ozaki's life, seeing her not as a bitterly disappointed author who gives up writing, as literary critics believed, but as a woman who continues to live her life with dignity, taking care of her sister's children, surviving the wartime period, and enjoying her life as it is. The film also touches on women's aging not as a one-dimensional development but as a complicated continuity interacting with the artistic creativity of the writer and her responsibilities toward her family members, as the conflicts between being an artistic creator and a responsible caregiver for family members are very often acutely experienced by women. In mosaic fashion, it integrates a cinematic realization of the writer's masterpiece *Wandering in the Realm of the Seventh Sense* (*Dainana kankai hōkō*),[27] experimental insertions of commentaries by feminist film and literary critics, and dramatic reconstructions of the writer's life. *Lily Festival* carried over several issues that *In Search of a Lost Writer* addressed but did not completely explore: the life paths of various women and their aging, the hetero-normative sexuality of later life, and female-to-female eroticized relationships. These issues of aging intersecting with gender difference and sexuality are presented in *Lily Festival* in a way unlike anything else found in other films on the aged. Their presentation can also be examined from the perspective of women's filmmaking in the porn film industry. In other words, such issues were approached and reinterpreted through Hamano's perspective on women's sexuality as a porn film director.

Being a female director in the porn industry is highly exceptional.[28] The hierarchy of the film crews is highly gendered, as directors and directors of photography are predominantly male. The genre is basically run by men (film crews, theater owners, and distributors), for men (viewers), and is about men's projection of sexual desire; women are subjugated to male sexual fantasy, youth is their absolute value, masculinity is reduced to strong sexual drive and penetration, violence is directed against women, and heterosexuality is the norm. Hamano has recollected her on-site experiences as an assistant director. She recounts being referred to as "mom," being expected to take up domestic chores including laundry and cooking, being teased about her breasts, and experiencing the inconvenience of her menstrual period. She states that she wanted to work as a man, and to become a man (Hamano 2005, 16). This is not an unusual experience for women who enter male-centered workplaces in general.[29] Because female workers are treated differently and expected to be different, they often hope to identify themselves with men. After first acknowledging their difference, they may attempt to overcome it by assimilating into the existing structure of gendered power relations. In doing so, the dominant norm is reinforced. In addition, women are not necessarily ready to help or ally with one another in such a male-oriented environment. However, Hamano established alliances with some female co-workers. One of them is Kazuko Shirakawa, who played Yokota in *Lily Festival* and Midori's younger sister in *In Search of a Lost Writer*. She is a former 1970s porn star whom Hamano came to know through her work. She supported Hamano in those days, and later fulfilled her promise to Hamano to appear in Hamano's own films.

As noted above, many of the conventions of porn and nonporn filmmaking are challenged in Hamano's works, especially in *Lily Festival*. This feminist female pornographer, who continues to direct both pink and nonporn features, challenges the dominant images of Japanese women and women's filmmaking.[30]

Conclusion

This chapter first introduced three highly gendered elements of popular cultural depictions of the aged: patriotic elderly men, overly dependent men leaning on their wives, and the "uselessness" of nonreproductive elderly women. It then provided a brief overview of contemporary Japanese films that focus on the issues of aging and the aged predominantly from the perspective of caregiving. Juxtaposing *Lily Festival* with the three popular cultural images of the aged, as well as other contemporary films, reveals the film's subversive approach to gender and sexuality. First, it provides lively, powerful female models of sexual desire often ignored in contemporary popular cultural discourse. Second, in contrast with other films' references to dementia as the primary theme or key to their plots, *Lily Festival* presents everyday life with trivial and familial conflicts, lies and deceptions, and varied relationships in a world where dementia and its care are not the center of the narrative. Rather, the center is occupied by sexuality, which is often denied of "elderly people" except in the context of nonreproductivity, as Governor Ishihara's comments suggest. The film challenges the norms of elderly female sexuality. There is a strong societal expectation of asexuality in women's aging, while paradoxically, their inability to reproduce is problematized. *Lily Festival* criticizes society's treatment of those who find themselves in the doubly discriminated position of "getting old" and "being a woman." In spite of its hetero-normativity, the film presents a set of unconventional narratives about and perspectives on sexual desire in elderly women, the failure of virility, an alliance between a "good wife" and a "fallen woman," and the lesbian continuum. While the issues related to women's aging are more often scrutinized, pathologized, and even mocked than men's issues, the film questions gender dichotomies and celebrates female sexual desire.

Finally, Sachi Hamano's directorship also serves as an arena for feminist negotiation of the politics of gender and sexuality, and the film can be seen as intertwined with her career experiences as a working and "aging" woman, and her history of subversive pornography making. *Lily Festival* relocates issues of aging and the aged in the context of popular discourse, contemporary Japanese cinema, and women's creativity by challenging social norms and stereotypes with its playful, deviant narrative.

Notes

1. The film was shown worldwide at film festivals, nonprofit screenings, and commercial theaters in Tokyo, Montreal, Turin, Hong Kong, London, New York, Paris, and other cities. The film won the Second Grand Prix award at the Ninth International Women's Film Festival (Turin, 2002); Best Feature Film (Lesbian Section) at the International Gay & Lesbian Film Festival (Philadelphia, 2003); and Best Feature Film at the Mix Brasil 11 Festival (2003).

2. There are a few studies that address cultural representations of the aging and the aged; see especially Featherstone and Wernick 1995, 1–15.

3. Kobayashi debuted in 1975. His best-known work, "Straight to Tokyo University" (*Tōdai icchoku sen*), is a representative work of the 1970s genre of nonsense comics (*gyagu manga*) that was serialized in a weekly comic magazine targeted at male youth.

4. The series was later published in multiple volumes by the Shogakukan publishing house. Numerous works of his containing social criticism are available in both comic and prose formats.

5. The term was chosen to represent the most expressive new word of the year in 1989, when it was awarded the "Grand Prix of Popular Coinage" (*Ryūkōgo taishō*). The award is bestowed by a selection committee after words are nominated in *Basic Knowledge of Modern Popular Usage of Words* (*Gendai yōgo no kiso chishiki*), published annually by Jiyūkokuminsha. The award-winning terms are reported in major media and gain wide recognition.

6. Kin Narita (1892–2000) and Gin Kani'e (1892–2001) were identical twin sisters. They became widely known after appearing in a TV commercial in 1991, serving as pleasant and auspicious symbols of longevity. They were frequently featured in the Japanese mass media during the 1990s.

7. Feminist and human rights activists sued Ishihara for his discriminatory remarks in 2003. The Tokyo District Court acknowledged that the remarks were sexist but dismissed the plaintiffs' demand for compensation and a public apology in February 2005. The plaintiffs appealed to the Tokyo High Court, but it upheld the District Court's decision in September 2005. Ishihara was reelected for a third term as governor in April 2007.

8. It is noteworthy that a popular weekly magazine comic strip by Machiko Hasegawa, *Obnoxious Old Woman* (*Ijiwaru baasan*, 1966–1971), could be seen as an excellent popularized image of a positive, strong elderly woman. The work has been occasionally adapted for television as a live-action drama and an animated series.

9. Two exceptions are the dramatic feature films *A Last Note* (*Gogo no yuigonjō*,

1995) and *I Want to Live* (*Ikitai*, 1999), both directed by Kaneto Shindō. Born in 1912, prominent postwar film director Shindō made these films at the ages of 83 and 87, respectively. The former introduces several days of vacation that an aging renowned stage actress spends in her summer house. A series of incidents forces her to ponder her own life as well as her friends' and late husband's lives. The latter film is about an elderly widower who is looked after by his daughter while his other two children ignore him. Also, while representations of the aged are found in their settings rather than in their central narratives, the following two contemporary films are noteworthy: *La Maison de Himiko* (*Mezon do Himiko*, directed by Isshin Inudō, 2005) and *The Mourning Forest* (*Mogari no mori*, directed by Naomi Kawase, 2007). The former introduces a nursing home for gay men, though the story focuses on a young woman and her relationship with her gay father. The latter explores the personal trauma of a female protagonist and a man and is set in a small assisted living institution for patients in the early stages of Alzheimer's. The latter film was directed by a female director who won awards at the Cannes Film Festival in 1997 and in 2007 (for *The Mourning Forest*).

    10. Earlier cinematic presentations of the aged in dramatic films have oscillated from a demonic, dehumanized old woman, for example, in *Onibaba* (directed by Kaneto Shindō, 1964), to a self-sacrificial old woman determined to take her own life for the sake of her son's family in *The Ballad of Narayama* (*Narayama bushi kō*, directed by Keisuke Kinoshita, 1958; remade by Shōhei Imamura, 1983), to the reserved, asexual, sagelike old father played by actor Chishū Ryū (1904–1993) in *Tokyo Story* (*Tōkyō monogatari*, directed by Yasujiro Ozu, 1953), which became a symbol of fatherhood in Japanese cinema.

    11. Iwanami Productions is a prominent documentary film studio associated with a prestigious publishing company of the same name. Toshie Tokieda (b. 1929) joined the studio in 1951 as its first female director, and she debuted in 1953 (Tokieda 2003, 3–4). Haneda began working in the photographic publication section at Iwanami before assisting in filmmaking. The first Japanese woman director of a dramatic feature was Tazuko Sakane (1904–1975), who was active as a director in the 1930s and 1940s. When women started to make films in the postwar era, they first made documentaries instead of dramatic features, because documentaries have lower budgets and their status in the industry is hierarchically lower than dramas, making them more open to women's employment. Still, the number of female directors in the industry has been very limited.

    12. For a summary of her career and works, see Makitsubo's website www.pao-jp .com.

    13. I am not able to provide the gender ratios of viewers at screenings, but anecdotally it is apparent that many more women came to the screenings and supported the films, reflecting the fact that, in most cases, it is women who look after elderly family members in Japan, as in other societies.

14. The ages of some characters of the film differ from those in the novel. This chapter refers to the ages used in the film.

15. The actors' ages varied from 54 to 75 years old in 2001, the year of the film's production. Their birth years are as follows: Kazuko Yoshiyuki (Miyano) was born in 1935; Kazuko Shirakawa (Yokota) in 1947; Chisako Hara (Namiki) in 1936; Sanae Nakahara (Satoyama) in 1935; Utae Shōji (Mariko) in 1929; Sachiko Meguro (Totsuka) in 1926; Hisako Ōkata (Kitagawa) in 1939; and Mickey Curtis (Miyoshi) in 1938.

16. The Ministry of Health, Labor, and Welfare announced that in 2004 Japanese women's average life span was 85.59 years, while men's was 78.64 (Mainichi Newspaper, July 23, 2005).

17. Mizoguchi questions this simplistic association between softness and lesbian sex, as it may stereotypically portray lesbian sexual practices as gentle. She also correctly points out that the film portrays Miyano and Miyoshi's sex more explicitly than lesbian sex. Unlike the heterosexual couple's sex, Miyano and Yokota's "naughtiness" is implied by showing only their kiss (Mizoguchi 2001, 18–19).

18. Additionally, the novel sarcastically describes his determination: "He looked as serious and determined as if he were about to jump off from a height to kill himself"; "Miyano became gradually moved by his seriousness" (Momotani 2000, 102). By stressing his struggle, the novel emphasizes his deteriorating health.

19. The cats' names are Haruki, Tomokazu, and Yūjirō—respectively, the novelist Haruki Murakami; Tomokazu Miura, an actor known for his charming portrayals of youth in 1970s films; and the late Yūjirō Ishihara, a 1950s youth film star.

20. For her career path, see Hamano 2005, 7–42, and her website www.h3.dion.ne .jp/~tantan-s/prof.html.

21. In Japan, it is not unusual for aspiring directors who are young and male to first enter the adult film industry to gain professional filmmaking experience since the declining studios no longer offer training or promotions to directorship, and then move on to mainstream filmmaking, as did Masayuki Suō, the director of *Shall We Dance?* (*Shall we dansu?* 1996), and Yōjirō Takita, who directed *Departures* (*Okuribito,* 2008).

22. Pink films are different from the Nikkatsu Roman Poruno series (1971–1988), another subgenre of porn film, which was launched by Nikkatsu, one of the major Japanese film studios with much higher budgets. Another distinct subgenre, contemporary adult video (nowadays often digitally produced and released on DVD) requires an even shorter shooting schedule and fewer staff. These are often shot within one day by handheld camcorder and have no story and poor editing. Production costs vary, starting around 100,000 yen (US$1,200). In contrast, pink films involve 35mm film (which requires more skill at directing, shooting, and editing), more crew members, a longer shooting schedule (though usually only three days), a strong scenario, and a greater cost, at around 4,000,000 yen (US$33,000). For the Nikkatsu series and some information on pink films, see Matsushima 2000.

23. Yamazaki Kuninori occasionally writes and directs gay porn films as well.

24. The images of these deviant women are often co-opted into conventional images of sexually active women that appeal to men, a phenomenon Hamano terms a "happy misunderstanding" on the part of theater owners and viewers (Hamano 2005, 41).

25. Some of her porn films have been shown at screenings exclusively for women at film festivals. They were also screened for the general public at the retrospective "An Overview of the Works of Film Director Sachi Hamano" (*Eiga kantoku Hamano Sachi no zenbō*, Kobe Art Village Center, August 2 and 3, 2008).

26. Williams introduces American feminist porn director Candida Royalle and discusses how her Femme Production films reenvision pornography. Though Royalle and Hamano target different audiences, both directors stand out in that they challenge the dominant narratives of the genre. See Williams 1999, 246–24, and Royalle 1993.

27. The novel, originally published in 1931, combines mock-botanical discussion of moss romance, female-to-female friendships, the protagonist Machiko's unrequited love, and an amusing depiction of her life looking after household chores for her eccentric brothers and their male cousin (Ozaki 1991). Judging from the names of the characters, the plot (a household of students who came to Tokyo from the countryside), and other components, the novel also reads as a parody of *Sanshirō* by Natsume Sōseki (1908).

28. Japanese women directors in dramatic features, too, are rare and work in a male-oriented workplace. The registered members of the Director's Guild of Japan include 580 males versus 23 females (Hamano 2005, 193). Moreover, the number of women registered includes those who directed only a few times.

29. The first Japanese female director of dramatic features, Tazuko Sakane, wore trousers and had her hair cut short, so that she was called a cross-dresser (*dansō*). She also attempted to work and act like a man so that she could assimilate into the workplace. For an overview of her life and career, see Hori 2005 and Ikegawa 2005.

30. In addition to producing several porn films a year, Hamano directed and produced a new nonporn film, *Cricket Girl* (*Kōrogi jō*), an adaptation of another Ozaki story, in 2006.

References

Featherstone, Mike, and Andrew Wernick, eds. 1995. Introduction. In *Images of aging: Cultural representation of later life*, 1–15. New York: Routledge.

Gee, Ellen M., and Meredith M. Kimball. 1987. The double standard of aging: Images and sexuality. In *Women and aging*, 99–106. Toronto: Butterworths.

Hamano, Sachi. 2005. *When a woman makes a film (Onna ga eiga o tsukuru toki)*. Tokyo: Heibonsha, 2005.

————. n.d. (Her career) www.h3.dion.ne.jp/~tantan-s/prof.html (accessed September 14, 2010).

Haneda, Sumiko. 2002. *Film and I* (*Eiga to watashi*). Tokyo: Shōbunsha.

————. 2005. (interview) *Yomiuri newspaper* (*Yomiuri shinbun*), April 19. www.yomiuri .co.jp/iryou/kyousei/sasaeru/20050419sq31.htm (accessed June 30, 2006).

Hori, Hikari. 2005. Migration and transgression: Female pioneers of documentary film-making in Japan. *Asian Cinema Journal* 16 (1): 89–97.

Ikegawa, Reiko. 2005. Japanese women film-makers in the Second World War: A study of Sakane Tazuko, Suzuki Noriko and Atsugi Taka. In *Japanese women: Emerging from subservience, 1868–1945*, ed. Hiroko Tomida and Gordon Daniels, 258–277. Folkstone, Kent: Global Oriental.

Inoue, Teruko, et al., eds. 1999. *Women's data book* (*Josei no dēta bukku*). 3rd ed. Tokyo: Yūhikaku.

Kitahara, Minori. 2000. *How feminists are hated* (*Femi no kirawarekata*). Tokyo: Shin-suisha.

Makitsubo, Tazuko. Pao Production Company official website (Kikaku seisaku Pao kōshiki hōmu peiji). www.pao-jp.com (accessed September 14, 2010).

Matsui, Hisako. 2004. *Turning point* (*Tāningu pointo: "Oriume" Hyakuman nin o tsumuida deai*). Tokyo: Kōdansha.

Matsumoto, Yumiko. 1996. *Women who made films* (*Eiga o tsukutta onna tachi*). Tokyo: Shinema hausu.

Matsushima, Toshiyuki. 2000. *History of Nikkatsu Studio porn series* (*Nikkatsu roman poruno zenshi*). Tokyo: Kōdansha.

Mizoguchi, Akiko. 2001. As a "versatile" lesbian (*Lezubian no "ribako" to shite wa*). In *Lily festival* (*Yurisai*; brochure), ed. Yurisai Production Committee. Tokyo: Yurisai Production Committee.

Momotani, Hoko. 2000. *Lily festival* (*Yurisai*). Tokyo: Kōdansha.

Ozaki, Midori. 1991. *Ozaki Midori*. Chikuma Collection of Japanese Literature (Chikuma Nihon Bungaku Zenshū). Tokyo: Chikuma shobō.

Rich, Adrienne. 1986. Compulsory heterosexuality and lesbian existence. In *Blood, bread, and poetry: Selected prose, 1979–1985*. New York: Norton.

Royalle, Candida. 1993. Porn in the USA. *Social Text* 37: 23–32.

Sedgwick, Eve. 1986. *Between men: English literature and male homosocial desire*. New York: Columbia University Press.

Tokieda, Toshie. 2003. Interview. *Documentary box*. Vol. 21, English edition, 3–13. Tokyo: Yamagata International Documentary Film Festival Organizing Committee.

Tsukamoto, Yasuyo. 2001. A gentle but invigorating "Rainy Night Discussion" (Kusugutta-kumo sōkai na "amayo no shinasadame"). *Lily festival* (*Yurisai*; brochure), ed. Yurisai Production Committee. Tokyo: Yurisai Production Committee.

Wada, Shuichi. 1995. Status and image of the elderly in Japan: Understanding the paternalistic ideology. In *Images of aging: Cultural representation of later life*, ed. Mike Featherstone and Andrew Wernick, 48–60. New York: Routledge.

Williams, Linda. 1999. *Hard core: Power, pleasure, and the "Frenzy of the Visible."* Rev. ed. Berkeley: University of California Press.

Yurisai (Lily festival). 2001. Directed by Sachi Hamano. 100 min. Tokyo: Tantansha.

II

Understanding and Misunderstanding the Verbal Behavior of the Elderly

6 The Value of Talk

Critical Perspectives on Studying the Speech
Practices of Elderly People in the United
States with Implications for Japan

Anne R. Bower

The Similarity of American and Japanese Aging Concerns

In 2004, the number of people over the age of 65 in Japan was 24.8 million, about 20 percent of the Japanese population. This is expected to increase to about 35 percent by 2050 (National Institute of Population and Social Security Research 2002). In 2000, the population over 65 in the United States was 35 million, about 12.4 percent of the total population. This number is expected to increase to about 20 percent in 2050, constituting a projected 79 million (United States Census Bureau 2004). Not surprisingly, Japan and the United States share similar concerns about how to meet the projected long-term care needs of their growing elderly populations (Chan 2005).

Importing Care Models

In an effort to meet the anticipated residential needs of its elderly population, Japan has investigated both Western and Asian industrialized nations' approaches to long-term care in a variety of areas. Of particular interest have been models for long-term care (Walker 1996; Nakane and Farevaag 2004), models for assessing quality of care (Watanabe et al. 1999) and quality of life (Tsutomu et al. 1998; Liang et al. 1992), architectural models for institutional residences (Links International 2003), direct care staff licensing and training requirements (Yamada and Sekiya 2003), dissemination of dementia care training programs (Chee and Levkoff 2001), and models for development of long-term care policies (AARP Global Aging Program 2003).

Importing Bias

Cross-cultural applications of this sort can be productive but are not without their hazards. Chief among those hazards is the problem of importing and replicating cultural bias from one setting into another. Here, "bias" refers to the culturally bound ways of thinking by which people ordinarily shape their experiences and attribute meaning. Biases emerge from deeply entrenched cultural beliefs and values. Whether explicit or implicit, they powerfully influence how we see and interpret the world around us. In cross-cultural settings, it is desirable that biases be made as explicit as possible to enhance the clarity and productivity of cross-cultural exchange.

There is a wealth of multidisciplinary literature addressing the differences between Japanese and Western perspectives on aging. Cultural similarities and differences in beliefs have been widely studied in caregiving for elderly people (Chi et al. 2001; Bengston et al. 2000; Long 2000; Liu and Kendig 2000), particularly with regard to Japanese and Western perspectives on "generational contract" (Izuhara 2002; Hashimoto 1996), residential preferences (Howe 2001), long-term care (McCormick et al. 2002; Bethel 1992; Kinoshita and Kiefer 1992), and palliative care (Fetters 2002). However, the American characterization of Japanese culture as one that "honors its elders" has been increasingly challenged as an idealization (O'Leary 1993; Palmore 1993; Tobin 1987; Ota and Giles, this volume), and a growing body of literature has begun to question the applicability of Western social constructs to Japanese cultural contexts (Murata 2007; Ryang 2004; Kozuki and Kennedy 2004; Goodman 2002). Developing culturally sensitive interpretations of the experience and meaning of aging has been an important objective in this literature, which is based on research involving Japanese families' nursing home visiting patterns (Fukahori et al. 2007), notions of caregiver burden (Asahara et al. 2001), and definitions of quality of life (Wu 2004).

In this realm of discourse, the risk of importing bias decreases because cultural difference in experience and interpretation is the explicit focus. Yet implicit cultural biases also exist in this discourse, and the risk of replicating them remains high because they are rarely readily apparent. The purpose of this chapter is to identify and explore one such implicit bias as it appears in the Anglo-American gerontological research and practice community and to consider its implications for Japanese gerontologists.

Researchers and practitioners in the Anglo-American community place a high value on talk—language and communication—as a means of understanding the physiological and social experiences of aging. Language and communication are regarded as diagnostic of both the disease processes associated with aging and the adaptive processes that accompany aging. With regard to disease processes, elders' language and speech practices are conceptualized as indicators of cognitive or physiological capability and discussed in terms of maintenance, preservation, or loss. With regard to adaptive processes, elders' speech practices are regarded as indicators of psychosocial adjustment and discussed in terms of successful or unsuccessful adaptation. This way of thinking about talk as a diagnostic of disease or adaptation proceeds from a confluence of cultural beliefs about language and age and how they are related to one another. In the Anglo-American context, talk is a valued form of individual self-expression and self-assertion. It conveys personal experience, thoughts, and feelings. Culturally, it is regarded as an important and enjoyable activity, and the absence of talk is perceived as potentially problematic. Meanwhile, aging—that is, growing old and being old—is conceptualized as an overarching experience of decrement, decline, and loss that cuts across work and social life, social and familial relationships, independence, cognitive ability, and health. Talk and aging intersect because talk represents a central mechanism through which all members of the culture experience and interpret aging.

The view of talk as diagnostic is deeply entrenched in the gerontological research and practice community as an appropriate starting point for the study of aging. It shapes the way research and practice are conducted. Because gerontological literature, with its deeply ingrained belief in the importance of talk, is the dominant means of elucidating the needs of elderly people, health care providers turn to this body of literature for direction in developing clinical treatment programs, caregiving plans, and long-term care policy. As a result, this notion profoundly influences the quality of care and quality of life for elderly people in community and institutional settings.

Yet the gerontological literature rarely reflects upon the beliefs and values about talk and aging that it brings to identifying significant research questions, conducting research, interpreting findings, and making recommendations. Further, implicit in its view of aging as loss is the primacy of the younger adult perspective as the normative base. With the best of intentions, the research and practice discourse describes, interprets, and explains aging and speech from vantage points implicitly grounded in the younger adult's experience and perspective. Thus, while elderly people serve as subjects of study and their linguistic and communicative activities constitute the data, *their* perspectives on their language and speech practices are rarely sought or addressed. This unconscious but systematic omission of elders' perspectives is an important manifestation of the bias.

For those who are considering cross-cultural applications of Anglo-American caregiving models, it is important to be aware that such a bias about talk and age exists, understand its shape and operation, and weigh the advantages and disadvantages of importing it into Japanese contexts.

To this end, this chapter attempts to explain the talk-as-diagnostic bias, provide a methodology for doing so, and suggest an alternative interpretation. It is to be hoped that this discussion will encourage researchers and practitioners in both Anglo-American and Japanese communities to reflect on the assumptions that shape their thinking about elders' language and speech practices (see also Matsumoto, this volume) and how these may affect their work with elderly people (see also Morita, this volume).

A Critical Gerontological Perspective on Language and Speech Practices

A critical perspective serves as one entryway into explicating the talk-as-diagnostic bias. Whether in gerontology, cultural anthropology, or literary studies, a critical approach typically challenges prevailing theories, methods, and interpretations. Its aim is to develop new insights into the field of inquiry and to identify new ways of conceptualizing, defining, and addressing problems.[1]

A central contention in critical gerontology is that shared assumptions about the world are encoded in the research process. These serve not only to shape the course of inquiry, but also to maintain or replicate societal values, roles, and structures. Luborsky and Sankar (1993) argue that such assumptions are located in and communicated by "scripts" buried in the analytic constructs of the field. Such scripts can be identified, examined, and used as a basis for further research that provides new insights into a given phenomenon.

The implicit bias of interest here—talk as diagnostic—is just such an embedded script in aging research and practice. It can be described and explored using the theories and methods of cultural anthropology.

The Ethnography of Speaking

Language and speech practices are cultural phenomena. As such, their form, structure, and meaning are open to discovery and description. Interpretation must proceed from and reflect members' experiences and perceptions of meaning in speaking and speech practices in a given culture. To this end, cultural anthropology offers an interpretative model known as the "ethnography of speaking" (Hymes 1972) or "ethnography of communication" (Saville-Troike 1989).

In the late 1960s, anthropologist and linguist Dell Hymes presented a model for describing language use and speech practices across cultures. In his now classic article entitled "Models for the Interaction of Language and Social Life" (1972), Hymes argued for the need to treat language and speech as situated practice, that is, as an activity located for participants in a physical and social environment at a given point in time. This makes it possible to discover and delineate the aspects of speech practice that participants regard as salient (Hymes 1972, 52).

The speaking model used in the ethnography of speaking is comprehensive, complex, and elastic. It was developed from an extensive study of speech use in 75 different societies (Sherzer and Darnell 1972). In addition to providing an analysis of speech and speaking, it also offers guidelines for the ethnographic study of other aspects of language use, such as beliefs about speech, the role of speech in the life cycle, the social control functions of speech, and cultural typologies of language use. The model identifies multiple components of speaking that may be used to analyze speech and speaking in any given society. These components include the social unit, social setting, and participants; the language variety and unit of study; the quantity, frequency, topic, content, tone, and manner of speech; the purpose and outcomes of speech, and the norms of interaction and interpretation of speech.

The content and salience of each component varies among social groups. The relationships among the components also varies. The identity of the components and the way in which they relate to each other constitute the ways of speaking for members of a culture. It is the objective of the ethnographer to show for a given sociocultural group what the components are, what their nature is, which components are salient, and how they relate to one another.

This model will explicate the talk-as-diagnostic bias in several ways. In the following section, the model is applied to the gerontological literature that addresses elderly people's language and speech practices in order to learn: first, what components of speech the research and practice community identifies as important; second, the nature of those components as perceived by that community; and third, the perceived relationships among the components of speech. The succeeding section shows how this process reveals the assumptions the community brings to its analysis of elders' speech practices and how it shapes understanding. Finally, the model is applied to select examples from the literature to show how a different set of assumptions results in a different understanding of the experience and meaning of old people's talk.

The Aging Research and Practice Literature

Researchers elect to study what they perceive to be salient aspects of a phenomenon, and those perceptions are derived in part from the cultural groups of which they are members. The scientists represented in this review are from the United States, Canada, Australia, Britain, Scotland, and Wales, constituents of a broader Anglo and North American culture. They are also members of various scientific or clinical communities, carrying out their work guided by the intellectual paradigms in which they were trained. Their scientific interest in and writing about aging in general and how language figures in the experience of aging reflect both Anglo-American values and the attitudes of their scientific and clinical communities. Thus, the research literature these scientists and clinicians produce can be viewed as cultural documents—as primary sources of cultural information about Anglo-American values and beliefs related to the elderly and their speech practices.

Clinical and social science literature about the experiences of elderly people in institutional, long-term care settings comprises a variety of theoretical perspectives and social agendas, quantitative and qualitative methodologies, and social and geographic groups. Much of this literature specifically addresses various aspects of elders' linguistic and communicative capabilities. In addition, a substantial body of work focuses on the social interactions of elderly people. While talk is not the main focus of these studies, they contain important information about talk nonetheless. Given the diffuse nature of this literature, it is a challenge to identify, synthesize, and interpret findings relevant to old people's talk. However, two central conceptualizations of the nature and meaning of elders' talk emerge in the literature—a biomedical formulation and a sociocultural formulation. The speaking model described in the preceding section provides a means for characterizing each formulation and relating it to a broader structure of cultural beliefs and values. Each is discussed below.

The Biomedical Formulation

The biomedical perspective is represented by neuropsychological, neurolinguistic, psycholinguistic, and other clinical research that studies the neurological and cognitive bases of language production and comprehension, in part by measuring speakers' ability to produce and comprehend linguistic forms and relationships.

Researchers have developed a wide range of clinical tools and standardized instruments to discern and measure linguistic capabilities. These instruments are employed across age groups and are typically used as diagnostic measures to identify the nature and extent of cognitive impairment among the elderly (Kim and Bayles 2007). As an object of study, language production and comprehension is largely removed from its social context. Testing is typically carried out in clinical or research settings, although less formal settings are increasingly included. Testing sessions vary considerably in length, depending on the subject's stamina.

The biomedical formulation operationalizes speakers' verbal utterances as a production phenomenon, such as a "verbal output continuum" (Ulatowska and Chapman 1991). The linguistic form is the central unit of investigation.[2] For data analysis, language forms are unitized and quantified. The number and frequency of forms produced by a speaker are the central dimensions for analyzing language competence and performance because number and frequency are regarded as indicators of linguistic complexity, for example, the number of words in a clause, the number of clauses in a sentence, the number of sentences in a story, and so on. Complexity is also defined in terms of the relationships among forms, as in syntactic relationships (active-passive voice, dependent-independent clause), syntactic structures (left and right branching structures), or discourse processes (topic, theme, coherence, cohesion). The time it takes a speaker to produce or comprehend a "verbal output continuum" is another important unit of measurement. It is conceptualized in terms of speed, that is, how fast a speaker can produce and comprehend language. From this perspective, the implicit standard of linguistic performance is the younger or middle-aged adult's production and comprehension ability (Coupland et al. 1991), while for the impaired elder, the implicit standard is the healthy elder's ability.

A substantial biomedical literature directly addresses the linguistic and communicative capabilities of elderly speakers.[3] Key findings from this literature are summarized and presented in the following profile of the biomedical perspective on elderly speakers' linguistic and communicative capabilities.

From the biomedical perspective, normal aging is regarded as having an overall deleterious effect on speakers' ability to competently produce and comprehend language. While there appears to be little clinically identifiable change in the phonological productions of elderly speakers, progressive decline in competence and performance is identified in most areas of language, including production fluency and the speed of speech production and comprehension. While studies indicate no changes in elders' prosodic features (e.g., intonation, stress), physiological changes in voice quality (e.g., hoarseness, creaky voice) are widely noted.

Similarly, elderly speakers' ability to retrieve and process words declines with regard to accuracy and performance time. Meaningful content decreases as "empty words" (e.g., pronouns lacking clear referents, indefinites), fillers (e.g., "uh," "you know," "okay"), and circumlocution increase. (See Hamaguchi, this volume.) Elderly speakers demonstrate increased difficulty in processing the complex logical or inferential relationships signaled by linguistic forms. There is a progressive decrease in elderly speakers' production and comprehension of complex syntactic structures (Kemper 1992). Sentences are shorter and less complex syntactically.

At the discourse level, elderly speakers' competence and performance in producing extended stretches of topically focused, thematically relevant talk decreases. Introduction of nonthematic material increases (Glosser and Deser 1992), as does the frequency of self-interruption, hesitation, revision, and repetition. Elderly speakers also are likely to have difficulty in comprehending topics across stretches of discourse (Ulatowska and Chapman 1991; Wingfield 1996). However, elders' discourse production skills are found to diminish less significantly in narrative (telling a story) than in other speech genres (e.g., description, giving instructions, conversation), and elders' narratives have been found to contain highly elaborate event and evaluative structures. Elderly speakers whose linguistic capabilities have diminished compensate for these limitations by drawing on their real-world knowledge about the speech situation to aid them in production and comprehension tasks (Bayles and Kaszniak 1987; Ulatowska et al. 2004).

This summary reflects findings for the "normal" aged in relatively good health. However, the diseases (e.g., Alzheimer's disease and other dementias, Parkinson's disease, stroke) and conditions (e.g., hearing loss, depression) associated with old age are felt to further compromise elderly speakers' language production and comprehension. Different diseases and medical disorders affect language production and comprehension in different ways (Ripich 1991). Alzheimer's disease appears to progressively affect a speaker's word retrieval capabilities and ability to manage coherence, while sparing syntactic complexity (Wingfield 2001). Verbosity, defined as a prolific and topically unfocused speech pattern often associated with age, appears to co-occur with declining frontal lobe performance (Gold et al. 1994).

In the biomedical formulation, a task- and performance-oriented vocabulary is used to assess, describe, and discuss language production and comprehension ability. Standardized assessment instruments are called "tests," "tasks," and "measures" (e.g., the Boston Naming Test, the Lexical Decision Task, or the FAS Word Fluency Measure). Speakers' capabilities, competence, and performance are evaluated along dimensions of "increase" and "decrease," and are described as "preserved" or "maintained," as "reduced" or "diminished," or "spared" by disease processes. Elders' speech performance is also glossed using cultural descriptions of speech styles, for example, "verbose," "tangential," "taciturn," or "perseverating." This vocabulary of decrement and decline has been widely noted in social and behavioral science research, and its link to broader cultural constructs has also been discussed (Coupland et al. 1991; Hamilton 1999; McHugh 2003). We will return to this link below.

The Sociocultural Formulation

A number of disciplines in the social and behavioral sciences are also concerned with aging, including social psychology, sociology, cultural anthropology, sociolinguistics, and communication science in the social sciences, and clinical psychology, social work, recreation therapy, and pastoral care in the behavioral sciences. Nursing is strongly represented in gerontology, encompassing both biomedical and sociocultural perspectives. Health care business, administration, and policy are also significant voices.

Referred to here collectively as *sociocultural*, these varied perspectives are united by their focus on the elderly person's physical, mental, social, and spiritual well-being. Adaptation, adjustment, and activity are key principles in conceptualizing late-life experiences (see also Doba et al., this volume, and Takahashi et al., this volume).[4] Adaptation theory, activity theory, and the role of adjustment in both have been expounded, examined, applied, and contested through several decades of gerontological research (George 2001; Atchley 2001; Achenbaum et al. 1996, 6–10), but it is generally agreed that language and communication are central to these processes (Hummert and Nussbaum 2001). Language enters into this discussion as "talk," a meaningful verbal exchange between individuals and a central component of social interaction. Referred to by a variety of terms, such as interpersonal interaction, social interaction, verbal interaction, communication, or conversation, talk also constitutes an activity in its own right. It encompasses and is embodied in a wide range of social actions.[5]

From the sociocultural perspective, the frequency, quantity, and quality of the speech activities in which an individual engages are regarded as important indicators of adaptation and adjustment. A large quantity of talk and frequent participation in speech activities is felt to result in higher levels of life satisfaction. Conversely, low levels of participation are felt to result in lower life satisfaction levels (Brent et al. 1984). Sociocultural researchers conceptualize the quality of talk in terms of topic and content, typically describing it as "high" or "low," "deep" or "superficial," "important" or "trivial." The tone of talk represents another indicator of quality, and is described as "engaged" or "disengaged," "involved" or "uninvolved," and so on. Thus, talk of high quality is felt to be directly related to positive adaptation and adjustment, while low-quality talk is felt to indicate the opposite.

In this formulation, both quantitative and qualitative methods are used to study elders' speech activities.[6] Sociocultural researchers regard speech activities as important means for studying adaptation because they have a concrete shape and their frequency and quantity can be unitized and quantified. However, the "quality" of talk, as revealed in topic, content, and tone of speech, is less easily quantified. As in the biomedical formulation, the younger or middle-aged adult's speech practices are the implicit basis for assessment and comparison.

The quality of life and care for elderly people living in long-term care settings has been a central focus in sociocultural research. It is generally agreed that this setting, particularly nursing homes, neither fosters nor supports the types of social interactions and speech activities that promote elderly residents' successful adjustment and adaptation (Ice 2002; Baltes and Wahl 1996; Grainger 1995; Nolan et al. 1995; Coupland and Ylanne-McEwen 1993; Nussbaum 1991; Lubinski 1984; Shield 1988; Gubrium 1975). A summary of findings from the sociocultural research and practice literature provides a snapshot of this perspective on the context and nature of elders' speech activities in nursing home settings.

The sociocultural literature consistently reports an overall "absence of conversation" as the normative state (Applegate and Morse 1994; Reed and Payton 1996; Sigman 1985), and the "paucity," "scarcity," and "lack" of speech activity is widely noted (Hubbard et al. 2002; Kaakinen 1992; Savishinksy 1991; Shield 1988; Gubrium 1975). Sociocultural researchers identify elements of the setting that impede opportunities for talk among residents. For example, residents' immobility or other-initiated mobility (e.g., staff) interferes with their ability to select and talk with compatible conversational partners and results in less social interaction (Smithers 1990). Because talk is regarded as an integral element of friendship between residents, residents who name few others on the unit as friends are felt to lack conversational opportunities (Bitzan and Kruzich 1990; Miller and Beer 1977). Researchers also observe that the norms of conversational address, polite conversation, and turn-taking are consistently suspended in the nursing home setting. Residents do not address each other by name, do not initiate conversations when in the presence of others, make poor eye contact with others, and respond with one- or two-word answers when spoken to or do not reply at all (Kato et al. 1996; Applegate and Morse 1994; Lubinski et al. 1981; Bennett 1963).

Researchers conclude that residents do engage in social interaction and speech activities with each other, but that the quantity and frequency of such interactions is low (Kato et al. 1996). As a result, the nursing home as a social setting is characterized as having "pockets of social interaction within the context of social isolation" (Hubbard et al. 2002; Sigman 1985).

While the quantity and frequency of speech activities as embodied in social interaction is a critical dimension of adaptation, the quality of speech activities is equally crucial. The topic and content of speech activities and their tone and conduct represent important indicators of quality. Overall, the quality of speech activities in the nursing home setting is widely regarded as "impoverished" along these dimensions (Lubinski 1995).

The content of speech activities on the unit is regulated by both residents and staff. Topic guidelines are clearly articulated. Residents say they talk about the weather, the behavior of other residents, feelings about living in the nursing home, food and eating, personal interests, family, formalities, and complaints (Reed and Payton 1996; Gutheil 1991). They identify a variety of topics that they perceive to be inappropriate for discussion, for example, dying, getting lonely, criticism of the nursing home, illness, and personal matters (Kaakinen 1992; Bennett 1963). Similarly, nursing home staff identify topics they regard as appropriate for discussion, such as sports, crime, and local politics. Topics felt by staff to be inappropriate for discussion include events outside the facility, personalities, residents' life before the nursing home, life, death, and religion (Hubbard et al. 2003; Hubbard et al. 2002). Sociocultural researchers regard this range of topics for talk to be "narrow" (Powers 1995) or "trivial," with an emphasis on biographical facts rather than character, interests, or personal details (Reed and Payton 1996). They report that residents themselves note the absence of "meaningful" conversation with other residents (Lubinski et al. 1981), saying they have nothing to talk about (Kaakinen 1992). Residents' overall participation in speech activities is widely described as "superficial" and "disinterested," with little attempt to acknowledge the other (Applegate and Morse 1994). Sociocultural researchers note that while residents do participate in speech activities, they rarely appear engaged. The tone of a social interaction may be cordial, but rarely intimate or intense (Reed and Payton 1996).

As in the biomedical formulation, the sociocultural vocabulary enlists a performative metaphor for assessing, describing, and discussing nursing home residents' social interactions. Adjustment and adaptation are achieved "successfully" or "well." Antonyms for "successful" (e.g., "failed," "unsuccessful," "maladjusted"), although implicit, are rarely used in this literature. Mitigated variants (e.g., "less successful," "lower level of quality of life," "less well-adjusted") are preferred. The value placed on quantity, frequency, and quality of talk is apparent in the vocabulary used in the sociocultural formulation to describe speech in the nursing home setting, including "absence," "lack," "scarcity," "paucity," and "impoverishment." We will further consider these values below.

Seeing the Script

Although characterized by different disciplines, theories, methods, questions, and goals in their study of aging and language, the biomedical and sociocultural research and practice communities are quite similar in how they conceptualize the language and speech practices of elderly people. Both communities place a high value on talk as a means of assessing the physiological and social experience of aging. The structural components of talk that are perceived as salient, the beliefs about talk that support perceptions of salience, and the norms for interpreting elders' talk are also nearly identical. Table 6.1 summarizes the elements of speaking identified by both formulations and displays them in alignment with components of the speaking model.

As we have seen, three components consistently emerge as central in both formulations: the quantity, frequency, and quality of speech. Speech is assessed along a greater-to-lesser continuum of quantity (from "a lot of talk" to "no talk"), frequency (from "often" to "never"), and quality (from "coherent" to "incoherent," from "deep" to "trivial"). The perceptions of quantity, frequency, and quality as salient components of talk reflect culture-based beliefs about language, as does the perception that their combinations and patterns have meaning. This meaning is also expressed as a continuum—from the presence of talk to the absence of talk.

Table 6.1. Elements of speaking identified by the biomedical and sociocultural formulations

Speaking model	Biomedical formulation	Sociocultural formulation
Unit of study	Linguistic form of talk, particularly lexical, syntactic, and discourse	Speech activities, particularly conversation
Context of study	Talk studied in an experimental context	Talk studied in the social setting
Quantity of speech	"A lot of talk" vs. "no talk"	"A lot of talk" vs. "no talk"
Frequency of speech	"Often" vs. "never"	"Often" vs. "never"
Quality of speech (topic and content)	Coherence and cohesion	Depth of content: "Deep" vs. "trivial"
Language belief: Quantity + frequency + quality = Meaning	Presence vs. absence "Talk" vs. "no talk" Speaking vs. silence	Presence vs. absence "Talk" vs. "no talk" Speaking vs. silence
Role of talk	Diagnostic (pathologizes speech practices)	Diagnostic (problematizes speech practices)
Norm of interpretation: Method of study	Count quantity and frequency; interpret quality	Count quantity and frequency; interpret quality
Norm of interpretation: Standard for evaluation	Middle-aged adults or healthy elderly in social interaction; evaluation based on performance and task	Middle-aged adults in social interaction; evaluation based on performance and achievement
Norm of interpretation: Findings	Varying quantity + frequency + less quality = decreased linguistic capability: decrement, decline, and loss	Less quantity + less frequency + less quality = "paucity" or "lack": unsuccessful adaptation

In the Anglo-American context, the absence of talk is often glossed as *silence*. Given the importance of talk and the absence of talk in the biomedical and sociocultural understanding of elderly people's speech practices, it will be useful to briefly consider some of the cultural beliefs about silence in the modern Anglo-American context. A cross-cultural, comparative literature offers important insights into the cultural meaning of silence (e.g., Kurzon 1997; Jaworski 1997; Enninger 1987; Tannen and Saville-Troike 1985) and consistently notes the high value Anglo-American cultures place on talk. Americans lead their British, Australian, and Anglo-Canadian counterparts in demonstrating a strong preference for active, overt, verbal exchanges about a range of topics with both intimates and strangers in a wide variety of public and private settings (Tannen 1985). For Americans particularly, talk is a highly valued form of self-expression and self-assertion through which individual experiences, thoughts, and feelings are conveyed.

Americans value a high quantity and frequency of talk. They report spending on average seven hours in conversation per day, compared to Japanese reports of approximately 3.5 hours of conversation per day (Bruneau and Ishii 1988). Americans are highly sensitive to the occurrence of periods of time in which no talk occurs. Speed of response is a critical element in the conversational exchange, and "no talk" is perceived as silence within a very narrow window of time (Walker 1985). Conversation analysts report that an "acceptable" period of silence in American conversational speech situations is 1.5 seconds. At three seconds, the period is perceived as "an extended silence" (Sacks et al. 1974; Davidson 1984). Listeners are rarely silent when others speak. While a speaker is talking, listeners continuously produce an array of verbal and nonverbal "back channel" cues such as "mhmm," "yes," "uh-uh," eye contact, nods, and physical proximity that both interlocutors construe as indications of engagement (Houck and Gass 1997).

Thus, for Americans, a highly salient experience of talk is in its absence, that is, silence. In American conversational settings, the preference for continuous talk is strong (Goffman 1971; Tannen 1985), and it is specifically required in settings where social relationships must be established or reestablished (Milroy 1980). Within this conversational context, silence is regarded as very likely to indicate trouble. Even the shortest periods of silence may signal a potential problem in the conversational exchange, such as a production error (e.g., an inaudible utterance) (Schiffrin 1987), a rejection of some aspect of the interaction (Davidson 1984), disengagement from the conversation (Goffman 1967), disagreement with the current speaker's statement (Pomerantz 1984), or a difference in sociocultural knowledge about conversational norms (Gumperz 1999). Silence is also widely considered evidence of negative affect, such as sorrow, embarrassment, or anger (Jaworski 1997; Tannen and Saville-Troike 1985). When silences do occur in a conversational setting, there must be a "legitimate excuse" for silence (McLaughlin and Cody 1982), such as being in an "open state of talk" in which speech can stop or start coincident with another activity (Goffman 1976). A "legitimate" silence may also occur in settings where the rapport or intimacy between participants is so great that "they have no need for words" (Saville-Troike 1989).

American culture is not alone in attributing meaning to silence. British, Australian, and Anglo-Canadian cultures share this value (Giles et al. 1992), although there are differences in its extent and intensity. However, in other cultures, the value of talk and the meaning of silence differ. For example, in the Paliyan culture of southern India, the value of talk and silence is virtually opposite that of Anglo-American culture: "Paliyans communicate very little at all times and become almost silent by the age of 40. Verbal, communicative persons are regarded as abnormal and often as offensive" (Gardner 1966, 398). In the Native American cultures of the Columbia River area in Oregon, silence represents a normative response to a question: "[They do] . . . not require that a question be immediately followed by an answer. . . . It *may* be followed by an answer but may also be followed by silence, or by an utterance that bears no relationship to the question. Then the answer to the question may follow as long as five or ten minutes later" (Hymes 1975, 31). Japanese and American beliefs about the value of talk and the meaning of silence also appear to be in opposition, and differences between the two cultures have been widely documented (Bruneau and Ishii 1988; Enninger 1987; Lebra 1987; Barnlund 1975; Doi 1974).

The presence of such beliefs and values about talk and silence has important implications for gerontological research and practice. Researchers and clinicians are first and foremost members of their cultures. Not surprisingly, then, they formulate questions, structure inquiries, and interpret their findings about elders' language and speech practices in light of their cultural beliefs about talk. The cultural orientation toward quantity, frequency, and quality as the salient components of talk and the presence or absence of talk as a meaningful pattern lead to the perception of talk as *diagnostic*. Cultural beliefs about the meaning of silence lead to an interpretation of the absence of talk as indicative of a potentially troublesome state or situation.

Thus, for biomedical researchers and clinicians who are concerned with disease and the aging process, talk becomes a *diagnostic of pathology*. This perception underpins biomedical research findings about elders' reduced quantity and frequency of talk, loss of content quality, and declining production and comprehension capability. Similarly, for sociocultural researchers and clinicians for whom the process of adaptation is central, talk becomes a *diagnostic of psychosocial adjustment*. The culture-based belief that silence is problematic supports the view that, for elderly people in social settings, "scarcity of conversation" and "long periods of silence in which no words are spoken" (Savishinsky 1991) are maladaptive conditions.

Just as these cultural beliefs about talk shape perceptions about what components of language and speaking are relevant for study, they also guide judgments about appropriate methods for study and standards for assessment and evaluation. Cultural beliefs about language intersect with beliefs about age, as when the speech of language and communicative behavior of younger adults serves as the standard for describing, assessing, and evaluating elders' talk.[7]

From an ethnographic perspective, however, culture-based ways of conceptualizing talk, identifying its presence and absence, interpreting silence, selecting methodologies, and establishing reference points for assessment all represent norms of interpretation. In his discussion of the speaking model, Hymes describes norms of interpretation as "conventional, consensual understandings about the meaning of verbal behavior" that are grounded in a community's belief system (Hymes 1972, 64). As such, they constitute the implicit bias or the embedded scripts described in the preceding section. Embedded scripts are simply collectively held norms of interpretation about some phenomenon—in this case, talk and the meaning it holds. Like most interpretative norms, they lie so deeply below the level of conscious awareness as to be invisible. They are rarely perceived as influential in shaping theory, method, hypotheses, and findings about elders' speech practices. They simply feel like the "right" way to think about language and aging.

Yet, these implicit biases serve to replicate and validate the conventional practice of gerontology that pathologizes and problematizes the quantity, frequency, and quality of elders' speech and interprets them in light of middle-aged adult linguistic and communicative behaviors. How nearly these formulations capture the elderly speaker's experience of language and speaking is questionable. We know little about how elders experience their language and speech activities and still less about the meaning their speech practices hold for them. As members of their culture, elderly people also hold beliefs and values about talk, silence, and age, but we know little about how these are the same or different from those of younger people. The power of the conventional wisdom is such that the elderly voice—when it is directly appealed to and reported on—is filtered through the prevailing scripts of pathology and problem. In research reports that discuss elderly persons' linguistic and communicative experience, it is difficult to distinguish between the elder's voice and the research voice. As a result, with the best of intentions, the conventional scripts that underpin the gerontological community's study of elderly people's language and speech practices obscure our view of elders' experience of talk and the meaning it holds for them (see also Matsumoto 2009). This can lead to inaccurate understandings of elders' experiences and can reduce the efficacy of the caregiving models and practices that are developed.

An Alternative Approach

The objective here is not to challenge the *accuracy* of the behavioral observations that gerontologists have made about the linguistic and communicative behaviors of elderly people. Indeed, elders' language and speech practices do appear to differ from those of younger adults, at least in form, quantity, and frequency. Elders do appear to speak less than their middle-aged counterparts. However, the prevailing scripts that pathologize and problematize the absence of talk among the elderly—particularly among the institutionalized elderly—have important implications for caregiving and so are worthy of challenge. These scripts limit our thinking and understanding with regard to elderly speakers' practice of silence, and this points to the need for an alternative approach.

To this end, an ethnographic approach is proposed. Applied to the study of elders' talk and silence, an ethnographic approach seeks to identify and describe elderly speakers' practice of silence and to discover the meaning it holds for them in their daily speech settings and situations. Three examples drawn from sociocultural studies of frail, elderly nursing home residents will illustrate how a critically applied ethnographic perspective can produce an analysis that challenges conventional interpretations of elders' silence as problematic. In each example, the "paucity" or "lack" of interaction between elders so frequently noted in the sociocultural formulation is recast in terms of the speaking model's components to arrive at a very different interpretation of elders' practice of silence.

Speech Situation: Paucity of Interaction or State of Open Talk?

In an ethnographic study of nursing home elders' talk about dying and death (Bower 1998), I reinterpret the phenomenon of "paucity of interaction." Nursing home residents spend many hours in the public areas of their facilities in silent company with other residents. The silence is punctuated at intervals by talk. However, I argue that, in the public social places on a residential unit of a nursing home, this clearly identified pattern of speaking (i.e., quantity and frequency) is more consistent with a *state of open talk* than indicative of problematic interaction. Following sociologist Erving Goffman's definition (1981), when an open state of talk obtains in a social setting, participants have the right—but not the obligation—to initiate talk with others, suspend talk with others, resume talk, or resume silence, depending on the activities unfolding in that setting at that moment. Thus, an open state of talk is characterized by periods of talk and periods of silence. Silences of varying lengths occur naturally and appropriately. The alternating periods of talk and silence are not perceived by those present to indicate new, interrupted, or concluded encounters but rather to constitute a whole, on-going conversation. I contend that the sociocultural formulation of such stretches of silence as a "dearth" of talk or "paucity of interaction" fails to grasp the complex nature of the speech situation. Such a characterization focuses on the absence of talk as the single defining component of the speech situation and extracts it from the context in which it occurs, thereby stripping it of its meaning. As a result, the speech situation as a whole is misconstrued and misrepresented. The elderly residents participating normatively and appropriately in this state of open talk are assessed as maladaptive.

Speech Acts: Paucity of Interaction or Shared Code?

In their 1994 qualitative study of personal privacy and interactional patterns in a Canadian veterans' nursing home, Applegate and Morse report on the "absence of conversation among residents," which they describe as "the most striking feature" of the nursing home unit they observed (1994, 418). They identify speech settings and speech situations in which they regard the absence of talk between residents to be particularly marked because these are occasions normatively expected to include speech activities, such as entry to and exit from public social spaces, meal times, or shared living quarters. In a compelling example of the absence of talk, they report that "two of the men greeted each other at every meal with the same expression: 'I see you made it' to which the second man replied, 'Yes, and I see you did, too.' Other than that exchange, no words were spoken during the meal" (422). Applegate and Morse characterize the topic and tone of this exchange as "superficial and trite," grouping it with other behaviors they take to indicate impersonal relationships, such as not making eye contact and not greeting others. In their view, this exchange is "depersonalizing."

This interpretation is certainly consistent with the sociocultural formulation, but it misses the opportunity to discern in the *absence* of talk the *presence* of something else. For example, it could be argued that the exchange between these two elderly veterans represents a communication that affirms their shared experience and articulates a sense of complicity. The linguistic form of this exchange, its content, and its occasion all suggest a phatic communication, that is, one whose primary function is to create or sustain a social contact rather than convey information or ideas (Malinowski 1935; Coupland et al. 1992). The linguistic form of this exchange is terse—12 words in all. The economy of linguistic form is characteristic of the coded message. Codes index shared identities and experiences in language that are typically brief (Bernstein 1972) and may serve either a phatic or referential purpose (Bower 2010). The content of the exchange between the two elderly veterans suggests a shared understanding of their past and present roles and circumstances. As co-residents in a nursing home, they are now comrades-in-arms, just as they might have been in the military. Life in the nursing home is their battlefield now. Each day at their meals, they see that the other has "made it" through yet another skirmish—another morning in the nursing home, another afternoon, another night—and is still alive to fight on, to continue living in the nursing home. The repetition of this exchange at each meal over an extended period of co-residence lends it a ritualistic character that supports its analysis as a phatic communication.

If this alternative interpretation of the veterans' exchange is accepted, then its outcome is the direct opposite of Applegate and Morse's "depersonalization." Rather, the outcome is an enhanced social connection between the two men. In the ceremonial exchange of these 12 words, the two elders articulate and affirm their experience and the meaning it holds for them. The social relationship that emerges is thus maintained and reinforced—at each meal, on a daily basis—by this coded communication embedded in the absence of other talk.

Although the alternative interpretation is grounded in the elderly veterans' actual language, both the "depersonalization" interpretation and the "social connection" interpretation are merely speculative. Good ethnographic practice recommends a return to those two speakers to talk with them about their exchange of the same 12 words each night at dinner in order to learn from them what they perceive their exchange to mean.

Topic and Frequency of Talk: Paucity of Interaction or Verbal Strategy?

A third example demonstrates how the absence of talk serves an important communicative function for elderly speakers. In his ethnographic study of social interaction in an American Jewish nursing home, Kahn (1999) discusses how elderly residents find ways to make a home for themselves in the institutional setting of a long-term care facility. He identifies one strategy for doing so, which residents call "making the best of it." For residents, a central aspect of "making the best of it" is de-emphasizing the negative aspects of nursing home life, a speech act Kahn describes as "downplaying." His description reveals that residents accomplish downplaying through control over the topic, quantity, and frequency of talk. He reports that residents are "willing to speak in great detail about losses related to their own health and previous life experiences" but that they make "few negative remarks about their living situation" and the negative remarks they do make are "not elaborated fully" (Kahn 1999, 123). Further, Kahn notes that his direct questions to residents about the difficulties or problems they encounter in their nursing homes were consistently met with "shrugs of apparent indifference." Thus, for these elders, an important means of "downplaying" the negative aspects of nursing home life is to *not* talk about them.

Kahn's data indicate that the quantity and frequency of talk on the topic of negative aspects of nursing home life combine to form a pattern of silence on the topic. This silence is intentional and topic related. It has meaning for these elderly residents, but not the meaning conventionally attributed by the sociocultural formulation. Here, silence supports a deliberate strategy for coping with life in a nursing home. It is directly linked to successful adaptation as it is defined and experienced by the elderly residents themselves, rather than indicative of a problem in social adaptation.

Conclusions

The presence or absence of talk as it occurs in the speech practices of elderly nursing home residents has been examined in terms of quantity, frequency, and content. A pattern of silence is evident in the speech data in each example, representing a pattern of speaking that the sociocultural formulation interprets as a "lack" of communication or a "paucity" of social interaction.

Drawing on a critical, ethnographic perspective, these data are reexamined and reinterpreted to arrive at an understanding of the absence of talk as naturally occurring in the context of "open talk," as a means of communicating and reinforcing a shared bond, and as a speech-based coping strategy, respectively. In each example, the "problem" meaning that the prevailing script laminates onto *silence* is peeled away. When it is, a very different perspective on the linguistic capabilities and communicative resources of the elderly speakers themselves emerges. Thus, a paradigm shift away from conventional scripted thinking and toward a critical, ethnographic inquiry into elders' language use and speech practices leads to a clearer vision of elderly speakers as competent, resourceful users of language.

Seeing the Script in One's Own Culture

In his discussion of the ethnographic description of speech practices, anthropologist Dell Hymes reminds us that speech and language are "not everywhere equivalent in role and value; speech may have different scope and functional load in the communicative economies of different societies" (1972, 39). It is easy to imagine this to be the case for other cultures, but it is considerably more difficult to believe about one's own.

The journey toward such insight is always a personal one. In my case, awareness of the patterns of silence and speech among elderly nursing home residents emerged in the course of my ethnographic fieldwork among them. The purpose of the fieldwork was to learn how dying and death is experienced by residents, care staff, families, and others in the nursing home setting. I was particularly interested in how elderly residents talked about dying and death: specifically, how and when the topic of death arose in elders' conversations, where such talk occurred, how the topic was managed by conversational participants, what its content was, and what talking about death meant for residents (Bower 1998; 2010). Care staff consistently reported an absence of talk about death among residents and attributed it to residents' fear of death and discomfort with talking about death. This interpretation was reflected in and supported by the sociocultural literature.

As my fieldwork unfolded, I spent time with the elderly residents, both in silence and in talking with them about many things in addition to their thoughts and feelings about death. I came to see that elders' verbal behavior was markedly different from that of younger speakers in terms of the quantity, frequency, and form of talk. No matter what the topic, the structure of their utterances was minimalist; they spoke fewer words and less often than the younger adults around them. It seemed to me that residents' talk about death could only be described and understood within this broader context of language use and speech practice. If reports about the "absence" of death-talk among elders were accurate, then it might be due less to their discomfort with the topic than with their overall pattern of silence and speaking in the nursing home speech setting. Further, if this alternative analysis was the case, then the substantial literature that described nursing home elders as fearful of death and unwilling to talk about it was based on an erroneous understanding of the meaning of elder people's silence. This realization led me to return to the sociocultural literature to reexamine its findings about nursing home elders' language and speech practices and to reconsider its interpretations. During this process, I discerned the pervasive, unquestioned script that has been the topic of this chapter.

The difficulty in "seeing" one's own culture is, of course, at the heart of "seeing" the implicit scripts in one's own research and practice paradigm. Research and practice in a cross-cultural context compounds these difficulties because there are multiple scripts to be discerned and constellations of supporting cultural beliefs and values to be discovered.

Implications for Japanese Gerontology

This discussion has focused on the communicative experience of elderly people living in nursing homes, a social setting of increasing importance in both Japan and the United States. In both countries, a central concern is where the growing population of elderly people will reside. For example, in 1990, a national survey conducted by the Japanese government revealed that the second most desired reform to the social welfare system was an increase in the number of residential and health care facilities for the elderly (O'Leary 1993, 5; Urata 1990). In 2000, the introduction of a national long-term care insurance program led to a higher than anticipated increase in applications for nursing home placement (Shirasawa 2004) and spurred a substantial increase in the construction of new nursing homes (Houde et al. 2007). The accruing pressure in Japan to expand long-term care options for the elderly is attributed to changing norms in intergenerational contract ("filial piety") that are expected to solidify over the next decades (Izuhara 2002; Mayhew 2001). In the United States, however, elders' residential preferences are shifting away from nursing homes and toward assisted living or home care alternatives. The number of people 65 years and older who lived in nursing homes increased by 29 percent between 1980 and 1990, but declined by 2.1 percent in the following decade (U.S. Department of Health and Human Services 2005).

It is clear that residential long-term care for the elderly in both Japan and the United States is very much in transition. Whatever form such care takes, elders' quality of life and quality of care will be the foremost considerations for long-term care providers. Because providers turn to the research and practice literature for guidance in developing their treatment programs, care models, and policies, it is incumbent upon our community to provide them with the most authentic and clearly delineated research possible.

At present, while the existing literature on the actual speech practices of Japanese elders living in long-term care settings is in its infancy, two important lines of inquiry are emerging: one regarding Japanese elders' communicative practices in general (Matsumoto 2009; Backhaus 2009; Okazaki 1999), and a second regarding interactional patterns between elderly residents in Japanese nursing homes and their care staff (Backhaus 2008; Kitamoto 2006;

Katō et al. 2004; Yoshikawa et al. 2003). This slender literature underscores the need for additional research about Japanese elders' speech activities and the need for research that is grounded in and reflective of the lived experiences of Japanese elders.

To this end, the intention of this discussion has been to encourage the gerontological research and practice community in Japan and in the West to adopt a critical perspective in their conceptualizations of the elderly, language, and aging and in how they identify their problems for study. For example, what cultural values and assumptions about language shape and support the research and practice communities in Japan? To what degree are they implicit or explicit? How are they scripted? How do they intersect with other cultural beliefs and values about aging and the elderly? What other cultural themes influence the perceived shape and value of talk in Japanese culture? How will the embedded scripts of the Japanese gerontological community affect the caregiving policies and provisions made for elders in long-term care settings? What are the speech practices of elderly Japanese people? How do they experience talk and silence in their daily lives? What does talk and speaking mean for them, from their perspectives, through their own actions and in their own words? How can the lived experience of elderly Japanese people be built into care models that reflect and respond to their communicative needs and wants?

While care models in both countries will always be grounded in cultural values and beliefs about the elderly and their needs, such models must be equally reflective of and responsive to the actual experiences of elderly people and the meaning their experiences hold for them. That experience is open to observation and description. The application of an ethnographic approach to describing and interpreting the speech practices of elderly people in nursing homes will assist gerontologists and health service providers in both cultures in identifying the outlines of the embedded scripts that implicitly guide their research and practices. It will free them to think *descriptively* about elderly people's talk rather than *prescriptively*. Enhanced descriptive clarity will, in turn, provide a solid basis for developing culturally sensitive and authentic caregiving models for elderly people in both countries. We will benefit from such critical thinking in exchanges regarding caregiving models, both within and across our own paradigms of theory and practice, and between our two cultures. The elderly people in both our cultures will be better served because of it.

Notes

I offer my sincerest thanks to two colleagues who helped me so much to complete this chapter: Yoshiko Matsumoto, who organized the "Masks of Aging" conference, conceptualized and edited this volume, and graciously brought it to completion, and who directed me to research related to Japanese elders' experiences in long-term care settings; and Susan Long, for reading the manuscript and generously sharing her knowledge about Japanese caregiving practices with me.

1. Over the past several decades, critical perspectives on the study of aging have generated discussions about the values and structures that shape gerontological theory and practice, for example, in the culture of dementia care (McLean 2006; Diaz-Moore 1999; Kitwood 1997) and in the treatment of late-life depression (Luborsky and Riley 1997) and end-of-life depression (Bower and Reifsnyder 2002).

2. Linguistic form and the relationships among forms at every level of complexity are examined, from phonological and prosodic units, morphological units (e.g., syllables), and lexico-semantic units (e.g., words and their meanings) to syntactic units (e.g., phrases, clauses, sentences) and the larger discourse units (e.g., stories, descriptions, instructions, conversation) and processes (e.g., topic and theme, coherence and cohesion). For example, phonological capabilities and lexical or semantic comprehension are assessed through word recognition and naming tests that require recognition, recall, and reproduction of target units (Ripich 1991). Speakers' abilities to formulate and comprehend sentences are examined through tests that require comprehension, interpretation, and reproduction of increasingly complex syntactic structures and relationships, as well as ungrammatical structures (Emery 1986; Kemper 1988). Speaker capabilities in producing and comprehending larger discourse units are assessed using both standardized tests and unstructured discourse tasks that require narrative construction, description activities, and informal conversation.

3. The findings of these studies vary and are often contradictory. For these reasons, their theoretical implications continue to be debated (Kemper and Kliegl 1999). Nonetheless, a consensus does emerge about the overall effect of aging on language.

4. *Adaptation* is defined as the fit between the individual and her social or physical environment. It is regarded as a highly complex and situated phenomenon, but a positive fit is felt to promote a satisfying emotional life and improve cognitive functioning (Parmalee 1982). *Adjustment* is a concept related to adaptation. It can be positive or negative, and is often discussed in terms of an individual's activity level and affect (Johnson et al. 1998). *Activity* refers to the domains of social action in which individuals engage each other. Activities are felt to promote social interaction. Social interaction, in turn, provides important support for elders' sense of self, helps to reinterpret and reinforce social roles, and mitigates the disruption of late-life losses (Kiely et al. 2000; Jerrome 1992). In this way, elders' perceptions of subjective well-being are enhanced and life satisfaction increases.

5. For example, talk refers to identifiable speech events that occur independently (e.g., conversation, gossip, shooting the breeze, reminiscing) or as part of another social activity (e.g., having dinner, playing cards, waiting). It refers to verbal strategies (e.g., joking, arguing, getting acquainted, showing off) as well as individual speech acts (e.g., exchanging greetings, asking for assistance). The purpose of talk may be sociable (e.g., getting acquainted, having companionship), practical (e.g., meeting a physical need), or expressive (e.g., releasing emotions), but its outcome includes increased social interaction.

6. The choice of method typically reflects individual discipline, so that cultural anthropologists are likely to employ ethnographic methods, while social psychologists and nursing researchers typically mix quantitative with qualitative methods. One-on-one interviews, participant observation, and structured observation (all at varying levels of structure, depth, and extent) are well represented. The majority of sociocultural research is highly contextualized as to setting. It is conducted in the locations where elderly people live or gather (e.g., in their homes and communities, at senior day centers, in volunteer organizations or interest groups, and in long-term care environments such as independent living, assisted living, and nursing homes). Elderly people and their families, friends, and caregivers are participants in the research, and their words and behavior represent the data (for example, see Hamaguchi, this volume; Matsumoto, this volume; and Traphagan, this volume).

7. This complex nexus of values has not been systematically explored ethnographically in the research and practice literature, but has been discussed by sociocultural researchers as an aspect of "intergenerational communication" (Giles et al. 2003; Okazaki 1999; Coupland et al. 1991; 1988).

References

AARP Global Aging Program. 2003. *AARP international forum on long-term care: Proceedings.* Washington, DC: AARP Global Aging Program.

Achenbaum, W., S. Weiland, and C. Haber. 1996. *Keywords in sociocultural gerontology.* New York: Springer.

Applegate, M., and J. Morse. 1994. Personal privacy and interactional patterns in a nursing home. *Journal of Aging Studies* 8 (4): 413–434.

Asahara, K., Y. Momose, S. Murashima, N. Okubo, and J. Magilvy. 2001. The relationship of social norms to use of services and caregiver burden in Japan. *Journal of Nursing Scholarship* 33 (4): 375–380.

Atchley, R. 2001. Activity theory. In *The encyclopedia of aging: A comprehensive resource in gerontology and geriatrics,* ed. G. Maddox, 10–13. New York: Springer.

Backhaus, P. 2008. *Resident-staff interaction in a Japanese elderly care facility.* Paper presented at Seoul International Conference on Communication in Health Care, September 26–27, in Seoul.

———. 2009. Politeness in institutional elderly care in Japan: A cross-cultural comparison. *Journal of Politeness* 5 (1): 53–71.

Baltes, M., and H. Wahl. 1996. Patterns of communication in old age: The dependent-support and independence-ignore script. *Health Communications* 8: 217–231.

Barnlund, D. 1975. *Public and private self in Japan and the United States.* Tokyo: Simul Press.

Bayles, K., and A. Kaszniak. 1987. Linguistic communication and normal aging. In *Communication and normal aging and dementia.* Boston: Little, Brown.

Bengston, V., K. Kim, G. Myers, and K. Eun. 2000. *Aging in East and West: Families, states and the elderly.* New York: Springer.

Bennett, R. 1963. The meaning of institutional life. *Gerontologist* 3: 117–125.

Bernstein, B. 1972. A sociolinguistic approach to socialization with some references to educability. In *New directions in sociolinguistics*, ed. J. Gumperz and D. Hymes, 465–497. New York: Holt, Rinehart, and Winston.

Bethel, D. 1992. Life on Obasuteyama, or, Inside a Japanese institution for the elderly. In *Japanese social organization*, ed. T. Lebra, 109–134. Honolulu: University of Hawaii Press.

Bitzan, J., and J. Kruzich. 1990. Interpersonal relationships of nursing home residents. *Gerontologist* 30 (3): 385–390.

Bower, A. 1998. *The topic is death.* Paper presented at the 31st annual meeting of the Gerontological Society of America, November 20–24, in Philadelphia.

———. 2010. *The topic is death: Discursive practices of elderly nursing home residents.* Unpublished manuscript.

Bower, A., and J. Reifsnyder. 2002. *Perceiving the dead: The value and meaning of sensing experiences for the dying and their caregivers.* Paper presented at the 35th annual meeting of the Gerontological Society of America, November 25, in Boston.

Brent, R., E. Brent, and R. Mauksch. 1984. Common behavior patterns of residents in public areas of nursing homes. *Gerontologist* 24 (2): 186–192.

Bruneau, T., and S. Ishii. 1988. Communicative silence: East and West. *World Communication* 17 (1): 1–33.

Chan, A. 2005. Aging in Southeast Asia and East Asia: Issues and policy directions. *Journal of Cross-Cultural Gerontology* 20 (4): 269–284.

Chee, Y., and S. Levkoff. 2001. Interdisciplinary cross-national program on dementia for health professionals in Japan: Shared lessons learned from the United States. *Gerontology and Geriatrics Education* 22 (1): 45–58.

Chi, I., K. Mehta, and A. Howe. 2001. *Long-term care in the 21 century: Perspectives from around the Asia-Pacific Rim.* New York: Haworth.

Coupland, J., N. Coupland, and J. Robinson. 1992. How are you? Negotiating phatic communion. *Language in Society* 21: 201–230.

Coupland, N., J. Coupland, and H. Giles. 1991. *Language, society, and the elderly.* Oxford: Basil Blackwell.

Coupland, N., J. Coupland, H. Giles, and K. Henwood. 1988. Accommodating the elderly: Invoking and extending a theory. *Language in Society* 17: 1–41.

Coupland, N., and V. Ylanne-McEwen. 1993. Discourse, institutions, and the elderly. *Journal of Aging Studies* 7 (3): 229–236.

Davidson, J. 1984. Subsequent versions of invitations, offers, requests and proposals dealing with potential or actual rejection. In *Structure of social interaction: Studies in conversation analysis*, ed. J. Atkinson and J. Heritage, 102–128. London: Cambridge University Press.

Diaz-Moore, K. 1999. Dissonance in the dining room: A study of social interaction in a special care unit. *Qualitative Health Research* 9 (1): 133–155.

Doi, M. 1974. Some psychological themes in Japanese human relationships. In *Intercultural encounters with Japan*, ed. J. Condon and M. Saito, 17–26. Tokyo: Simul Press.

Emery, O. 1986. Linguistic decrement in normal aging. *Language and Communication* 6: 47–64.

Enninger, W. 1987. What interactants do with non-talk across cultures. In *Analyzing cross-cultural communication*, ed. K. Knapp, W. Enninger, and A. Knapp-Potthof, 267–302. Berlin: Mouton de Gruyter.

Fetters, M. 2002. Cancer disclosure and family involvement with Japanese patients in the United States. In *Innovations in end-of-life care: Practical strategies and international perspectives*, ed. M. Solomon, A. Romer, and K. Heller, 93–101. Larchmont, NY: Mary Ann Liebert.

Fukahori, H., et al. 2007. Factors related to family visits with nursing home residents in Japan. *Archives of Gerontology and Geriatrics* 45 (1): 73–86.

Gardner, P. 1966. Symmetric respect and memorate knowledge: The structure and ecology of individualistic culture. *Southwestern Journal of Anthropology* 22: 389–415.

George, L. 2001. Adaptation. In *The encyclopedia of aging: A comprehensive resource in gerontology and geriatrics*, ed. G. Maddox, 13–15. New York: Springer.

Giles, H., N. Coupland, and J. Wiemann. 1992. "Talk is cheap . . ." but "My word is my bond": Beliefs about talk. In *Sociolinguistics today: International perspectives*, 218–243. London: Routledge.

Giles, H., K. Noels, A. Williams, T. Lim, S. Ng, E. Ryan, and L. Somera. 2003. Intergenerational communication across culture: Young people's perceptions of conversations with family elders, non-family elders, and same-age peers. *Journal of Cross-Cultural Gerontology* 18 (1): 1–32.

Glosser, G., and T. Deser. 1992. A comparison of changes in macrolinguistic and microlinguistic aspects of discourse production in normal aging. *Journal of Gerontology: Psychological Sciences* 47: 266–272.

Goffman, E. 1967. *Interaction ritual.* New York: Anchor Books.

———. 1971. *Relations in public.* New York: Harper Colophon.

———. 1976. Replies and responses. *Language and Society* 5: 237–313.

———. 1981. *Forms of talk*. Philadelphia: University of Pennsylvania Press.

Gold, D., D. Andres, T. Arbuckle, and A. Schwartzman. 1994. Measurement and correlates of verbosity in elderly people. *Journal of Gerontology: Psychology and Sciences* 43: 27–33.

Goodman, R. 2002. *Family and social policy in Japan: Anthropological approaches*. Cambridge, UK: Cambridge University Press.

Grainger, K. 1995. Communication with the institutionalized elderly. In *Handbook of communication and aging research*, ed. J. Nussbaum and J. Coupland, 417–436. Mahwah, NJ: Erlbaum.

Gubrium, J. 1975. *Living and dying at Murray Manor*. New York: St. Martin's.

Gumperz, J. 1999. On interactional sociolinguistic method. In *Talk, work and institutional order: Discourse in medical, mediation and management settings*, ed. S. Sarangi and C. Roberts, 453–472. Berlin: Mouton de Gruyter.

Gutheil, I. 1991. Intimacy in nursing home friendships. *Journal of Gerontological Social Work* 17 (1–2): 59–73.

Hamilton, H. 1999. *Language and communication in old age: Multidisciplinary perspectives*. New York: Garland.

Hashimoto, A. 1996. *The gift of generations: Japanese and American perspectives on aging and the social contract*. Cambridge, UK: Cambridge University Press.

Houck, N., and S. Gass. 1997. Cross-cultural back channels in English refusals: A source of trouble. In *Silence: Interdisciplinary perspectives*, ed. A. Jaworski, 285–308. Berlin: Mouton de Gruyter.

Houde, S. R., Gautam, and I. Kai. 2007. Long-term care insurance in Japan: Implications for U.S. long-term care policy. *Journal of Gerontological Nursing* 33 (1): 7–13.

Howe, A. 2001. Lessons learned, questions raised. *Journal of Aging and Social Policy* 13 (2–3): 233–241.

Hubbard, G., A. Cook, S. Tester, and M. Downs. 2002. Beyond words: Older people with dementia using and interpreting nonverbal behavior. *Journal of Aging Studies* 16: 155–167.

Hubbard, G., S. Tester, and M. Downs. 2003. Meaningful social interactions between older people in institutional care settings. *Ageing and Society* 23: 99–114.

Hummert, M. L., and J. Nussbaum. 2001. *Aging, communication and health: Linking research and practice for successful aging*. Mahwah, NJ: Erlbaum.

Hymes, D. 1972. Models of the interaction of language and social life. In *New directions in sociolinguistics*, ed. J. Gumperz and D. Hymes, 37–71. New York: Holt, Rinehart, and Winston.

Hymes, V. 1975. The ethnography of linguistic intuitions at Warm Springs. In *The second LACUS forum*, ed. Peter A. Reich, 29–36. Columbia, SC: Hornbeam.

Ice, G. H. 2002. Daily life in a nursing home: Has it changed in 25 years? *Journal of Aging Studies* 16: 345–359.

Izuhara, M. 2002. Care and inheritance: Japanese and English perspectives on the "generational contract." *Ageing and Society* 22 (1): 61–77.

Jaworski, A. 1997. *Silence: Interdisciplinary perspectives.* Berlin: Mouton de Gruyter.

Jerrome, D. 1992. *Good company: An anthropological study of old people in groups.* Edinburgh: Edinburgh University Press.

Johnson, B., G. Stone, E. Altmaier, and L. Berdahl. 1998. The relationship of demographic factors, locus of control and self-efficacy to successful nursing home adjustment. *Gerontologist* 38 (2): 209–216.

Kaakinen, J. 1992. Living with silence. *Gerontologist* 32 (2): 258–264.

Kahn, D. 1999. Making the best of it: Adapting to the ambivalence of a nursing home environment. *Qualitative Health Research* 9 (1): 119–132.

Kato, J., M. Hickson, and L. Worrall. 1996. Communication difficulties of nursing home residents. *Journal of Gerontological Nursing* (May): 26–31.

Katō, S., T. Abe, T. Yabuki, Y. Abe, and N. Nagashima. 2004. Shōkibo kea ni okeru kōkateki kainyū moderu no sakusei (Developing an effective intervention model for small-size care). In *Chihōsei kōreisha oyobi kaigo kazoku no seeikatsu no shitsu no kōjō ni kansuru kenkyū jigyō* (Research on the improvement of life quality for demented elderly and their families), ed. Kōreisha chihō kaigo kenkyū kenshū Sendai sentaa, 117–170. Sendai: Kōreisha chihō kaigo kenkyū kenshū Sendai sentaa.

Kemper, S. 1988. Geriatric psycholinguistics: Syntactic limitations of oral and written language. In *Language, memory, and aging,* ed. L. Light and D. Burke. New York: Cambridge University Press.

———. 1992. Language and aging. In *Handbook of aging and cognition,* ed. F. Craik and T. Salthouse, 213–270. Hillsdale, NJ: Erlbaum.

Kemper, S., and R. Kliegl. 1999. *Constraints on language: Aging, grammar, and theory.* New York: Springer.

Kiely, D., M. Simon, R. Jones, and J. Morris. 2000. The protective effects of social engagement on mortality in long-term care. *Journal of the American Geriatrics Society* 48: 1367–1372.

Kim, E., and K. Bayles. 2007. Communication in late stage Alzheimer's disease: Relation to functional markers of disease severity. *Alzheimer's Care Quarterly* 8 (1): 43–52.

Kinoshita, Y., and C. Kiefer. 1992. *Refuge of the honored: Social organization in a Japanese retirement community.* Berkeley: University of California Press.

Kitamoto, K. 2006. Sōsharu wāku ni okeru komyunikeeshon bunseki: Tokubetsu yōgo rōjin hōmu ni okeru seikatsu bamen o chūshin ni (An analysis of social work communication: On daily life conversation at a nursing care home for senior citizens). *Bulletin of the Graduate School of Jōsai International University* 9: 49–64.

Kitwood, T. 1997. *Dementia reconsidered: The person comes first.* Philadelphia: Open University Press.

Kozuki, Y., and M. Kennedy. 2004. Cultural incommensurability in psychodynamic psychotherapy in Western and Japanese traditions. *Journal of Nursing Scholarship* 36 (1): 30–38.

Kurzon, D. 1997. *Discourse of silence*. Amsterdam: John Benjamins.

Lebra, T. 1987. The cultural significance of silence in Japanese communication. *Multilingua: Journal of Cross-Cultural and Inter-language Communication* 6 (4): 343–357.

Liang, J., J. Bennett, H. Akiyama, and D. Maeda. 1992. The structure of PGC Morale Scale in American and Japanese aged: A further note. *Journal of Cross-Cultural Gerontology* 7 (1): 45–68.

Links International. 2003. *Homes for senior citizens*. Barcelona: Links International.

Liu, W., and H. Kendig. 2000. *Who should care for the elderly: An East-West value divide*. Singapore: Singapore University Press.

Long, S. 2000. *Caring for the elderly in Japan and the United States: Practices and policies*. New York: Routledge.

Lubinski, R. 1984. The environmental role in communication skills and opportunities of older people. *Aging and communication: Problems in management*, ed. D. Beasley and G. Davis, 139–145. New York: Haworth.

———. 1995. State-of-the-art perspectives on communication in nursing homes. *Topics in Language Disorders* 15 (2): 1–19.

Lubinski, R., E. Morrison, and S. Rigrodsky. 1981. Perceptions of spoken communication by elderly, chronically ill patients in an institutional setting. *Journal of Speech and Hearing Disorders* 46: 405–412.

Luborsky, M., and E. Riley. 1997. Residents' understanding and experience of depression: Anthropological perspectives. In *Depression in long-term and residential care*, ed. R. Rubinstein and M. P. Lawton. New York: Springer.

Luborsky, M., and A. Sankar. 1993. Extending the critical gerontology perspective: Cultural dimensions. *Gerontologist* 33 (4): 440–444.

Malinowski, B. 1935. *Coral Gardens and their magic: A study of the methods of tilling the soil and of agricultural rites in the Trobriand Islands*. London: Allen and Unwin.

Matsumoto, Y. 2009. Dealing with changes—Humorous self-disclosure by elderly Japanese women. *Ageing & Society* 29 (6) (Special issue on "Discourse, identity and change in mid-to-late life: Interdisciplinary perspectives on language and ageing," edited by Justine Coupland): 929–952.

Mayhew, L. 2001. *Japan's longevity revolution and the implications for health care finance and long-term care*. London: Pensions Institute.

McCormick, W., C. Ohata, J. Uomoto, H. Young, and A. Graves. 2002. Similarities and differences in attitudes toward long-term care between Japanese Americans and Caucasian Americans. *Journal of the American Geriatrics Society* 50 (6): 1149–1155.

McHugh, K. 2003. Three faces of ageism: Society, image, and place. *Ageing and Society* 23: 165–185.

McLaughlin, M., and R. Cody. 1982. Awkward silences: Behavioral antecedents and consequences of the conversational lapse. *Human Communication Research* 8 (4): 299–316.

McLean, A. 2006. *The person in dementia: A study of nursing home care in the United States.* Ontario: Broadview Press.

Miller, D., and S. Beer. 1977. Patterns of friendship among patients in a nursing home setting. *Gerontologist* 17: 269–275.

Milroy, L. 1980. *Language and social networks.* Baltimore: University Park Press.

Murata, K. 2007. Unanswered questions: Cultural assumptions in text interpretation. *International Journal of Applied Linguistics* 17 (1): 38–59.

Nakane, J., and M. Farevaag. 2004. Eldercare in Japan. *Perspectives* 28 (1): 17–24.

National Institute of Population and Social Security Research. 2002. *Summary of the Japanese population projection.* www.ipss.go.jp/pp-newest/e/ppfj02/suikei_g_e.html.

Nolan, M., G. Grant, and J. Nolan. 1995. Busy doing nothing: Activity and interaction levels amongst differing populations of elderly patients. *Journal of Advanced Nursing* 22: 528–538.

Nussbaum, J. 1991. Communication, language, and the institutionalized elderly. *Ageing and Society* 11 (2): 149–165.

Okazaki, S. 1999. I can't drive: Painful self-disclosure in intergenerational talk. In *Language and communication in old age: Multidisciplinary perspectives,* ed. H. Hamilton, 233–266. New York: Garland.

O'Leary, J. 1993. A new look at Japan's honorable elders. *Journal of Aging Studies* 7 (1): 1–24.

Palmore, E. 1993. Is aging really better in Japan? *Gerontologist* 33 (5): 697–699.

Parmalee, P. 1982. Social contacts, social instrumentality, and adjustment of the institutionalized aged. *Research on Aging* 4: 269–280.

Pomerantz, A. 1984. Agreeing and disagreeing with assessments: Some features of preferred/dispreferred turn shapes. In *Structure of social interaction: Studies in conversation analysis,* ed. J. Atkinson and J. Heritage, 57–101. London: Cambridge University Press.

Powers, B. 1995. From the insight out: The world of institutionalized elderly. In *The culture of long-term care: Nursing home ethnography,* ed. J. Henderson and M. Vesperi, 176–196. Westport, CT: Bergin and Garvey.

Reed, J., and V. Payton. 1996. Constructing familiarity and managing the self: Ways of adapting to life in nursing and residential homes for older people. *Ageing and Society* 16: 543–560.

Ripich, D. 1991. Differential diagnosis and assessment. In *Dementia and communication,* ed. R. Lubinski, 188–215. Philadelphia: B. C. Decker.

Ryang, S. 2004. *Japan and national anthropology.* New York: Routledge.

Sacks, H., E. Schegeloff, and G. Jefferson. 1974. A simplest systematics for the organization of turn-taking in English. *Language* 50: 696–735.

Saville-Troike, M. 1989. *The ethnography of communication.* Oxford: Blackwell.

Savishinsky, J. 1991. *The ends of time: Life and work in a nursing home.* New York: Bergin and Garvey.

Schiffrin, D. 1987. *Discourse markers.* Cambridge, UK: Cambridge University Press.

Sherzer, J., and R. Darnell. 1972. Outline guide for the ethnographic study of speech use. In *Directions in sociolinguistics: The ethnography of communication,* ed. J. Gumperz and D. Hymes, 548–554. New York: Holt, Rinehart, and Winston.

Shield, R. 1988. *Uneasy endings: Daily life in an American nursing home.* Ithaca, NY: Cornell University Press.

Shirasawa, M. 2004. The evaluation of care management under the public long-term care insurance in Japan. *Geriatrics and Gerontology International* 4: S167–S168.

Sigman, S. 1985. Conversational behavior in two health care institutions for the elderly. *International Journal of Aging and Human Development* 12 (2): 137–153.

Smithers, J. 1990. A wheelchair society: The nursing home scene. *Journal of Aging Studies* 4 (3): 261–275.

Tannen, D. 1985. Silence: Anything but. In *Perspectives on silence,* ed. D. Tannen and M. Saville-Troike, 93–112. Norwood, NJ: Ablex.

Tannen, D., and M. Saville-Troike, eds. 1985. *Perspectives on silence.* Norwood, NJ: Ablex.

Tobin, J. 1987. The American idealization of old age. *Gerontologist* 27 (1): 53–58.

Tsutomu, M., K. Tomita, and N. Mike. 1998. A support system to make care plan of elders. *Medinfo* 9 (1): 117–120.

Ulatowska, H., and S. Chapman. 1991. Discourse studies. In *Dementia and communication,* ed. R. Lubinski, 115–132. Philadelphia: B. C. Decker.

Ulatowska, H., S. Olness, A. Samson, M. Keebler, and K. Goins. 2004. On the nature of personal narratives. *Advances in Speech Language Pathology* 6 (1): 3–14.

United States Census Bureau. 2004. *We the people: Aging in America.* www.census.gov/prod/2005pubs.

United States Department of Health and Human Services. 2005. *Current population reports.* www.census.gov/prod/2006pubs.

Urata, N. 1990. *Chōju shakai to danjō no yakuwari-ishiki* (The aged society and the perception of gender roles). Tokyo: Ministry of Finance Publications.

Walker, A. 1985. The two faces of silence: The effect of witness hesitancy on lawyers' impressions. In *Perspectives on silence,* ed. D. Tannen and M. Saville-Troike, 55–76. Norwood, NJ: Ablex.

Walker, C. 1996. An overview of the role of government in the organization and provision of health services in Japan. *Australian Health Review* 19 (2): 75–93.

Watanabe, M., K. Kono, K. Miyata, K. Nakaya, and K. Kawamura. 1999. An investigation of the disabled elderly in a geriatric health services facility in an urban area of Japan and attitudes of their family caregiver. *Asia Pacific Journal of Public Health* 11 (1): 39–44.

Wingfield, A. 1996. Cognitive factors in auditory performance: Context, speed of processing, and constraints of meaning. *Journal of American Academy of Audiology* 7:
175–182.

———. 2001. Language comprehension. In *The encyclopedia of aging: A comprehensive
resource in gerontology and geriatrics*, ed. G. Maddox, 582–583. New York: Springer.

Wu, Y. 2004. *Care of the elderly in Japan.* New York: Routledge Curzon.

Yamada, Y., and M. Sekiya. 2003. Licensing and training requirements for direct care
workers in Japan: What can the United States and Japan learn from each other? *Journal of Aging and Social Policy* 15 (4): 113–129.

Yoshikawa, Y., K. Sugai, and Y. Abe. 2003. Kaigoshoku to shisetsu nyūkyoshakan no
hatsuwa kōdō ni kansuru kenkyū (Research on conversational behavior between
caring staff and residents). In *Kōreisha chihō kaigo kenkyū kenshū Sendai sentaa
kenkyū nenpō 3* (Third annual research report of the Sendai Center for Research and
Training on Elderly Dementia Patients), ed. Kōreisha chihō kaigo kenkyū kenshū
Sendai sentaa, 59–66. Sendai: Kōreisha chihō kaigo kenkyū kenshū Sendai sentaa.

7 Kimochi

Capturing Elderly Japanese Dialysis Patients' Experiences
Natsumi Morita

Kidney Disease in Japan

In many different fields of practice, nurses encounter people with chronic illnesses who must change their lifestyles. Chronic kidney disease, one of the most common chronic illnesses in Japan, is one such condition. Patients with chronic kidney disease suffer from decreased function of the kidneys to filter out wastes and excess fluid from their bodies; as the term "chronic" suggests, the condition cannot be cured but can only be managed. When chronic kidney disease progresses into end-stage renal disease (ESRD), patients are forced to choose from one of three options: undergo kidney transplantation, receive kidney dialysis for the rest of their lives, or continue to deteriorate from ESRD and die.[1]

Treatment Options for Kidney Disease Patients

In 2007–2008, there were about 303,000 ESRD patients in Japan (Nihon Ishoku Gakkai Kōhō Iinkai 2008; Nihon Tōseki Igakukai Tōkei-chōsa Iinkai 2008). Among them, 93 percent went on to receive dialysis,[2] whereas fewer than 7 percent underwent kidney transplantation.[3] There are a number of cultural factors behind the extremely small number of patients who undergo kidney transplantation in Japan. In 1997, the Law Concerning Human Organ Transplants (Law No. 104 of July 16, 1997) was enacted in Japan. The purpose of this law was to clarify the legal definition of death and cadavers so as to increase the number of organ donations. The enactment of this law was the fruit of decades-long discussions in Japan on the issues of brain death and organ transplantation (Akabayashi 1997; Ōta 1998; Bagheri 2003; 2005). Still, in spite of legal support, organ donation from cadavers has not increased to any significant extent. Kaji

(*Sankei Shinbun*, April 30, 2009) points out that this is because Japanese people are reluctant to donate the organs of a dead family member. Kaji notes that the current Japanese views on death are not conducive to the idea of organ donation. In Japan, for thousands of years, the body was buried as a whole. This is because, according to Confucian and Buddhist traditions, the deceased are expected to return to meet with their living families during periodic religious rituals held long after death. Against such a backdrop, a great majority of ESRD patients in Japan end up receiving dialysis for the rest of their lives.

Aging of Dialysis Patients in Japan

In 2008, approximately 37,700 new patients started dialysis in Japan. About 62 percent were over 65 years old, and the average age of new patients was 67.2 (Nihon Tōseki Igakukai Tōkei-chōsa Iinkai 2008).[4] The ten-year survival rate of Japanese dialysis patients was close to 26 percent (ibid.).[5] These numbers indicate that the majority of ESRD patients in Japan receiving dialysis are seniors and that they are living longer. It is projected that in the future, nurses in Japan will face an increasing number of elderly dialysis patients.

The Experience of Dialysis Patients

Simply stated, dialysis is a process during which a machine removes wastes and excess fluid from patients' bodies through blood filtration. To be successful, treatment must achieve precise control and maintenance of the dialysis process, which often takes time and, occasionally, much trial and error over the course of weeks or even months, depending on the patient's condition, tolerance, and other individual attributes.

However, dialysis patients are not inanimate objects merely to be cleaned by machines; rather, dialysis patients must live with changes. When patients begin dialysis, many elements in their lives need to be restructured, some slowly and others abruptly. First, a special device, called a shunt, is implanted, often in the arm, for the insertion of dialysis tubes; patients must be careful to protect this site. Simultaneously, the person beginning dialysis is confronted with often severe dietary and fluid restrictions. Dialysis patients may be required to measure and record the amount of fluid they ingest each day. Furthermore, securing available dialysis time is not an easy task for everyone. Dialysis patients without exception must receive treatment, which can last three or four hours a day up to three days a week, at dialysis hospitals and clinics, which are not always close by. For dialysis to be successful, this routine must be strictly maintained.

The most profound change for all dialysis patients is that their lives completely depend on their intermittent connection to the dialysis machine. In other words, if the patients want to live, then they must continue getting dialysis treatment at a prescribed frequency for the rest of their lives. Beginning a life with dialysis is a far more complicated process than, for example, simply learning what foods to avoid. Dialysis patients go through a tremendous amount of change in their lives and live under an enormous amount of pressure. Nurses who care for dialysis patients must understand their experiences in order to better assist this group of people to continue to cope with their requirements.

Nursing

The goal of nursing practice is to achieve the most desirable patient care outcome (Morita and Ōnishi 1997). For example, the concept of patient-centered nursing has been the goal for some time (Matsumoto and Morita 2009). To achieve patient-centered nursing, nurses pay attention to each individual patient's needs. Attentiveness to patients' needs is not limited to their physical and biomedical needs but extends to their personal, social, emotional, and psychological needs as well.

In order to achieve the most desirable outcome for each patient, nurses first identify the health problems of each patient. The data are analyzed and the resultant nursing diagnosis is used to establish a course of action, often called a nursing care plan. The outcomes of nursing interventions are then evaluated to see whether the problems first identified have been resolved. Thus, a fundamental aspect of nursing practice is the objective identification and evaluation of each patient's problems.

Unfortunately, in this process of objectively evaluating their patients' problems, nurses often become immersed in medical and technical language, which is different from the language that patients feel comfortable using in their everyday lives (Wilkinson and Ahern 2009). The terminology used in modern nursing practice is not always patient friendly. There is a gap between the clinical nursing terminology that aims to objectively evaluate, monitor, and analyze patients' conditions and the words used by patients, who do not share the language used by their nurses.

This is not to say that nurses are not interested in the experiences of their patients. On the contrary, nurses have always been concerned about the experiences of patients living with a multitude of health issues (Matsumoto and Morita 2009). "Psychological care," "emotional support," and "holistic nursing" all point to the way in which nurses emphasize their patients' inner experiences (see also Ota and Giles, this volume).

Unlike a physical condition, which can be seen, nurses cannot know patients' inner experiences. One of the most popular approaches used by nurses to learn about the patients' inner experience is to ask, or more formally, to interview the patients. However, when nurses casually approach their patients with clinical language, an inevitable gap is created. For example, in Japan, if a nurse asks a patient "please describe your psychological status," it is more likely than not that the nurse will get a blank stare from the patient (see Bower, this volume). Hopefully, no nurse will ever use such an expression; yet, at the same time, it is perhaps equally unrealistic to assume that all nurses use patient-friendly language when they are actually trying to learn about the patients' inner experiences. Nurses must be aware of the need for a better bridge to connect nurses and patients.

Tapping into the Dialysis Patients' Experiences

In order to understand the inner experiences of dialysis patients, I have adopted the theoretical framework of feelings and progression of feelings proposed by Carl R. Rogers (Rogers 1958; Walker et al. 1960). Using Rogers's Person-Centered Approach (Kirschenbaum 2007), I propose that if dialysis patients can be open to their experiences, it will lead to an acceptance of their world, which includes dialysis treatment. At the same time, openness to their experiences will also help dialysis patients to improve their sense of well-being despite the multitude of heavy demands that weigh upon their lives.

The Structure of the Word *Kimochi*

In Japanese conversational contexts, the experience of a person's changing reality is best captured by the word *kimochi*. *Kimochi* denotes feeling, emotions, sentiment, and thoughts, all of which make up the core of a person's mindset or the inner world of a person. *Kimochi* is an everyday word, not an academic or scientific term, and it is used in ordinary Japanese conversations. The word *kimochi* has two parts, *ki* and *mochi*.[6] The character for *ki* is frequently translated as energy flow, air, or breath. There are literally hundreds of Japanese expressions that contain the character for *ki*, and these Japanese expressions have meanings associated with mind, heart, feeling, atmosphere, energy, or flavor (Kindaichi et al. 1997). The latter part, *mochi*, is a form of the word *motsu*, which means "to have" or "having." Hence, *kimochi* means a person's holding, or having, mind, heart, feeling, atmosphere, energy, or flavor. *Kimochi*, therefore, refers to the feeling or experience that arises from the center of a person and a person's will to live.

Understanding *Kimochi*

In Japan, the expression "understand a person's *kimochi*" is often heard. This is not merely to recognize a person's static emotional or psychological status. In order to understand someone's *kimochi*, one must have a grasp of the person's entire experience behind his or her superficial emotions. This requires empathetic involvement on the part of the listener in order to gain an understanding of the person's inner experience. For example, merely recognizing and saying that someone is sad because the person is crying does not meet the criterion of "understanding someone's *kimochi*." However, if the observer of the crying person decides to get emotionally involved with compassion, and if the crying person reveals the totality of his or her experience behind overtly expressed sadness, then the listener might come to "understand the person's *kimochi*."

In the purest sense, when someone understands a person's *kimochi*, there is no blame, criticism, analysis, or attempt to rectify problematic situations. In this regard, it may be argued that in a Japanese sense, the understanding of *kimochi* is, in and of itself, an end product, which has its own meaning for the person who is being understood. The experience of being understood gives the person a sense of satisfaction, comfort, and even of reconciliation and resolution regarding his or her situation.

When a person uses the expression "to understand *kimochi*," the word *kimochi* does not necessarily refer to short-term emotions that change every minute. *Kimochi* indicates a person's deeper existential experience. In other words, *kimochi* has a more complex, ontological meaning. Therefore, a person's "current *kimochi*" can be happiness if someone has just won a lottery. But the same person may also have another *kimochi* toward his/her lifelong struggle with alcoholism, for example.

In a typical conversation in Japan, under normal circumstances, the expression "understand *kimochi*" requires no further explanation. When someone approaches another person and says, "tell me your *kimochi*," in a sense, the conversational tone is set. The listener is expressing his or her desire to appreciate and understand the other person's experience. The listener does not want to talk about the weather. He or she wants to know the inner experience of the other person.

For this reason, *kimochi* can be seen as a tool or process that enables a person to freely communicate his/her felt realities, for example, regret, hope, or doubt. These attributes of the concept of *kimochi* make it a highly useful term in interviews of dialysis patients. As such, *kimochi* has become the key word in facilitating conversations between nurses and dialysis patients.

Interviews and Analysis

From 1985 to 2006, I conducted more than 150 interview sessions with approximately 50 Japanese dialysis patients in four research projects (Maeda 1986; Morita 2002; 2005; 2006; 2007; 2008).[7] The common purpose of these interviews was to understand the nature of the dialysis patients' *kimochi* through open interviews. The age range of these patients was from 28 to 84 years old; eight of them were above the age of 65. There were approximately equal numbers of male and female patients.

Prior to each study, the patients were informed about the research and their official consent was obtained. The interviews were conducted during the patients' dialysis sessions; during the interviews, patients were lying on their back on their dialysis beds, while the author sat at their bedside in a chair. Each interview lasted from about half an hour to two hours. The patients were asked the question: "Please tell me about your *kimochi*." The interviews were conducted according to the approach proposed by Rogers (1957).[8] According to Rogers's theory, when an interviewer maintains congruence, empathetic understanding, and unconditional positive regard, patients will be increasingly open to their own experiences (Rogers 1957).

About half the interviews were tape-recorded and later transcribed.[9] From the transcribed narratives, descriptions that seemed to capture the essence of an individual patient's *kimochi* were extracted. When numerous *kimochi* were identified, these were examined and further classified into groups of similar *kimochi* experiences. The results of this analysis were divided into two sections—the *kimochi* of all the dialysis patients and the *kimochi* of the elderly dialysis patients.

The *Kimochi* of the Dialysis Patients

I identified 12 *kimochi* experiences of the patients: (a) What? Me?; (b) I really don't want to do it; (c) I wish I had done better; (d) I may not make it; (e) I'm so frustrated; (f) It's no small deal; (g) I'm not a disabled person; (h) It can't be helped; (i) I gotta hang in there; (j) I'm doing it; (k) I'm thankful; (l) This is my life.

"What? Me?"

This *kimochi* was expressed by patients when their kidney function deterio-rated and, finally, dialysis became inevitable. This *kimochi* corresponded to their experience during the first stage of living as a dialysis patient. The patients who revealed this *kimochi* could not have and had not foreseen the possibility of needing dialysis despite the progression of their disease symptoms, medi-cal data, and other personal experiences of illness. Because of their inability to comprehend their situation and have foresight, the patients experienced what seemed to be a sudden new reality. This *kimochi* expressed the confusion and surprise that occurred because of the gap between the patients' understanding of their past and present.

> I was hospitalized and getting treatment, but my doctor suggested that I get the shunt, just in case. So I thought I was going home, but my data became worse and worse, and my doctor said, "Let's do dialysis." [. . .][10] I cried. It was such a shock to me. (65-year-old female with six months of dialysis experience)

> For seven years, it [her condition] didn't change much. So I absolutely didn't think I was going to be so bad that I [. . .] would need dialysis. I was just so surprised. (55-year-old female with 14 years of dialysis experience)

"I really don't want to do it"

The patients who expressed this *kimochi* did not explicitly state the words, "I really don't want to do it." However, it became clear to the author that, using different phrases, several patients were saying the very same thing as "I really don't want to do it." It is an honest and naked feeling that arises when dialysis becomes necessary for one to live. Intellectually and logically, perhaps the pa-tients understood the need for the dialysis, yet they still could not deny the ooz-ing truth deep inside of them—that dialysis was not their real choice.

> I tell you, as a chronic kidney disease patient, I don't even want to hear the word "dialysis." I don't even want to learn what that means. I guess I'm in denial, simply. (45-year-old female with 14 years of dialysis experience)

> Think about it. Nobody wants to do dialysis. I come here three times a week, but I never want to do it. But I have to. If I didn't have to, I would never do it. (55-year-old female with 20 years of dialysis experience)

As these patients expressed, every dialysis patient was exposed to the word "dialysis" earlier in their illness experiences, yet many felt it was irrelevant to their individual situations. When dialysis became inevitable, the patients reflected upon their personal experiences surrounding the word "dialysis." These personal experiences included their knowledge about dialysis, the condition of the other patients in the room when they were admitted to the hospital for their first dialysis, and personal acquaintances who were on dialysis. Some of these memories evoked negative images of dialysis, and ironically, when these negative images were juxtaposed with the picture of their own current situation and future, this eventually led to the patient's strong sense of disgust. It is a haunting reality—one that small children might protest by crying and stomping; as adults, these dialysis patients had to agree to lifelong dialysis treatment in order to survive.

"I wish I had done better"

Up until the point when the patients had started to receive dialysis, many of them showed certain levels of acceptance and understanding about the ways they had lived their lives. However, when faced with the reality of dialysis, the patients began to fear that something they had done in the past, or even that the way they had lived their lives, had caused them to need dialysis.

> [Because I was caring for my mother], I didn't have the time to rest. So, I think I caused this, you see? (65-year-old female with six months of dialysis experience)

> Come to think of it, I should've gone to the hospital then. I regret that now. (43-year-old male with one month of dialysis experience)

Many of these patients felt at times that they had not undertaken sufficient therapeutic action or behavioral modification. Once they ended up receiving dialysis, they were left regretting their past actions. If they could not find any cause, then it seemed as though they had to make one up. It was as if they needed some reason or logic to explain their plight.

"I may not make it"

Many patients, prior to dialysis, had a vague notion about their longevity, even if that notion did not come with a concrete number.[11] However, with the introduction of dialysis, some patients felt that they might not live to their expected age, whatever it may have been. This was the experience of facing one's own death. The patients described the feeling of having an uncertain future. This, in turn, gave them a sense of dread that their lives were going to be cut short.

> I always felt that I might die, even though I tried everything. [. . .] It's scary to face death. I do wonder when I will die. (64-year-old male with one month of dialysis experience)

> My nephew [who was on dialysis] eventually died. [. . .] I really had a sense of—how can I say?—hate and fear. (66-year-old male with six months of dialysis experience)

It should be noted that many people in Japan avoid the use of words that evoke a bad omen, and "death" is one of them. Still the patients were able to describe the existential experience of facing their own deaths.

> Oh my, I thought that was going to be it. [. . .] I wonder how my last moment is going to be. It would be nice if I can go suddenly, just "poof." (84-year-old female with two years of dialysis experience)

> When dialysis became inevitable, I decided that I wouldn't live long. [. . .] That was such a shock, that I wouldn't see my sixty-sixth birthday. (65-year-old female with six months of dialysis experience)

> The dialysis itself was okay. I could deal with it. But the feeling that I may not make it—that anxiety was always there. (63-year-old male with ten years of dialysis experience)

"I'm so frustrated"

As described above, dialysis often requires a severe limitation of food and fluid intake. Fluid intake is monitored by weight. Immediately before and after each dialysis, the patient's weight is recorded. The amount of extracted fluid and the level of pain experienced during each dialysis depends on the weight patients have gained since their last dialysis. Generally speaking, adult dialysis patients can have liquid in the amount of two water bottles between two dialysis sessions. When a patient has consumed more fluid than the prescribed amount, his or her next dialysis is longer and physically tougher. The patients vividly described how demanding life with dialysis is.

> You know, the water [. . .] that's all I thought of [. . .] for about 7 or 8 years. [. . .] I'm telling you, it was really hard that you can't drink water. (45-year-old female with 14 years of dialysis experience)

The patients soon discovered that they must learn to get better at living with dialysis, yet even the learning process was in and of itself a challenge. Many dialysis patients tried to take matters into their own hands by searching for information in books or in the words of health care providers. However, the information they sought was often not available, or was available but not helpful to their own situations.

> There is this gap between reality and the books, you know? [...] Then there are things that are not even written in the books. I learned those things after I began my dialysis. (54-year-old male with one year of dialysis experience)

"It's no small deal!"

This *kimochi* was one of the most frequently expressed by many of the dialysis patients, regardless of age and gender. In a Japanese context, it means that things are neither normal nor desirable. It also conveys a sense of being overwhelmed, overtaxed, and unprepared. From one perspective, everything that came with dialysis was "no small deal" for many patients. The entire scope of the multidimensional requirements, from commuting to the treatments three times a week, to measuring the drinking water in a cup and recording every ounce of it, all contributed to this *kimochi*.

> Once you begin, then you are stuck for the rest of your life. Oh, my ...
> (40-year-old female with two months of dialysis experience)
>
> Rain or shine, I gotta get here. What am I gonna do?! (40-year-old female with two months of dialysis experience)
>
> The more I learn, the more I realize that my condition is a tough one. [...] It really is a big deal. It's heavy on my shoulders. (38-year-old male with one month of dialysis experience)
>
> I just can't seem to get it. (57-year-old male with one year of dialysis experience)

"I'm not a disabled person"

In Japan, a dialysis patient with ESRD, by law, receives the designation of a Class I Disability. This entitles the dialysis patients to receive all essential health care, free of charge if necessary. Class I certified patients also receive a booklet which works as a ticket they can use to receive a multitude of social welfare services, including taxi fare on the day of dialysis, special discounts on airfares, and special admission rates to enter various places, including movie theaters, for example.

Although a Class I title enabled the dialysis patients in the study to receive much-needed services, it also created a particular morale issue among some of them. That is, if the patients had any negative images about disabled people, the designation of a Class I Disability might evoke the feeling that they are no longer "healthy, normal people." The image of a disabled person as being someone who is less desirable may have led to the patients' *kimochi* of "I'm not a disabled person." The patients faced the reality of dialysis and struggled to live with this perceived gap between their own negative preconceptions of being disabled and their current condition of fully qualifying as Class I Disabled, a designation that was forced upon them.

> It's all about being a disabled person. I'm that disabled person. I don't want people to know that. I don't mean to be bigoted, but . . . (28-year-old male with eight months of dialysis experience)

> I never knew anybody who was on dialysis. I had this bias that those people cannot live like normal people . . . it's just an image. (65-year-old female with six months of dialysis experience)

Relating to this gap between the image of disability and the image of their current selves was yet another gap that existed between the patients' current image of who they were and their ideas of how they may look from the outside. The commonly accepted image of productive adults is that they are in the workforce. Therefore, when the dialysis patients became unable to live up to this image because of the demands of dialysis, they had to deal with the changing image of the self as a social agent. Also, once they started dialysis, their relationships with others had to change, and they had to cope with a new self-image projected upon them by other people.

Many patients said that they did not want other people to know that they were on dialysis. At times, the normal expressions of sympathy shown by other people, which were intended as caring acts or words, made the patients feel down.

> I didn't want other people to know that I was on dialysis. [. . .] For about a year I felt doomed. (55-year-old female with 14 years of dialysis experience)

> Healthy people can't really understand a sick person's pain. [. . .] It's hard for me to say that I don't feel well [to a healthy friend]. [. . .] I don't want any

sympathy, so I try to keep it to myself. (57-year-old female with 13 years of dialysis experience)

I don't want sympathy. But sometimes I need it. But I don't want it (45-year-old female with 14 years of dialysis experience).

"It can't be helped"

Many patients expressed their experience of hitting rock bottom after their dialysis had started. In the simplest terms, they experienced a sense of deep depression. In general, this was an experience of the lowest kind for many of the patients. They had to figure out how to get out of the pit. When the patients figured out that there was an opening in their seemingly stymied world, they were able to acknowledge the inevitable—a life with dialysis.

In Japanese, the *kimochi* "it can't be helped" is not necessarily an active acceptance of one's situation. Rather, it is a sense of resignation, but with the chance of a slightly positive twist. It is a confirmatory expression of one's determination, identification, and recognition of one's current situation. In fact, the ability to say "it can't be helped" can often be interpreted as a virtue in Japanese culture.

Now I'm in this position, and there is nothing I can do. (28-year-old female with one month of dialysis experience)

No sense being mopey. [. . .] No matter what, what I've got is what I've got. [. . .] Time will solve everything. [. . .] They say "even the saddest tears will eventually dry out," you know. (55-year-old female with 14 years of dialysis experience)

"I gotta hang in there"

This *kimochi* was often expressed along with the *kimochi* "it can't be helped." However, the patients reflected upon this *kimochi* not by simply acknowledging their inevitable situation, but instead by taking a more positive action in their world of uncertainty. It showed, in a sense, the attempts of the patients to affirm a sense of determination in the face of many difficulties. There was a strong sense of awareness, as the patients determined to take the first step on their own.

I'm resigned to it. [. . .] It can't be helped, because it's done. When I told myself to give it up, I finally felt some energy inside me. (55-year-old female with 14 years of dialysis experience)

My oldest son said, "I know that you are doing your best, mom, but we too have been trying. You have to keep going." [...] So with that one word [...] I thought I gotta hang in there for my kids. (55-year-old female with 13 years of dialysis experience)

"I'm doing it"

The dialysis patients faced many ups and downs in the course of their treatment regimen. Looking back, some patients were able to reflect upon the achievements they had made. They realized that they had actually made some progress.

My husband told me to take a cab, but I took a train. I was totally fine! (40-year-old female with two months of dialysis experience)

It became so real. [...] I'm doing okay. [...] So, the key is that I have to do what I can, so from now on I'm going to live and have fun in my life. (55-year-old female with 13 years of dialysis experience)

This *kimochi* of "I'm doing it" emerged when the patients realized that they were beginning to successfully manage the prescribed treatments. The awareness of their progress gave them a sense of future possibility, something they could not see when dialysis first began. Because of this discovery, it was as if the gap between their old understanding of their world (i.e., "I'm not doing it right") and their current understanding of their world (i.e., "I'm doing it") became smaller. When the patients were able to see the positive results of their efforts, they were encouraged and more inclined to take the initiative while living with dialysis. Eventually, the patients reached the point where they were more secure and confident about upcoming and future events, instead of feeling lost and worried about what might happen to them in the future.

"I'm thankful"

Despite the difficult lives they led, many dialysis patients expressed a sense of gratitude and appreciation for what they still had. They were thankful for the social welfare system and for assistance from health care providers and families; they were also grateful that they were better off than other patients with more serious conditions. All of these sentiments led them to the deeper realization that, after all their trepidations, difficulties, and stresses, they were still alive.

Unlike cancer, I can still live. (Several patients)

I have to use one day for dialysis, but then I have the next day for myself. (40-year-old female with two months of dialysis experience)

The needles are painful, but with that I can live three more days. (43-year-old male with one month of dialysis experience)

When the dialysis patients first began their treatment, calibrating the machine to match the individual patient's needs often took time. However, as their physical condition stabilized through properly calibrated dialysis, the patients often felt an immediate and immense sense of physical improvement and a sense of enhanced morale. This gave the patients time to reflect upon the fact that their lives were saved, and that they could continue to live.

If we put a price tag on the cost [of dialysis], [...] in seven years, [...] we can buy a small condominium. This is incredible. [...] We are allowed to live. I am thankful. [...] You know, thanks to everybody. (54-year-old female with seven years of dialysis experience)

"This is my life"

This *kimochi* was expressed by patients with several years of dialysis experience. As the months and years of dialysis go by, some dialysis patients became better able to accept the unavoidable reality that although they did not choose to be on dialysis, they had to live with it. In doing so, they transcended all the aforementioned negative *kimochi* to some extent. In other words, no matter how many problems the patients described, their sense of resoluteness became visible in this one line. "This is my life" was an affirmative statement.

At the beginning, I just hated it. But now I feel more okay about it. [...] I didn't choose to be like this [...] but this is my life. [...] If I think of it that way, I can live like this. (54-year-old female with seven years of dialysis experience)

This is the life I was given. (55-year-old female with 20 years of dialysis experience)

Through these words, the patients showed a general sense of acceptance of the fact that although they had not chosen to be sick, and regardless of why they became sick, they had found a way to come to terms with their situation and actively live their lives. This *kimochi* was not simply about choosing one thing over another. It was the experience of believing, and it showed how the patients tried to see their experiences in the best possible light. It should be noted, however, that some patients had the urge to make sure that the interviewer knew their real *kimochi* by noting simultaneously their resolute attitude to accept the current condition and their true feeling of not wanting to live with dialysis.

> This is the life that was given. The key is how to live in this life cheerfully and positively. [. . .] But the truth is, living with dialysis is a big deal. It's unbelievably hard. I'm sure nobody wants to do it if they don't have to. (55-year-old female with 14 years of dialysis experience)

The *Kimochi* of the Elderly Dialysis Patients

I identified five *kimochi* experiences of the elderly patients: (a) "I never thought I would live this long"; (b) "I don't want to be a burden to my family"; (c) "I've got something to do"; (d) "Half is my age, half is my illness"; (e) "I feel terribly lonely."

"I never thought I would live this long"

Simply, this was a *kimochi* that could not have come from the younger adult dialysis patients. For older patients, many friends in their cohort have already died. They may have seen the financial, physical, and social misfortunes of others that did not make it. They may have witnessed the last world war, which devastated the country. In a sense, those elderly patients wore their seniority medals with pride—a sense that was reflected in their narratives.

> I didn't think that I'd live to be over 80 years old. Not many of my friends are still alive. (84-year-old female with two years of dialysis experience)

> Because I get my pension, I don't have problems with money. My life is stable and it's pretty good. You see, I am who I am. I don't worry about my illness any more. (75-year-old male with four years of dialysis experience)

"I don't want to be a burden to my family"

Healthy elderly people experience a normal aging process, which includes a reduction in physical capacity and susceptibility to sickness. Eventually they require the help of their children or other people outside their family. The comments of the elderly dialysis patients showed that they were no exception. In fact, unlike the younger adult dialysis patients, the elderly dialysis patients were more dependent on their family members because, in addition to simply being old, they had the extra problem of being on dialysis. For some elderly patients, encouragement from their family members was an important factor in their decision to go on dialysis. But they were mindful of their family members who were shouldering extra weight because of their dialysis treatments. With or without encouragement, some elderly dialysis patients were keenly aware that their lives had to be considered in light of their family members' needs. (See also Doba et al., this volume, and Traphagan, this volume, for elders' relationships with their family members.)

> When I heard "dialysis," I said that they would have to kill me before I agreed to that. [. . .] But then again, I realized that if I didn't, my daughters were going to suffer. (77-year-old female with five years of dialysis experience)

"I've got something to do"

One of the notable differences between the younger adult dialysis patients and elderly dialysis patients was that many of the latter had retired after working for a number of years. It is easy to see how this detachment from social roles can lead to isolation from society and an increased difficulty in keeping the simple rhythm of everyday life. Interestingly, whereas one of the younger adult patients was troubled by the fact that he could no longer be the productive social agent he used to be, some elderly dialysis patients cherished the predictable lifestyle that was imposed by their dialysis treatment. Despite their old age, these patients were able to maintain their connection with the outside world through dialysis.

> I hated dialysis because I have to come to the clinic every other day for the rest of my life. But now I think that this gives me an opportunity to live a well-regulated life, because if I didn't have dialysis, I'd have nothing special to do. (82-year-old female with two years of dialysis experience)

> When I retired, I felt bored, but now coming here is giving me a rhythm in my life, and this may rescue me. (75-year-old male with four years of dialysis experience) (See also Doba et al., this volume.)

"Half is my age, half is my illness"

In Japan, aging has been accepted as more or less a normal course of living. As one ages, there is nothing one can do to stop the aches, joint pain, and reduction of stamina—what most Japanese would consider to be normal issues that "can't be helped." Therefore, in a sense, if a patient's condition is caused by aging—a condition that everyone gets—then one just needs to deal with it. Not so, however, if one has an illness that not everybody gets, for it is not seen as normal.

Unlike their younger counterparts, elderly patients had the unique tendency to view life with dialysis in light of the physical aspects of aging. In other words, some elderly dialysis patients attributed their physical condition to both their illness and the aging process. By introducing the dual nature of life with dialysis, it was as if these elderly patients were better able to accept the unplanned aspects of their situation.

> When I first got here, I wondered why everybody was walking so slowly, but then soon I was doing the same thing! [. . .] I always try to tell myself that half of my condition is from my aging and the other half is from my illness. (75-year-old male with four years of dialysis experience)

"I feel terribly lonely"

The elderly patients were not simply old in their chronological ages. As they lived each year, they lost more of their friends. Their children, if they had any, became independent and often moved away. The patients' physical condition slowly deteriorated, both from aging and from their illnesses. All of these elements contributed to their decreased capacity to socialize. Moreover, life with dialysis left them with more issues to face. No matter what happened in their lives, one fact remained: they had to keep going back to dialysis, three times a week, for the rest of their lives. It is not impossible to change one's dialysis clinic. However, there is no doubt that leaving one's current clinic requires an enormous amount of determination on the part of the patient and coordination among health care providers, simply because dialysis is a highly complex and individualized treatment. Perhaps even unconsciously, the patients felt as if they were tethered in place as the lives of others around them continued to change, leaving them behind. Some elderly patients felt lonely, and this distinctive sense of loneliness was commonly observed among elderly patients.

> I feel terribly lonely. [. . .] I feel emptiness that I cannot describe. When I was young, I never felt this way. (84-year-old female with two years of dialysis experience)

Discussion

The Kimochi *of the Elderly Dialysis Patients*

Two elements were identified in the analysis of the dialysis patients' *kimochi*, namely the *kimochi* of dialysis patients in general and the *kimochi* of elderly dialysis patients. The core *kimochi* commonly expressed among many dialysis patients appeared to be the gap between the self of the past and the self of the present. The patients had to learn a regimen that included newly imposed limits on food and water intake and affected their everyday living in general. The words of the patients illustrated how this process took place in their lives. However, the patients gradually became used to the concrete realities of life with a machine. And in the process, they described how they found hope and became able to articulate their experiences.

The patients' words showed that they had gained a sense of mastery in their struggle to live with dialysis. Once accustomed to their routine of living on dialysis, they had some room to reexamine their situation from a new, more objective point of view. The long-term dialysis patients were able to observe their experiences not only from the inside, but also from the points of view of other people and society in general. Their narratives showed that they continued to realistically accept the limitations imposed upon their lives by dialysis treatment.

However, even patients with a long history of dialysis who commented that "this is my life"—those who showed the appearance of acceptance—still maintained deep inside that they "really don't want to do" dialysis. Caregivers for dialysis patients should never forget this subtle but important *kimochi* expressed by even the most veteran of dialysis patients.

The analysis of *kimochi* related to aging makes it clear that the impact an illness has on a person can be different depending on his or her age. Younger patients generally assumed that they had endless years ahead of them. The younger patients also took an active role in their community. Because of this, they showed increased concern about how they were viewed by other people.

The elderly patients, on the other hand, had generally fulfilled their social roles, and many of them had the satisfaction of having lived to a certain age. For those elderly patients who were generally healthy prior to becoming dialysis patients, however, going into dialysis was doubly stressful, as they had to deal with the normal deterioration of their physical condition in addition to the illness-related deterioration of their mental and physical capacities. Furthermore, the *kimochi* of some elderly dialysis patients indicated that they experienced a particular sense of loneliness from being removed from active social life and from the realization that their life was shortening, while others acknowledged increased opportunities for social communication through dialysis treatment.

Everyday-Language Labeling of Kimochi

As discussed at the beginning of this chapter, nurses have a tendency to rely on professional terms in order to objectively and scientifically assess and evaluate their patients; this is their primary role in any clinical setting. However, it is also important for nurses to remember that patients are not necessarily privy to the type of language used in hospitals and clinics.

To illustrate how nurses objectify their patients' experiences, let us examine the *kimochi* "I really don't want to do it." Some nurses can, for example, describe and chart this *kimochi* as the patient's "denial." Similarly, the *kimochi* "What? Me?" can be labeled as "confusion" or "surprise"; "I wish I could have done better" can be seen as "regret"; "you really can't know what's coming next" can be construed as "anxiety"; and "it can't be helped" can be taken as "resignation." In these examples, it can be argued that the *kimochi* expressed by the patients is not always captured with accuracy. The use of objective and oversimplified expressions may be acceptable in some clinical settings, such as a fast-paced emergency room, where saving patients' lives is the priority. In any other setting, however, this should not become the standard for nursing care.

Furthermore, some *kimochi* expressed by the dialysis patients cannot simply be reduced to more objectified terms. For example, "I think this might have been a good thing that I did" expressed the complex emotional and existential experiences of patients who were living with dialysis. It may convey elements of resoluteness, satisfaction, relief, or even resignation. Similarly, several patients said: "I wonder how my last moment is going to be." This may not indicate a simple "fear of death." It might signal acceptance of the patients' world, or it might disclose a cry for help. Or it may be that the patients were simply reflecting upon their experiences and lives in general. There are many other expressions of *kimochi* that cannot be simply reduced to mere one-dimensional, fixed meanings.

As these examples show, capturing the profound experiences of patients in the fullest sense is not an easy task, and the use of objective, abbreviated terms to describe the patients' experiences does not effect a better understanding. Takeo Doi (1977), a Japanese psychiatrist, pointed out that language is not merely a method of expressing our emotions; rather, the words we use in our daily lives form our very psychologies. By using everyday-language labeling—

that is, by using the language used by patients in its original form—nurses are more likely to be able to capture the essence of patients' experiences, which, in turn, should help improve the care of those patients.

Implications for the Care of Elderly Patients

This investigation has examined the impact of using the concept of *kimochi* in communication between nurses and dialysis patients. This investigation may be useful in the following respects.

First, this investigation should help nurses become more aware of how they communicate with their patients. Nurses may become more sensitive to their choice of words as they communicate not only with dialysis patients, but also with patients who have other diagnoses. This suggestion is based on the assumption that if nurses can better understand the *kimochi* of their patients, better communication between nurses and their patients will result. With a renewed awareness of their choices of words, nurses should be able to provide better care for patients, all of whom hold highly individualized worldviews.

Second, as pointed out above, nurses tend to use objective or scientific terms to assess and monitor their patients' condition, including their nonphysical or psychological condition. However, because the valuable world of patients' experiences might get lost in the process of translation, there is a risk involved in this act of reducing the significance of patients' experiences. Also, there may not be sufficiently succinct terms to capture some of the complex and profound experiences of the patient. When no corresponding description of *kimochi* is found in nursing diagnostic terms, it is possible that the nurses are not recognizing the *kimochi* of the patients. This is a problem for the patients, but not for the nurses, as they cannot know what is not recorded in patients' charts, and they cannot improve what they cannot know.

For this reason, it is argued here that everyday-language labeling, as demonstrated in this chapter through special attention to the *kimochi* of the dialysis patients, should help nurses to properly understand and record their patients' experiences. The introduction of the concept of everyday-language labeling should promote communication between nurses and their patients on a wide scale.

Third, it would be a mistake to think that because nurses may be able to tap into their patients' profound inner experiences, the purpose of such acts is aimed at understanding psychological or psychiatric diagnoses and treatments. After all, the purpose of this investigation was not to promote a particular type of psychiatric nursing or psychological counseling. Instead, patients' *kimochi* and the use of everyday-language labeling were the foci of this investigation insofar as they may prove useful to nurses who care for elderly patients. It is important for patients to perceive that their feelings are accurately understood and recognized by nurses and others, because this enables patients to continue to feel valued as individuals. This sense of value enables patients to better honor their own lives and leads to better self-care over the course of continued kidney dialysis. Everyday-language labeling should be useful in helping nurses to become aware of their elderly patients' *kimochi*, which in turn deepens the nurses' understanding of the patients' experiences. This should lead to better nursing care and intervention for elderly patients.

Limitations of This Chapter

In this chapter, the narratives extracted from the interviews with Japanese dialysis patients were used to investigate the *kimochi* expressed by those patients. Because the contents had to be translated into English, the fine nuances that exist in experiences of *kimochi* in a Japanese cultural context may not have been properly preserved and conveyed. From a slightly different angle, there may be subtle yet significant misinterpretations or misunderstandings among readers because of their cultural and linguistic assumptions. This is not to say that readers are at fault, but instead, that this is a limitation of any cross-linguistic investigation. Still, the use of everyday-language labeling in the assessment of elderly patients' *kimochi* might prove potentially useful in an English-speaking culture, as well as in other cultures. Further studies are needed to deepen our understanding of elderly patients' experiences, regardless of their health status.

With regard to methodology, following the interview approach based on Rogers's theory may prove problematic (Rogers 1957). Full commitment to his approach may require formal training. Also, because most nurses simply do not have enough time to fully implement Rogers's methodology, a modified clinical application of this interview approach is needed to make it more practical and useful. Therefore, for nursing applications, an optimum way for nurses to take advantage of Rogers's Person-Centered Approach in actual clinical settings must be identified. This will require further investigation.

Implications for Future Nursing Research

In the future, research approaches based on everyday-language labeling with a focus on patients' *kimochi* should be applied not only to ESRD patients, but also to patients with other chronic illnesses, such as liver diseases, diabetes, and lung diseases. The healthy elderly population may also be the focus of future investigations.

Furthermore, the impact of everyday-language labeling on patient care outcomes needs to be investigated. We must ask the following questions: Will the use of everyday-language labeling improve the outcome of nursing intervention, and if so, how exactly? Are there any other benefits or problems that arise in the use of everyday-language labeling? Insights obtained from this line of investigation may also be used in the education of clinical nurses, who have daily interface with their patients (Morita 2009a; 2009b).

Notes

The publication of this chapter was made possible by support from the following individuals: Yoshiko Matsumoto, who offered me the opportunity to present at the "Faces and Masks of Aging" conference and gave me the chance to publish in this book; Junko M. Mills, who gave me tremendous assistance in all areas of manuscript construction, editing, and translation; Margaret H. Kearney, who encouraged me and taught me the importance of contributing to science across borders; Grace H. Klein, who has given me many years of guidance in the area of Carl Rogers's Person-Centered Approach.

1. The main purpose of dialysis is to remove toxins and excess fluid from a patient's body through machine filtration.

2. This particular number denotes hemodialysis. Another common dialysis method is peritoneal dialysis. The difference between them is not relevant to this chapter.

3. During the same time period, there were about 527,000 ESRD patients in the United States, approximately twice the number in Japan. However, unlike Japanese ESRD patients, about 70 percent of the U.S. patients received kidney dialysis and 30 percent chose kidney transplantation (National Institutes of Health 2009a; 2009b).

4. By comparison, in 2007, there were 111,000 new dialysis patients in the United States. About 50 percent were over 65 years old, and the average age of new patients was 58.3 (National Institutes of Health 2009a; 2009b).

5. By comparison, in the United States, the 10-year survival rate was about 6 percent (National Institutes of Health 2009a).

6. Japanese characters: ki (気), mochi (持ち).

7. These studies (Morita 2005; 2006; 2007) were funded by Keio Gakuji Academic Development Funds in 2003, 2004, and 2005.

8. The author attended the Rogers Counselor Certification Program offered by Japan Women's University and was certified as a Class II Counselor in 1991.

9. Not all of the interviews were recorded, since they were conducted more than 20 years ago, and the original research design did not include recording requirements.

10. An ellipsis within brackets ([. . .]) indicates that sections of the patients' words have been omitted. An ellipsis without brackets (. . .) denotes a pause.

11. In 2008, the average life expectancy in Japan was 79.29 for males and 86.05 for females (Kōsei Tōkei Kyōkai 2009).

References

Akabayashi, Akira. 1997. Japan's parliament passes brain-death law. *Lancet* 349 (9069): 1985.

Bagheri, Alireza. 2003. Criticism of "brain death" policy in Japan. *Kennedy Institute of Ethics Journal* 13 (4): 359–372.

———. 2005. Organ transplantation laws in Asian countries: A comparative study. *Transplantation Proceedings* 37: 4159–4162.

Doi, Takeo. 1977. *Hōhō toshite no mensetsu* (Interview as a method). Tokyo: Igaku Shoin.

Kindaichi, Kyōsuke, Tadao Shibata, Kenji Sakai, Yasuo Kuramochi, and Akio Yamada, eds. 1997. *Shin meikai Kokugo jiten* (Shin Meikai Japanese dictionary). 5th ed. Tokyo: Sanseidō.

Kirschenbaum, Howard. 2007. *The life and work of Carl Rogers*. Ross-on-Wye, UK: PCCA Books.

Kōsei Tōkei Kyōkai (Health and Welfare Statistics Association). 2009. Kokumin eisei no dōkō, dai 2 hen: Eisei no shuyō shihyō (Annual statistical report of national health conditions, Section 2: Main index of health and welfare). *Journal of Health and Welfare Statistics* 59 (9): 71.

Maeda, Natsumi. 1986. *Ketsueki tōseki ryōhō no tame ni nyūin shita mansei jinfuzen kanja no keiken sekai no moderuka: Dōnyū mae kara gairai tōseki ni ikō suru jiki* (A model for the realm of experience seen in patients treated with hemodialysis for end-stage renal disease: From before the start of inpatient hemodialysis treatment to the beginning of outpatient treatment). M.S.N. thesis, St. Luke's College of Nursing.

Matsumoto, Makoto, and Natsumi Morita, eds. 2009. *Shinpan: Kango no tame no wakariyasui keesu sutadii* (Case study: From theme-setting to report writing for nursing, new edition). Tokyo: Shōrinsha.

Morita, Natsumi. 2002. Mansei ketsueki tōseki kanja no "kimochi" no tankyū hōhō— Katari bunseki no kokoromi (Approaches to the inquiry into *kimochi* of patients with chronic hemodialysis: Analysis of narratives). *Journal of St. Luke's Society for Nursing Research* 6 (2): 30.

———. 2005. Ketsueki ryōhō o ukete seikatsu suru seijin mansei jinfuzen kanja no kimochi no tankyū (Inquiry into *kimochi* of adult patients with chronic hemodialysis). *Keio Gijuku Academic Development Funds Report of the Year 2003*: 161–162.

———. 2006. *Ketsueki tōseki ryōhō o ukete seikatsu shite iru mansei jinfuzen kanja no "kimochi" no kōzō* (Structure of *kimochi* in patients living with hemodialysis for end-stage renal disease). PhD diss., St. Luke's College of Nursing.

———. 2007. Ketsueki tōseki ryōhō o ukete seikatsu suru kōreishya no karei to byōki, tōseki ni taishite idaku kimochi no tankyū (Inquiry into *kimochi* of elderly patients with chronic hemodialysis). *Keio Gijuku Academic Development Funds Report of the Year 2005*: 129–130.

———. 2008. Ketsueki tōseki ryōhō o ukete seikatsu suru mansei jinfuzen kanja no "kimochi" no kōzō (Structure of *kimochi* in patients living with hemodialysis of end-stage renal disease). *Journal of St. Luke's Society for Nursing Research* 12 (2): 1–13.

———. 2009a. Mansei jinfuzen kanja no "kimochi" o rikai suru tame no kangoshi ni taisuru kyōiku puroguramu no kaihatsu (Development of educational program to train nurses to understand ESRD patients' *kimochi*). *Keio Gijuku Academic Development Funds Report of the Year 2007*: 156–157.

———. 2009b. Mansei jinfuzen kanja no "kimochi" o rikai suru tame no kangoshi ni taisuru kyōiku puroguramu no hyōka (Evaluation of educational program to train nurses to understand ESRD patients' *kimochi*). *Keio Gijuku Academic Development Funds Report on the Year 2008*: 148.

Morita, Natsumi, and Kazuko Ōnishi, eds. 1997. *Rinshō kangogaku sōsho: 2, Keika betsu kango* (Clinical nursing 2: Nursing according to the clinical stage of patients). Tokyo: Medical Friend Sha.

National Institutes of Health. 2009a. Vol. 2 of *United States renal data system, annual data report*. www.usrds.org/adr.htm.

———. 2009b. Vol. 3 of *United States renal data system, annual data report*. www.usrds.org/adr.htm.

Nihon Ishoku Gakkai Kōhō Iinkai (Communications Committee of the Japan Society for Transplantation). 2008. *Zōki ishoku fakuto bukku, Part III, Jinzō* (Organ transplant fact book, Part III, the kidneys), 14–23. www.asas.or.jp/jst/pdf/fct2008.pdf.

Nihon Tōseki Igakukai Tōkei-chōsa Iinkai (Statistical Survey Committee of the Japanese Society for Dialysis Therapy). 2008. *Zusetsu wagakuni no mansei tōseki ryōhō no genkyō* (Current state of chronic dialysis treatment in Japan, illustrated). http://docs.jsdt.or.jp/overview/index.html.

Ōta, Kazuo. 1998. Strategies for increasing transplantation in Asia and prospects of organ sharing: The Japanese experience. *Transplantation Proceedings* 30: 3650–3652.

Rogers, C. R. 1957. The necessary and sufficient conditions of therapeutic personality change. *Journal of Counseling and Psychology* 21: 95–103.

———. 1958. A process conception of psychotherapy. *American Psychologist* 13: 142–149.

Walker, A. M., R. A. Rablen, and C. R. Rogers. 1960. Development of a scale to measure process changes in psychotherapy. *Journal of Clinical Psychology* 1: 97–85.

Wilkinson, Judith M., and Nancy R. Ahern. 2009. *Prentice Hall nursing diagnosis handbook: With NIC interventions and NOC outcomes.* 9th ed. Upper Saddle River, NJ: Pearson Education.

8 Beyond Stereotypes of Old Age

The Discourse of Elderly Japanese Women

Yoshiko Matsumoto

IN CONTRAST to numerous discourse analytic and sociolinguistic studies of young adults and children, studies of the discourse or the language used by the elderly are rare, despite the already sizeable and increasing elderly population in developed countries. It is conceivable that the paucity of research arises from a perception of old age as a less significant stage of one's life after the peak of adulthood, one that represents decline from full physical, social, and linguistic competence. Similar to other socially categorized groups of people, the elderly do not seem to escape being stereotyped by the more dominant groups in society. Such a perception, if it is responsible for the relative neglect of the elderly by researchers, would ignore the fact that old age can be a period in which an individual benefits from the wealth of accumulated personal history to develop an identity of her or his own.

Notable studies on elderly discourse have disputed the decrement view of aging and have provided a valuable foundation for further research (e.g., Coupland, Coupland, and Giles 1991; Coupland and Nussbaum 1993; Hamilton 1994; 1999). These studies also show the significant influence of old-age stereotypes in intergenerational verbal communication involving the elderly. In their seminal work on verbal interaction of the elderly, Coupland, Coupland, and Giles (1991) described a characteristic phenomenon in the speech of the elderly as "painful self-disclosure (PSD)." In PSD, elderly speakers reveal unhappy personal information on their ill health, immobility, or bereavement, and describe themselves in terms of negative stereotypes, such as "grumbling," "egocentric," or "disengaged." However, further studies on PSD (Coupland, Coupland, and Grainger 1991; Coupland, Coupland, and Giles 1991) revealed that the PSD of elderly speakers was, in fact, often interactionally engendered by the younger conversational partners. That is, the younger interlocutors led the conversations with the expectation that elderly people should be experiencing certain hardships and asked questions that led to PSD by the elderly. The interactional nature of language use was also persuasively argued for in Hamilton's (1994) study of an elderly Alzheimer patient's conversations. Communicative success and breakdown with the patient were not solely dependent on the patient's ability or disability, but were crucially influenced by the (healthy) interlocutor's conversational moves.

Negative stereotypes that affect communication are further evidenced in "patronizing speech," a type of speech used toward the elderly that includes exaggerated pronunciation, slow speech, and repetition (e.g., Ryan et al. 1991; Hummert and Shaner 1994), and also in negative evaluation of the elderly by younger adults in different cultures, including Japan (e.g., Harwood et al. 1996; Ota et al. 2002; Cuddy et al. 2004; Ota and Giles, this volume). While positive stereotypes of older people do exist, negative stereotypes are found to be more prominent and influential (Hummert and Shaner 1994; Hummert et al. 2004). For example, when elderly people behave incompetently, they are viewed warmly, reflecting consonance with expectations (e.g., Cuddy and Fiske 2002; Cuddy et al. 2005).

A question that presents itself is whether these stereotypical perceptions of the elderly are consistent with their actual lives and linguistic behavior. I will consider this question by examining naturally occurring conversations among elderly Japanese women, comparing the content and the manner of their conversations with three commonly held perceptions about the elderly and their verbal behavior. The first of these is the already mentioned expectation of painful self-disclosure. Second, from common beliefs about Japanese culture and the place of old women in society, conversations among elderly Japanese women may be expected to include gender-neutral expressions and other indications of asexual attitudes, reflecting the speakers' place outside the (hetero)sexual market. Such an expectation is nicely exemplified in an essay by the Japanese actress and writer Momoi Kaori, who wrote that she looked forward to being 70 years old since she believed that, at that age, life becomes free of sexual and gender complexities and one's appearance becomes androgynous (Momoi 2002). A third expectation with respect to elderly women is that they should embody (Confucian-influenced) "good wife" behavior toward their husbands, since that was the normative female moral attitude until at least the end of World War II

(Lebra 1984) and should have been inculcated in them as part of the education of women who are now elderly.

In contrast to these three stereotypes of elderly identity, the actual verbal interactions of elderly Japanese women that I observed reveal a different reality. The data show that the topics and contents of elders' conversations reflect their current life stage and their past experiences, which are different from those of younger generations. The data also show that PSD is used in expressions of friendship and that the desires to be independent and to be sexually attractive are common issues across generations (see also Hori, this volume).

While the conversations in my data are in no way representative of the speech of all elderly Japanese women, the portrayal that emerges from my data is one of individuals who are aware of various worrisome changes around them, yet resilient and less inhibited than suggested by the stereotypes. Just as recent studies of language and gender in Japan have shown that normatively female speech is a social construct that does not accurately reflect reality (e.g., Okamoto and Shibamoto Smith 2004), the actual behavior of the elderly people discussed in this chapter does not coincide with the common beliefs, or stereotypes, about the elderly in general. An examination of verbal presentations by elderly speakers among their peer acquaintances should provide insight into an aspect of their lives rarely available to younger people. The observations obtained here, it is hoped, will lead to a better understanding of social situations in which older people are placed and of their patterns of communication, and ultimately reduce misunderstandings in intergenerational communication.

The Discourse of Elderly Japanese Women

Previous studies on the discourse of elderly Japanese women have predominantly been carried out in English-speaking contexts (e.g., Coupland, Coupland, and Giles 1991; Coupland and Nussbaum 1993; Hamilton 1994; 1999; Williams and Nussbaum 2001) or were quantitative studies of cross-cultural intergenerational communication (e.g., Giles et al. 2002; Ota et al. 2002). In-depth linguistic studies of Japanese elderly discourse are few (Hamaguchi 2001; this volume; Matsumoto 2005; 2007; Backhaus 2009), despite a large and growing population of elderly in Japan. According to official statistics, over 20 percent of the population of Japan is made up of people over 65 years of age, a share that is estimated to rise to almost 40 percent by 2050 (Kōsei Rōdō Shō 2006). These figures alone would make Japan's elderly an important group of people who need to be understood better, rather than being dismissed on the basis of stereotypes.

According to a 2002 survey by the Naikakufu (Cabinet Office), 47 percent of the Japanese aged 65 or older consider themselves to be in "good" health and another 25 percent say they are in "normal" health with no need for nursing, meaning that three-quarters of the Japanese elderly population are in relatively good mental and physical condition (Naikakufu 2002). This suggests that the target of aging studies should not be confined to the ill or institutionalized members of the elderly population. The elderly should be better understood in the many facets of their lives, not just from the perspective of categories that may be most contrastive to the young and healthy groups in society.[1]

This study is part of an endeavor to elucidate discourse practices of elderly individuals as whole persons by examining the language of elderly Japanese women, paying particular attention to ways in which age, gender, and individual personae are reflected and presented in their verbal interactions. Specifically, verbal interactions of the elderly are qualitatively examined in contexts of informal peer interactions among friends and acquaintances. The data, which were collected between summer 2001 and summer 2004, are of the speech of elderly women (above 65 years of age) who were in relatively good health and who, to varying degrees, shared a common background.[2] The women did not gather specifically for the purpose of having their conversations recorded, but had preexisting reasons for getting together. The topics in the conversations varied—they were not focused on age-related painful events, such as death or health conditions of friends and families, but were mostly about experiences of past travels and plans for future trips, food, shopping, sports, and books. One common feature noticeable in the ten audiotape recordings (each between 60 and 90 minutes) of the peer interactions is the participants' frequent laughter.

From common beliefs about Japanese culture and the place of old women in society, it might be expected that the conversations would include not only many instances of speech featuring (1) negative self-representations through "painful self-disclosure," but also (2) indications of (Confucian) good wife behavior toward their husbands, as well as (3) asexual attitudes and their attendant gender-neutral expressions, a reflection of the speakers' existing outside the (hetero)sexual market. Contrary to expectations based on these common beliefs, the collected conversations indicated that responses of (1) "painful self-disclosures" are often accompanied by humor and a sense of friendly understanding based on shared similar experience;[3] that (2) women happily compete in criticizing their husbands' selfish behaviors; and that (3) women make physical and romantic comments about themselves and men.

The present data reveal the complexity of old-age identity and illustrate that references to age and decline need not be understood as expressions of complaint and unhappiness, but may convey images of awareness, lessened inhibition, and self-analysis regarding the adjustment of one's persona to changing reality.

Conversations among Elderly Japanese Women

The following conversational examples reveal peer discourse practices that do not fit into stereotypical expectations. They include a recounting of brain malfunction and memory loss told with laughter and a comical moment at the time of a husband's death (both discussed in the section immediately following); complaints about a husband's one-sided communication and the independence of women (in the section "Subservient Good Wife"); and a story of a handsome young man at a European spa and a happy teasing of a well-figured friend (both in the section "Physical Attractiveness and Heterosexual Context").

"Painful Self-Disclosure" with Humor and Laughter

Perhaps the most surprising feature in the collected peer conversations is the frequency of laughter among the speakers. While no laughter was observed when "painful" topics regarding a third party were dealt with, it is striking that laughter accompanies the majority of self-disclosures of topics that are similar to those found in PSD in the sense used in Coupland, Coupland, and Grainger (1991). This illustrates that even when "painful" topics are discussed they are not presented by the speakers as gloomy and depressing, as stereotypical interpretations may suggest. The following extracts from conversations among various members from three different peer groups exemplify how laughter and humor are used, and how impressions quite different from the stereotypical image are conveyed in talking about presumably age-sensitive issues (see also Matsumoto 2005; 2007).

The first excerpt is from a conversation among five women who had traveled overseas together. Three were in their late sixties to early seventies at the time of recording, while K, the main speaker in this example, and N were in their mid-seventies.[4]

In the midst of the conversation about their past trips to Europe, K began to disclose her worry about her recent forgetfulness, which she presented as a possible sign of dementia, an impairment often associated with advanced age.

This excerpt is in fact one of several instances of similar stretches of discourse. (See the Appendix on page 216 for the transcription conventions used.)

(1) Recent forgetfulness

K1:   demo atashi ne:, <cough>

K2:   koo huu ni, mukashi no bun wa kooyatte omoidasu [kedo nee
X2:   [un

K3:   saikin no koto tashikani moo ne

K4:   ISSHU NO CHIHOO JA NAI KA [TO OMOO.
N4:   [[iya atashi soona no yo
T4:   [iya iya minna on[[nashi ne

K5:   KATAPPASHI KARA [WASURE CHAU [[NO YO. <laughter>
M5:   [onnashi onnashi
T5:   [[ie, minna hontoni, ne

K6:   [[DAKARA NANNEN NI DOKO ITTA KA MO WASURECHATTERU NO
        <laughter>
M6:   [onnashi [[onnashi
T6:   moo [shashin nannka

Translation

K1:   but I, you know, <cough>

K2:   like this, I can recall things from way in the past, [like this, but
X2:   [mm

K3:   in terms of recent things, I really don't

K4:   [[I ALMOST THINK IT'S A KIND OF [DEMENTIA[[
N4:   [[I am like that, y'know
T4:   [It's like every[[one, right?

K5:   [[I FORGET ONE AFTER [ANOTHER[[[[<laughter>
M5:   [same here, same here
T5:   [[everyone, really, right.

K6:   [[SO, I'VE FORGOTTEN WHERE I WENT IN WHICH YEAR [[<laughter>
M6:   [same here, [[same here
T6:   y'know, [photos and all

When K mentions the possibility of her developing dementia, others jump into the conversation, repeatedly confirming that they all experience the same symptoms. These overlaps indicate the participants' involvement in the interaction. K's allusion to dementia and further reference to her forgetfulness can be understood as a serious self-disclosure of age-related health problems, but the possible gravity of the matter is lightened by the accompanying chuckle, sounding as though she were just reporting somewhat disturbing facts that were not really serious.

The second excerpt is from a comical narrative given by a widow in an interaction at which both her peers and the researcher were present.

(2) N's husband's death

N1:   [chanto sensei ga [[moo teha [[[tehai-shite kudasatte[[[[
M1:   [a [[a, mo, oishasan mo [[[chanto shite, [[[[aa
T1:   [[[[haa

N2:   de sensei ga sugu tondekite kudasutte [kangofu-san to [[
M2:   [a [[a:
T2:   [a:

N3:   sorede nee, nakunatte ne, nijikan hodo shite odenwa ga [kakatte
M3:   [a:
T3:   [a:

N4:   de dodesuka tte sensei mo nijikan mae ni nak=

N5:   =sore mo hontoni ne, sobani itemo wakan nai gurai.

N6:   un to mo [sun <laughter> to mo kyun to mo iwanai de ne
M6:   [<laugh>

N7:   ano <laugh> watashi [mo shirooto desu kara ne, [[
M7:   [<laugh> [[<laugh>

N8:   iki ga tomatteru nante,

N9:   yome ga ne, soba ni ite, otoosama ne, iki shite rassharanai mitai desuyo tte kara=

N10: =[eeee (animated) <laughter> nante yutte ne [[
M10: [<laughter> [[<laugh>

N11:   SOIDE kooshite, nn shinzooni na:n to mo wakannai n desu ne,=

N12:   =soide raifu puranningu sentaa ni sugu denwa shimasita no.

N13:   soshitara ne <laugh>

N14:   nanka ano: are tisshupeepaa o ne hana no shita ni nokkete [kuda.
M14:   <laugh> [ee

N15:   no:kketemo ne ugoiteru ka ugoitenai ka wakan nain desu.

Translation

N1:   [The doctor [[had already [[[made arrangements [[[[
M1:   [mm [[mm already [[[a doctor was already arranged to be sent,
       [[[[hmm
T1:   [[[[I see

N2:   and the doctor rushed to my house [with a nurse [[
M2:   [ah [[hmm
T2:   [ah

N3:   and y'know, about two hours after my husband passed away, I got a
       [phone call
M3:   [mmm mm
T3:   [mmm mm

N4:   and, the doctor asked me "how is he?" (so I said) "two hours earlier."=

N5:   =and it was really, you wouldn't have noticed even if you were right next
       to him

N6:   (my husband) didn't say "ah"<laughter> OR DIDN'T EVEN GO "PEEP"
M6:   [<laugh>

N7:   WELL <laughter> SINCE I [AM A LAY PERSON, YOU KNOW, [[
M7:   [<laugh> [[<laugh>

N8:   I couldn't imagine that he stopped breathing.

N9:   my daughter-in-law was right beside us and said "Father (in-law) doesn't
       seem to be breathing," so=

N10:   =["GEE, REALLY?" (animated voice) <laughter> I SAID [[
M10:   [<laughter> [[<laugh>

N11:   SO, like this, um, (I touched) his heart, but I couldn't tell anything,=

N12:   =so, I called the Life Planning Center right away.

N13:   THEN Y'KNOW <laugh>

N14:   they told me that I should put a tissue paper under my husband's [nose.
M14:   [<laugh> [MM

N15:   even when I put the tissue paper on him, I couldn't tell if it was moving.

In this excerpt, N recounts what happened at the time of her husband's death ten years earlier. Her narrative becomes animated and comical, as shown in the above excerpt, when she describes the specifics of her experience at the time of her husband's death, and how she did not notice exactly when he died.[5] In her utterance numbered N6, after saying "*un to mo sun to mo*" "[he] didn't [say] 'ah'" (i.e., he didn't say anything), she continues by adding "*kyun to mo iwanai*" or didn't even go 'peep'" (i.e., he did not even make any sound). The association of a small creature's squeaks with one's husband's last moment, which would normally be expected to be described with dignity, is humorous, especially because it is embedded in N's otherwise polite and careful speech in the old-fashioned upper-middle-class style exemplified by her frequent use of honorific predicates and referential terms. Her use of onomatopoeia in this utterance as well as frequent use of direct quotes from her daughter-in-law (see line N9), herself (N10), and someone at the Life Planning Center (N14) make N's narrative vivid. The lapse of time since her husband's death and the peaceful way in which he died may or may not be determining factors allowing her to talk about the event calmly and comically, but it certainly is the case that speaking of bereavement itself does not necessarily imply that the topic is heavy or depressing.[6]

Studies of English-speaking females in their late teens to thirties suggest that humorous self-disclosure serves as a means to display friendship and solidarity (Rubin 1983; Ervin-Tripp and Lampert 1992; Hay 2000). As I have noted elsewhere (Matsumoto 2005), one aim of self-disclosure in conversations of elderly Japanese female friends seems to be to reinforce solidarity, a function not easily predictable from the stereotypical characterization of speech of the elderly. This appears to be the case in Excerpt (2). Although the events and situations referred to in such conversations could be considered painful and negative, the recorded conversations reveal that the stories were told comically and without apparent solicitation of sympathy.

"Subservient Good Wife"?

The speakers in the recorded conversations received at least elementary education before or during World War II, when the gender ideology of *ryōsai kenbo* ("good wife and wise mother"), an amalgam of Confucianism and the Western cult of domesticity (see, e.g., Tamanoi 1990), was dominant in Japanese society, and when the normative femininity focusing on modesty, elegance, and tidiness was inculcated in young women (Lebra 1984). In comparison to women educated after the end of World War II, who have been given more choices in their lives to resist this ideology (Fujimura-Fanselow and Kameda 1995; Imamura 1996), women of the generation of the speakers in this study are stereotypically thought of as remaining within the bounds of the old tradition, being respectful and subservient toward their husbands. The excerpts below provide a different perspective on their attitudes, revealing them as outspoken about their husbands' uncommunicative behavior and about independence that women should have.

(3) *One-sided communication by husbands*

K1:   dakara, chotto chooshi ga ii to omoeba moo hontoni

K2:   sonna koto itta oboe wa na::: i toka [tte donarushii ne,
T2:   [<laughter>

K3:   kiite nai zo::: tte [yu:shi sa
T3:   [<laughter>

K4:   [sonna donara nakutta tte ii ja nai no to omou n dakedo ne=
T4:   [<laughter>

K5:   =sore ga bin bi::n tto hairu to ne=
T5:   =un, okashiku naru?

K6:   dakara kikanai yooni kikanai yooni shitara [konogoro ne=
T6:   [un

K7:   =nanka terebi no oto made ne, kikoe [naku <laughter> natte kichatta ki ga [[suru.
T7:   [<laughter> [[chotto mimi ga

K8:   nna mimi ga ne, are kik kikumai kikumai to yuu huu ni [hataraku n ja na:i?
T8:   [un. so: ne,

. . .

K9:   [atashi,

T9:   mo watashi mo [kikoenai de iru no ga honto ni ne

K10:   [u:n,

T10:   dooshite ne, ko kotti wa, shaberu no [wa nannimo kiite kurenai desho,

K11:   soo yuu wake de [sho. [[soo, arega iya ne[[[e:

T11:   mukoo wa ikkura demo [un, daka[[ra ne, [[[unn,

T12:   dakara kikoenai tteyuu no wa komaru wa yo

T13:   mimi mo komaru shi me mo komaru shi <laughter>

Translation

K1:   so, when things are going sort of well, then, y'know, he starts

K2:   shouting something like "I don't remember [saying that!" or
T2:   [<laughter>

K3:   like "You didn't tell [me that!"
T3:   [<laughter>

K4:   [I don't think he needs to shout like that, you know, but=
T4:   [<laughter>

K5:   =when I hear that ringing voice=
T5:   =uh, go crazy?

K6:   so I've kept trying not to listen to him, and then, [these days=
T6:   [uhuh

K7:   =I feel like I can't even [hear <laughter> the sound of the [[TV.
T7:   [<laughter> [[um ears

K8:   um my ears must be working hard not to hear that thing, [don't you
      think?
T8:   [ah. right,

. . .

K9:   [I,
T9:   y'know, I also [can't hear things, really

K10:   [really

T10: why, y'know, he doesn't listen to me, [none of what I say

K11: exactly, he says it, [right? [[right, I hate that, [[[[y'know
T11: but, everything he wants, [yes, so [[y'know, [[[right,

T12: but it's a problem if you can't hear well

T13: it's a problem either way, if you can't hear, or if you can't see <laughter>

In the first half of the excerpt, K complains to her friend T that her husband shouts when he disagrees with her. With some laughter, she attributes her recent difficulty in hearing to her attempt to ignore his shouting. Later in the conversation, T echoes the complaint and mentions that her own husband says whatever he wants but never listens to her. Empathy between them in criticizing their husbands' unreasonable verbal behavior is clear in these lines, especially in K11 and T11, where K co-constructs a sentence with T by filling in a verb and finishing T's line. Subservient wives may be expected only to listen to their husbands and not be treated equally, but K and T's conversation here clearly illustrates that this is not how they behave with peers.

In other conversations, a different group of elderly women comically depicted their individual experiences of taking care of their ill or healthy husbands and the various predicaments that ensued. At one stage, one person started to talk about her tactic to get back at her selfish husband, which led her and others to say that as long as they had financial independence it would be perfectly fine to divorce. They decided to turn off the tape recorder when they began to express agreement on this view.

(4) Nothing wrong about getting divorced

W1:   ima no wakai hito wa iitai koto yuu shi, rikon wa hayai shi ne:.

. . .

H10: [[aru aru aru,
W10: soosuruto:, jibun de, ano:, [kutte ikeru no ne. [[hitori de.
K10: [seikatsuryoku ga aru no ne, uuun.[[

W11: a: soreja: ne:, mendokusai wa [ne:.
K11: [soo yo ne.

H12: [SOREJA MENDOKUSAI,
W12: [<laughter>
K12: <laughter>

R12:   [<laughter>

H13:   <laughter>
W13:   <laughter> DO, DOOSHITE KANA:,
K13:   <laughter>
R13:   <laughter>

H14:   <laugh>
W14:   [otoko nante iranai yo honto.
R14:   <laugh> zeitaku na koto osshatteru [shi:,

H15:   [nee, otoko [[nante.
W15:   [[ne, iranai.
K15:   ira[nai wa ne.

H16:   [honto.[[
W16:   [[<laugh>
K16:   [<laugh>
R16:   <laughter>[

W17:   da korekara no hito wa ne:,

W18:   yappari mo: otoko ga mo: honto otoko shakai datta kara,

W19:   iroiro kirai toka itte okori dashitari suru kara

W20:   moo sassa to rikon shite ii to omoo.

Translation

W1:   young people nowadays say whatever they want, and they get divorced
       quickly.

. . .

H10:   [[she can, she can.
W10:   then, she can, by herself, um, [earn her own bread, right? [[on her own
K10:   [she can support herself, can't she? I see [[

W11:   oh, if that's the case, it's a bother [isn't it
K11:   [I agree

H12:   [(. . .) IF THAT'S THE CASE, IT'S A BOTHER,
W12:   [<laughter>
K12:   <laughter>[

H12: [<laughter>

H13: <laughter>
W13: <laughter> i, i WONDER WHY
K13: <laughter>
R13: <laughter>

H14: <laugh>
W14: [don't need a man, really.
R14: <laugh> you have a high expectation [then,

H15: [right, you don't need [[a man.
W15: [[right, you don't need a man.
K15: you [don't need a man, right.

H16: [true. [[
W16: [[<laugh>
K16: [<laugh>
R16: <laughter> [

W17: people now,

W18: don't need men—it's been a men-centered society,

W19: as people get mad, finding points they don't like

W20: I think they should get divorced right away

Although these assertions and agreements were made with much laughter, which has the effect of lightening the force of the assertions and the possibility of labeling them as just jokes, these conversations and others, such as Excerpts (3) and (4), certainly demonstrate that at least some women in this age cohort, who were raised under strict Confucian guidelines before World War II, do not simply follow the stereotypical ideal of women, at least when among friends.

Physical Attractiveness and Heterosexual Context

Concern for an attractive body image has been most commonly associated with adolescent and younger women and not with older women (Hurd Clarke 2001). Combined with the modesty emphasized in traditional femininity training (Lebra 1984), elderly Japanese women may seem to be indifferent to showing interest in and concern for body image and attractiveness. The following examples show the contrary.

In Except (5), N is relating an incident that occurred at a spa in Europe, where a beautiful young man—presumably a spa attendant—brought a towel/robe to cover her when she had on a loose, oversized swimsuit that she had acquired locally. This embarrassed her and made her self-conscious, but she concludes in line N15 that everyone should have this type of experience. Her friend M agrees, in line M16, that it was a lot of fun.

(5) *Handsome young man at a spa in Europe*

N1:   deteku to, suteki na booya [ga ne, [[oo:, a, hansamu na booya ga
M1:   [hansamu na [[ne,

N2:   shiro[i, ookina taoru o [[kakete kureru no yo.
K2:   [aoi me no booya ga [[s

N3:   moo atashi hajime . . .
M3:   de N-san ga sore ga hazukashii [hazukashii tte yuu no
E3:   [<laughter>

N4:   sore ga san . . . sore ga [[saisho no toki ni ne
M4:   sore ga san #### dakara hazuka[shii [[datte [[[ne.
T4:   [<laughter> [[[inai

N5:   <laughter> saisho no toki ni hitori datta desho, onna, atashi ga hitori de.
M5:   <laughter>
T5:   <laughter>

N6:   [de otto wa dooshita no ka na? aa otto wa sassa to icchau kedo atashi
M6:   [un,
E6:   haa. [

N7:   sore ga hazukashiku te sore [ga anata buka buka no [[mizugi nan da.
M7:   [[<laughter>
K7:   [<laugh>

N8:   mizugi mottekanaku[te katta no [[yo.
M8:   [sorega ne,
K8:   <laugh>
E8:   [[aaa. <laugh>

N9:   [so:re:ga ookiku te ne kochira ni moo moratte [[moratta no. anmari ookikute.

K9:   o [ooki sugi chatta no ne.

E9:   [[<laughter>

N10:   sorede moo konnani natteru, mizugi de sore ga moo hazukashikute.

M11:   sore ga masshiro no ne, [gaun ga atatamete aru [[no.

K11:   <laughter> [[so,

T11:   [hazukashii. [[hee.

N12:   [[kakete kureru,

M12:   sore o ne, [niko niko to koo kakete [[kureru no.

K12:   [<cough, cough, cough>

T12:   [[huun,

N13:   kiree na otokonoko ga [kakete [[kurete. [[[<laughter>

M13:   [[[<laughter>

K13:   [[<cough, cough>

E13:   [<laughter>

N14:   soide mo[o anna hazukashii omoi shita koto nai no.

K14:   [######ne. <cough, cough, cough>

N15:   [demo mina san ne, [[soo yuu omoi mo shita hoo ga [[[ii to omotte.

M15:   [[ne.

K15:   <laughter> [[[soona no.

E15:   honto[o.

T15:   ###.

N16:   [minna ... soto de [[obachan tachi [[[oyoide ta [[[[kedo ne.

M16:   soo [tanoshi katta wa yo ne, [[go nin de ne. [[[[soide:

E16:   [[[hunn

Translation

N1:   when I got out, a lovely boy [was, [[bi::, ah, handsome boy was

M1:   [handsome [[yes,

N2:   whi[te, big towel, [[he was putting it on me.

K2:   [the blue-eyed boy was [[p

N3:   really I was, at first ...

M3:   then N-san was saying that that [was really embarrassing
E3:   [<laughter>

N4:   that was . . . that was [[at the beginning
M4:   that was #### so, it was embarrass[ing [[you [[[know.
T4:   [<laughter> [[[nobody was there

N5:   <laughter> at the beginning I was alone, a woman, I was the only one
      there,
M5:   <laughter>
T5:   <laughter>

N6:   [and I wonder where my husband was, h, he quickly went off, but I
M6:   [uhuh,
E6:   I see. [

N7:   it was so embarrassing, I had, [y'know, a totally loose [[swim suit on.
M7:   [[<laughter>
K7:   [<laugh>

N8:   I didn't bring a [swim suit with me [[so I bought one.
M8:   [that one was
K8:   <laugh>
E8:   [[aah <laugh>

N9:   [bu::t it was large, and I asked her to [[take it since it was really so big
K9:   t [too large, as it turned out
E9:   [[<laughter>

N10: and the swim suit was really like this, and it was so embarrassing, and

M11: and pure white [robe was warmed for [[us.
K11: <laughter> [[I see
T11: [embarrassing. [[hmmm.

N12: [[he covers us with it,
M12: and then [with smile he covers us [[with it.
K12: [<cough, cough, cough>
T12: [[I see

N13: the beautiful boy [put it [[on me [[[<laughter>
M13: [[[<laughter>

K13:   [[<cough, cough>
E13:   [<laughter>

N14:   and [really I had never felt so embarrassed as much as I did then
K14:   [######right <coughcoughcough>

N15:   [but everyone should [[have a chance to feel that way [[[I do think.
M15:   [[sure
K15:   <laughter> [[[is that so
E15:   real[ly
T15:   ###.

N16:   [everyone (pause) outside [[the middle-age women [[[were swimming
       [[[[you know
M16:   right [it was so much fun, [[with five of us [[[[a::nd
E16:   [[[I see

The same group of speakers, in a different stretch of conversation, talk about
the shapely figure of one of the members, M, in her tight-fitting sweater. In their
lively discussion sprinkled with laughter, they repeatedly use the slang word
boin ("big boobs, busty") to describe how she looks. The word *boin* is in italics
in the excerpt.

(6) Shapely figure

M1:   suggoku [nobite [[iino yoo.
T1:   [ii desho [[kore.
A1:   [[un, ii, ii.

T2:   oshare de[sho?
A2:   [un, [[M san ni,
N2:   [[iro ga ii wa.

M3:   tada mo:, . . . u[[n.
T3:   [ne.
A3:   M san ni yoku au sono iro ga.[. . . [[un.
I3:   u[[n.

M4:   [ne:.
T4:   [ne. [[motto.
A4:   akaruku naru wa,[sono hen, shiro [[dashi,

I4:   [un, [[uun,

M5:   [nde kimochi ga ii no [[yo:,
N5:   de M san ittsu[mo kuroppoi no,
I5:   un, [[u:n,

M6:   pitaaa tto shi[te.
T6:   [[dee hora, sugoi, *boin boin*,
N6:   [aa [[soo.

M7:   chigau, *boin* ja nai no ni *boin* rashiku mie chau no.
N7:   *boin* dakara nee.

M8:   [[honto wa *boin* demo [[[nan demo [[[[nai no.
T8:   [mie nai wa yo sore [[wa, [[[sugoi [[[[wa yo ne.
N8:   iya, [*boin* ni mieru wa yo.
I8:   [[[[un:::.

M9:   [[nandemo nai.
T9:   nandemo naku nai [wa yo, [[[ne::.
N9:   [nandemo nai [[wai urayamashii gurai [[[*boin* ja nai.
I9:   nnn.

M10:   nn nan[de. . . . [[baka yun ja nai,
T10:   [sukoshi poko tto tsukete morai tai [[wa.
N10:   [[sooooo,

M11:   BAKA YUN JA NAI.
N11:   <laughter>
M11:   <laughter>
I11:   <laughter>

Translation

M1:   extremely [stretchy [[so it's great.
T1:   [great [[isn't it
A1:   [[yes, it is

T2:   isn't this sty[lish?
A2:   [yes, [[great for M,
N2:   [[the color is good

M3:   it's really,[. . . [[yes.

T3: [right.
A3: that color suits M[... [[yes.
I3: y[[es.

M4: [right.
T4: [right [[even more
A4: it makes you look brighter, [it's white [[there,
I4: [uhuh, [[yes,

M5: [and it feels nice [[really,
N5: and M always [wears dark colors,
I5: ah, [[yes,

M6: it fits snug [and.
T6: [[and see, really, *busty busty*,
N6: [yes [[that's right.

M7: no, I'm not *busty*, but it looks as though I were *busty*.
N7: you are *busty*, so

M8: [[I'm not *busty* [[[or anything [[[[like that.
T8: [it's not that you just [[look, [[[you really [[[[are.
N8: yes [you look *busty*.
I8: [[[[yeeees.

M9: [[I'm not at all
T9: not that you are not [really, [[[you are.
N9: [you are not? [[I am envious [[[how *busty* you are
I9: yes.

M10: uh in what [way. [[stop saying such silly things,
T10: [I'd like to get some of that [[plump
N10: [[ME TOO,

M11: STOP SAYING SUCH SILLY THINGS
N11: <laughter>
M11: <laughter>
I11: <laughter>

In addition to the transcripts, the audio recordings of both Excerpts (5) and (6) illustrate how happy and vivacious the participants are in engaging in these conversations. Even though the speakers are generally considered far beyond the prime age for what is called the "heterosexual market"—remember the comments made by Momoi Kaori, referred to at the beginning of this chapter—they are extremely conscious of male existence and their appearance to men, as presented in Excerpt (5). The speaker recounts how bashful she was in a way that is reminiscent of teenage girls' chats, and how the young man's appearance did not escape her attention. Excerpt (6) shows that having a feminine body shape is desirable and sought after, and that talking about it is accepted, even when the speaker uses the slang word *boin* "big boobs, busty," which is not generally used in polite company. There is a tendency to consider elderly people as having transcended sexuality, body, and romantic images. My peer conversation data, however, indicate that this common image may best be described as existing more in the younger generation's imagination, rather than in the reality of older women's lives (see also Hori, this volume).

There has been a common belief that elderly women use or should use gender-neutral or asexual expressions, as reflected in some popular dramas, in which older women's utterances lack the typical characteristics of so-called feminine speech.[7] A similar point is discussed by Kitagawa (1977, 288–290), who states that the usage of the pragmatic particle *wa* has a "conspicuous constraint": when used "by an older woman (in her sixties or seventies, for example) it is liable to embarrass those around her" because it "embodies a sense of coquettish overture." These observations may be supported by saying that the absence of *wa* would reflect the speakers' position outside of the (hetero)sexual market (see, e.g., Eckert and McConnell-Ginet 1992), where the use of expressions indicating femininity in a social context is considered relevant.

Contrary to the expectation that older women should not use gendered expressions, the conversation excerpts analyzed in this chapter definitely do exhibit characteristics of so-called female speech (e.g., Okamoto and Sato 1992). Focusing only on the uses of the pragmatic particle *wa*, which has been most prominently associated with femininity and female speech in Japanese gender ideology for its gentle assertiveness, we can observe its use in the excerpts above, such as in (4), a discussion about independence of women; in (5), which recounts an event at a spa; and in (6), in chatting about one of the speakers' full figure.

These observations suggest, first, that sexuality may not be irrelevant to older women, and second, that the assumption that these expressions are solely relevant to the concept of youth-based sexuality is not correct. The mixed uses of forceful and attenuated expressions (which are stereotypically associated with speech of men and women, respectively) by middle-aged mothers in Tokyo (Matsumoto 2002; 2004a; 2004b) suggest that the choices of expressions in the conversations analyzed are also motivated by the content of the utterances and by the individual speaker's negotiation of the personae that portrays, rather than simply being determined by the characteristic of the speaker's age or gender.

Conclusion

In this chapter, I have examined several peer conversations among elderly Japanese women to see whether they reflect elderly stereotypes. Three common beliefs about the elderly in general and about traditional Japanese women in particular were focused on: (1) negative self representation through "painful self-disclosure"; (2) indications of (Confucian) good wife behavior toward their husbands; and (3) asexual attitudes and gender-neutral expressions, reflecting the speakers' position outside the (hetero)sexual market. Contrary to these common beliefs, the collected conversations indicated that (1) "painful self-disclosures" are often made with humor and a sense of friendly understanding based on shared similar experience; that (2) women happily compete in criticizing their husbands' selfish behaviors; and that (3) women make both physical and romantic comments about themselves and men.

The data also showed that, although the topics and contents of elderly women's conversations and the attitudes expressed reflect their current life stage and their past experiences—which as a matter of fact are different from those of younger generations—expressions of friendship through mutual complaints, a desire to be independent, and an interest in being sexually attractive are common across generations. The topics of health concerns and death, which appear among other more common and innocuous subjects, are certainly relevant and of keen interest to the speakers, as the topic of successful or unsuccessful romantic relationships is to young adults, and the topic of babies' diapers is to new parents. We may say that, for elderly adults, death and illness are not taboo subjects, just as topics surrounding diapers are not for parents of infants, while such topics may offend others in generationally mixed company. Setting a norm at the social and physical peak of adulthood only leads to discriminatory treatment of other age groups, including the elderly.

The examples discussed demonstrate the multiple interpretations that can be given to specific discourse practices and the methodological importance of data collection across diverse contexts. It is hoped that this study indicates the depth and breadth of verbal interaction among older speakers, providing counterexamples to ageist stereotypes and emphasizing the importance of examining naturally occurring data from a variety of contexts in order to gain insights into language use and what it says about the speakers' lives.

Appendix: Transcription Conventions

ISSHU NO	Small capitals indicate utterances with a laughing voice.
<laughter>	What is inside of < > is a sound element that is not a word.
(animated)	Description of conduct is indicated within parentheses.
[	Left square brackets on parallel utterance lines by different speakers indicate the onset of overlap. The second onset of overlap is marked by [[, the third by [[[, and the fourth by [[[[.
:	A colon following a vowel indicates a nonlexical elongated vowel sound.
::	Longer nonlexical elongated vowel sound.
,	A comma indicates continuing intonation.
.	A period indicates a final intonation contour.
. . .	Three dots indicate a pause.
##	Multiple hatches indicate linguistic elements that the transcriber could not comprehend.
(I said)	What is given inside of ( ) in translation is an expression that is not said in Japanese but added in English for the purpose of clarity.

A: latched=
B: =utterances
A line consisting of three centered dots indicates omitted dialogue.

Notes

This chapter was originally published in *International Journal of the Sociology of Language* 200 (2009): 129–151. It is reprinted here, with stylistic modifications, with permission of Mouton de Gruyter. It is an extended and revised version of a paper of the same title which I presented at the Annual Meeting of the Linguistics Society of America, San Francisco, 2006. I am grateful for the comments I received from the audience at the meeting as well as those from audiences who listened to other versions of this paper. I am also thankful to the editors and an anonymous reviewer for their helpful comments and suggestions. The research was partially supported by the Japan Foundation and the Center for East Asian Studies at Stanford University.

1. Coupland (2004, 71) argues that, even though not all old people are targets of ageism, sociolinguistic research "should be interested in documenting and modeling the changing social and ideological configurations of late life, as mediated by language" because "social inequality is not the only motivating issue for sociolinguistics."

2. As discussed by Eckert (1984), biological age is not necessarily an indication of a person's social age reflected in language, but I used 65 years of age for convenience in data collection.

3. The occurrence of laughter and humor do not necessarily mean a happy and lighthearted situation, as they are also found when the speakers are defensive (Ziv 1984) or experiencing extreme awkwardness (Chafe 2007). Although the multiplicity of functions of laughter and humor is itself an important issue, the interpretation that the laughter and humor that are found in the data I investigate indicate "non-seriousness" (Chafe 2007) and lighten the situation seems well supported in the given contexts, in which no serious interpersonal power struggle or psychological pressures are observed.

4. The use of initials is for convenience in discussing individual examples. The initials are neither reflective of the actual speakers' names nor do the same initials in different examples necessarily represent the same speakers.

5. According to Coupland, Coupland, and Giles (1991), the usual time to start recounting the way someone died seems to be five to ten years after bereavement.

6. It may be thought that, since many Japanese women of the generation focused on in my investigation did not have a love marriage, a narrative of the husband's death, such as in Excerpt (2), cannot be an example of bereavement. Although this is an arguable point, it is also reasonable to consider that an intimate relationship can be fostered during many years of marriage and a genuine sense of loss may be felt. For example, the extract given in (2) is surrounded by N's narrative expressing how grateful she was to the doctor who took exceptionally good care of her husband. In such a context, it would be difficult to imagine that the speaker is simply recounting a funny story. Complexity of emotions and of their expressions has been shown to be an important characteristic of elderly communication (see also Carstensen et al. 2000).

7. The expectation that older women should use fewer gendered forms can be seen in constructed dialogues. For example, the utterances of an older woman (65 years old), the wife of a semiretired middle-class man and the mother of middle-aged daughters, are mostly given in gender-neutral forms (which are sometimes associated with male speakers), while those of the middle-aged daughters are gendered expressions (associated more with female speakers) in a well-received TV drama *Ashura no gotoku* (Like Asura, aired in 1979), written by Kuniko Mukoda, an award-winning popular writer of essays, fiction, and drama scripts. Examples include the following pair of utterances (Mukoda 1985, 137), in which the relevant parts are in italic.

Mother: Huton tariru *ka nee*   "I wonder if we have enough futons."
Daughter: Moohu de ii *wa yo*   "Blankets will do."

References

Backhaus, Peter. 2009. Politeness in institutional elderly care in Japan: A cross-cultural comparison. *Journal of Politeness Research* 5 (1): 54–71.

Carstensen, Laura L., Monisha Pasupathi, Ulrich Mayr, and John R. Nesselroade. 2000. Emotional experience in everyday life across the adult life span. *Journal of Personality and Social Psychology* 79 (4): 644–655.

Chafe, Wallace. 2007. *The importance of not being earnest: The feeling behind laughter and humor.* Amsterdam: John Benjamins.

Coupland, Justine, Nikolas Coupland, and Karen Grainger. 1991. Intergenerational discourse: Contextual versions of aging and elderliness. *Aging in Society* 11: 189–208.

Coupland, Nikolas. 2004. Age in social and sociolinguistic theory. In *Handbook of communication and aging research,* ed. Jon F. Nussbaum and Justine Coupland, 69–90. Mahwah, NJ: Erlbaum.

Coupland, Nikolas, Justine Coupland, and Howard Giles. 1991. *Language, society and the elderly: Discourse, identity and ageing.* Oxford: Basil Blackwell.

Coupland, Nikolas, and Jon F. Nussbaum, eds. 1993. *Discourse and lifespan identity.* Newbury Park, CA: Sage.

Cuddy, Amy J. C., and Susan T. Fiske. 2002. Doddering but dear: Process, content, and function in stereotyping of older persons. In *Ageism: Stereotyping and prejudice against older persons,* ed. Todd D. Nelson, 3–26. Cambridge, MA: MIT Press.

Cuddy, Amy J. C., Susan T. Fiske, V. S. Y. Kwan, P. S. Glick, S. Demoulin, and J.-Ph. Leyens. 2009. Is the stereotype model culture bound? A cross-cultural comparison reveals systematic similiarities and differences. *British Journal of Social Psychology* 48: 1–33

Cuddy, Amy J. C., Michael I. Norton, and Susan T. Fiske. 2005. This old stereotype: The pervasiveness and persistence of the elderly stereotype. *Journal of Social Issues* 61 (2): 267–286.

Eckert, Penelope. 1984. Age and linguistic change. In *Age and anthropological theory,* ed. David I. Kertzer and Jennie Keith, 219–233. Ithaca, NY: Cornell University Press.

Eckert, Penelope, and Sally McConnell-Ginet. 1992. Communities of practice: Where language, gender, and power all live. In *Locating power: Proceedings of the Second Berkeley Women and Language Conference,* vol. 1, ed. Kira Hall, Mary Bucholtz, and Birch Moonwomon, 89–99. Berkeley, CA: Berkeley Women and Language Group.

Ervin-Tripp, Susan M., and Martin D. Lampert. 1992. Gender differences in the construction of humorous talk. In *Locating power: Proceedings of the Second Berkeley Women and Language Conference,* vol. 1, ed. Kira Hall, Mary Bucholtz, and Birch Moonwomon, 108–117. Berkeley, CA: Berkeley Women and Language Group.

Fujimura-Fanselow, Kumiko, and Atsuko Kameda, eds. 1995. *Japanese women: New feminist perspectives on the past, present, and future.* New York: Feminist Press at the City University of New York.

Giles, Howard, Hiroshi Ota, and Kimberly A. Noels. 2002. Challenging intergenerational stereotypes across Eastern and Western cultures. In *Linking lifetimes: A global view of intergenerational exchange*, ed. Matthew Kaplan, Nancy Henkin, and Atsuko Kusano, 13–28. Honolulu: University Press of America.

Hamaguchi, Toshiko. 2001. *Co-construction of meaning in intergenerational family conversations: A case of the Japanese demonstrative pronoun "are."* PhD diss., Georgetown University.

Hamilton, Heidi E. 1994. *Conversations with an Alzheimer's patient: An interactional sociolinguistics study.* Cambridge, UK: Cambridge University Press.

———, ed. 1999. *Language and communication in old age: Multidisciplinary perspectives.* New York: Garland.

Harwood, Jake, Howard Giles, Hiroshi Ota, Herbert Pierson, Cindy Gallois, Sik Hung Ng, Tae-Seop Lim, and Lilnabeth Somera. 1996. College students' trait ratings of three age groups around the Pacific Rim. *Journal of Cross-Cultural Gerontology* 11: 307–317.

Hay, Jen. 2000. Functions of humor in the conversations of men and women. *Journal of Pragmatics* 32 (6): 709–742.

Hummert, Mary L., Teri A. Garstka, Ellen B. Ryan, and Jaye L. Bonnesen. 2004. The role of age stereotypes in interpersonal communication. In *Handbook of communication and aging research*, 2nd ed., ed. Jon F. Nussbaum and Justine Coupland, 91–114. Mahwah, NJ: Erlbaum.

Hummert, Mary L., and Jay L. Shaner. 1994. Patronizing speech to the elderly as a function of stereotyping. *Communication Studies* 45: 145–158.

Hurd Clarke, Laura. 2001. Older women's bodies and the self: The construction of identity in later life. *Canadian Review of Sociology and Anthropology* 38 (4): 441–464.

Imamura, Anne E., ed. 1996. *Re-imaging Japanese women.* Berkeley: University of California Press.

Kitagawa, Chisato. 1977. A source of femininity in Japanese: In defense of Robin Lakoff's *Language and a woman's place. Papers in Linguistics* 10 (3/4): 275–298.

Kōsei Rōdō Shō (Ministry of Health, Labor, and Welfare). 2006. *Nihon no shōrai suikei jinkō (Heisei 18-nen 12-gatsu suikei)* (Japan's estimated future population [December 2006]). www.mhlw.go.jp/shingi/2007/01/dl/s0119-6c.pdf (accessed May 21, 2009).

Lebra, Takie Sugiyama. 1984. *Japanese women: Constraint and fulfillment.* Honolulu: University of Hawaii Press.

Matsumoto, Yoshiko. 2002. Gender identity and the presentation of self in Japanese. In *Gendered practices in language*, ed. Sarah Benor, Mary Rose, Devyani Sharma, Julie Sweetland, and Qing Zhang, 339–354. Stanford, CA: CSLI Publications.

———. 2004a. Alternative femininity: Personae of middle-aged mothers. In *Japanese language, gender, and ideology: Cultural models and real people*, ed. Shigeko Okamoto and Janet Shibamoto Smith, 240–255. Studies in Language and Gender. Oxford: Oxford University Press.

————. 2004b. The new (and improved?) language and place of women in Japan. In *Language and woman's place: Text and commentaries*, rev. and exp. ed., ed. Robin T. Lakoff and Mary Bucholtz, 244–251. Studies in Language and Gender. Oxford: Oxford University Press.

————. 2005. "We'll be dead by then!"—Comical self-disclosure by elderly Japanese women. In *Proceedings of the 30th annual meeting of the Berkeley Linguistics Society*, ed. Marc Ettlinger, Nicholas Fleischer, and Mischa Park-Doob, 268–279. Berkeley, CA: Berkeley Linguistics Society.

————. 2007. Dealing with changes: Discourse of elderly Japanese women. In *Japanese/Korean Linguistics* 15, ed. Naomi H. McGloin and Junko Mori, 93–107. Stanford, CA: CSLI Publications.

Momoi, Kaori. 2002. Kakkoii to omou yo, 70-sai no watashi wa (I think I'll be cool when I'm 70 years old). In Watashi ga iru jikan—gozen 4-ji (The hour when I am in—4 AM). *Asahi Shimbun* (September 22).

Mukoda, Kuniko. 1985. *Ashura no gotoku* (Like Asura). Tokyo: Shinchōsha.

Naikakufu (Cabinet Office). 2002. *H14 kōreisha no kenkō ni kansuru ishiki chōsa kekka* (2002 survey results on the health conditions of the elderly). www8.cao.go.jp/kourei /ishiki/h14_sougou/pdf/0-1.html (accessed May 21, 2009).

Okamoto, Shigeko, and Shie Sato. 1992. Less feminine speech among young Japanese females. In *Locating power: Proceedings of the Second Berkeley Women and Language Conference*, vol. 2, ed. Kira Hall, Mary Bucholtz, and Birch Moonwomon, 478–488. Berkeley, CA: Berkeley Women and Language Group.

Okamoto, Shigeko, and Janet Shibamoto Smith, eds. 2004. *Japanese language, gender, and ideology: Cultural models and real people*. Studies in Language and Gender. Oxford: Oxford University Press.

Ota, Hiroshi, Giles Howard, and Cindy Gallois. 2002. Perceptions of younger, middle-aged, and older adults in Australia and Japan: Stereotypes and age group vitality. *Journal of Intercultural Studies* 23 (3): 253–266.

Rubin, Lillian B. 1983. *Intimate strangers: Men and women together*. New York: Harper & Row.

Ryan, Ellen B., Richard Y. Bourhis, and Uus Knops. 1991. Evaluative perceptions of patronizing speech addressed to elders. *Psychology and Aging* 6: 442–450.

Tamanoi, Mariko Asano. 1990. Women's voices: Their critique of the anthropology of Japan. *Annual Review of Anthropology* 19: 17–37.

Williams, Angie, and Jon F. Nussbaum. 2001. *Intergenerational communication across the life span*. Mahwah, NJ: Erlbaum.

Ziv, Avner. 1984. *Personality and sense of humor*. New York: Springer.

9 Family Conversation as Narrative

Co-constructing the Past, Present, and Future

Toshiko Hamaguchi

> *Imagine a world without narrative. Going through life not telling others*
> *what happened to you or someone else, and not recounting what you read in*
> *a book or saw in a film. Not being able to hear or see or read dramas crafted*
> *by others. No access to conversations, printed texts, pictures, or films that*
> *are about events framed as actual or fictional. Imagine not even composing*
> *interior narratives to and for yourself. No. Such a universe is unimaginable,*
> *for it would mean a world without history, myths or drama; and lives*
> *without reminiscence, revelation, and interpretive revision.*
>
> **Ochs (1997, 185)**

IN THIS VIEW OF NARRATIVE, everyday conversation, our most mundane interaction, is "the most basic and universal form of narrative" (185). Just as we cannot imagine a world without narrative, we cannot imagine life without conversation. In Japan, the family is considered the basic unit of society, and conversation involving older family members is still common. Conversation requires cooperation on the part of the interlocutors, and narrative is also an interactive product requiring the narrator's and co-participants' collaboration for sense-making to take place. In this chapter, I examine family conversation as a type of narrative and emphasize the co-construction (Jacoby and Ochs 1995) of family history and identity through the everyday exchange of experiences.

Since a family by definition shares a history, it may be the case that whatever a family talks about automatically becomes part of its shared history. Nevertheless, family conversations as narrative are not simply the recounting of family events. Rather, family conversations as narrative require constant instantiation, adjustment, and recognition of family identity across generations. Such intergenerational activity manifests a range of responsibilities on the part of aging individuals who transmit the family history as its senior members. It also reveals the linguistic and cognitive capabilities that remain in the individual. Furthermore, narratives formed through intergenerational interactions provide opportunities for younger members to fill in and imagine their histories with both present and projected future events, while accommodating the declining cognitive and linguistic abilities of the elderly. (Also see Doba et al., Traphagan, and Ota and Giles, this volume, on intergenerational communication.) Analyzing discourse with the elderly in everyday settings by undertaking qualitative research based on naturally occurring interactions with the elderly helps to illuminate what people may face in aging societies.

Data

In order to analyze microlevel discourse strategies for co-constructing family identity, I will use a variety of discourse data collected between 1993 and 2004, including face-to-face conversations and telephone conversations. All the interactions involve a single elderly woman for whom I use the pseudonym "Natsuko." Natsuko was born in Tokyo in 1912 and raised in a wealthy family. She was married and then widowed during the Second World War. She lived independently and was quite active until 2001, when she was hospitalized for shingles that developed into meningitis. She was finally discharged after four months, but her doctor told Natsuko's daughter Sumiko that living alone was "not desirable [for Natsuko] anymore." Since then, Natsuko has been living with Sumiko.

Even before this change in her living situation, Natsuko had always been in close touch with her daughter and her two granddaughters, Rika and myself (Toshi). Face-to-face conversations between us were tape-recorded during casual interactions that often took place at meal or tea time. I also recorded several telephone conversations between Natsuko and myself when I was in graduate school in the United States. I collected Natsuko's life story in 1994 and again in 2003 for research purposes. These exchanges were tape-recorded in a conversational setting, rather than in an institutional or experimental setting. Although I was a researcher, I was also a participant in all of the interactions; the participant-observer technique provides the researcher with contextual information that is otherwise unobtainable. In the following sections, I will illustrate how each participant played a role and took responsibility for the creation of the past, present, and future in these conversations that shaped family identity. Except for my name, all the names of people and places have been changed.

Story-Sharing

The sharing of stories occurs frequently in family conversation. Topics range from daily occurrences to past events. In intergenerational family conversation, a particular kind of story-sharing can juxtapose similar experiences that happened in different time periods. In other words, family members talk sequentially about "the way it was" and "the way it is." Thus the speaker's past or present story becomes a trigger for another to tell stories of the past or the present.

The first example is taken from a conversation between Natsuko and Toshi (myself) at Natsuko's place over tea. Prior to this, we were talking about Natsuko's visit to Washington, D.C., where Toshi was studying. Natsuko said she was quite shocked when Toshi's Spanish roommate, Teresa, greeted her with a kiss:

(1)

1. Natsuko: kyonen wa: shinakatta noni
2. Toshi: iya dakara kyonen WA: =
3. Natsuko: =un
4. Toshi: hajimete datta desho?=
5. Natsuko: =un
6. Toshi: kotoshi wa shitteta kara yo.
7. Natsuko: so: yo ne dakara mo: sukkari
8. Toshi: nareta kara ne
9. Natsuko: mukashi. Sento Sofi ni Rosita to Maria no kyo:dai tte iunoga itano yo.
10. Toshi: fu:n
11. Natsuko: de Maria tte iuno wa ima Igirisu ni ite kekkonsite s- ano: oba:chama gurai no hito ga ne?
12. Toshi: un.
13. Natsuko: de Rosita tte iu no wa ro:jinho:mu mitai na toko de nakunatte kawaiso: ni dannasama to futari de sonna toko e haittete
14. Toshi: fu:n
15. Natsuko: de nakunatta no yo.

Translation

1. Natsuko: She didn't do that last year.
2. Toshi: No, so last year=
3. Natsuko: =uh-huh
4. Toshi: she was meeting you for the first time, right?=
5. Natsuko: =Right.
6. Toshi: This year, because she knew you already
7. Natsuko: You're right. So she was totally
8. Toshi: (feeling) familiar with you.
9. Natsuko: A long time ago, there were these sisters called Rosita and
              Maria at Saint Sofia.
10. Toshi: Uh-huh.
11. Natsuko: And Maria is now in England, married, and uh, she is about
              my age.
12. Toshi: Uh-huh.
13. Natsuko: And as for Rosita, she passed away at a senior home or some-
              place like that. Poor thing, with her husband, she was living in
              such a place.
14. Toshi: Uh-huh.
15. Natsuko: And passed away.

In this example, Natsuko brings up her own experience with two Spanish sisters, Maria and Rosita, following the discussion about Teresa, who is Spanish and Toshi's roommate and classmate. Maria and Rosita in line 9 had also gone to school with Natsuko. This merging of two time periods by putting the similar experiences side by side was initiated by the elderly woman. Tannen (1989) calls this interactional phenomenon "allo-repetition" (repetition of others), which serves as an involvement strategy in discourse, and which is exercised by sharing of personal experiences cross-generationally. It plays a significant role in family conversation since it makes the older person's life experiences visible and sharable with younger family members. Such experiences may otherwise remain concealed in the older person's memory.

The next example illustrates the way a granddaughter initiates the juxtaposition of the past and present. It is noteworthy that Natsuko's granddaughter Rika first ratifies Natsuko's story and then takes it as a resource for her own story. At the end of the segment, the two co-narrate the story. This conversation took place at the lunch table. Natsuko, her daughter, and two grandchildren are eating traditional New Year's dishes. Natsuko begins to comment on the black beans that Rika made. Black beans are a common New Year's dish and are known to be difficult to cook:

(2)

1. Natsuko: Sakakura-san ja nakutte nante iundakke, ne ano sensei no mata dai sensei
2. Rika: nandakke nandakke
3. Natsuko: ano ano Yanagihara-san.
4. Sumiko: a: Yanagida-san?
5. Rika: a:!
6. Natsuko: ano are ga omame no nikata o itte te mukashi wa tenjo: ni ho:ri nagete pishatto kuttsukeba sore de ii tte iundatta kedo=
7. Toshi: ha ha ha!
8. Rika: =nanka dokka nimo kaite atta na: dokka no ryo:tei no nimame no nikata toka itte shu:kanshi ni kaiteatta n dakedo
9. Sumiko: aso?
10. Rika: So: so: sorede pishatto nareba do:nok:no tte=
11. Natsuko: =nakanaka muzukashii no yo ne? omame wo ko: niruno tte=
12. Rika: =un.

Translation

1. Natsuko: Not Mr. Sakakura but what's his name, uh, the master teacher of the teacher [a famous chef]
2. Rika: What's his name, what's his name.
3. Natsuko: Uh, uh, Mr. Yanagihara.
4. Sumiko: You mean, Mr. Yanagida?
5. Rika: Yes!
6. Natsuko: Uh, so, he was talking about how to cook beans, in old times, we used to say that if you throw a bean to the ceiling, and if it goes "pisha!" [sticks firmly], it's done.=
7. Toshi: ha ha ha! [laughter]
8. Rika: =I think I read that somewhere. It says "The cooking method at such and such Japanese-style restaurant." It was in a magazine.
9. Sumiko: Oh yeah?
10. Rika: Yeah, yeah, and it says, "If it goes "pisha!" it's something something.=

11. Natsuko: =It's pretty difficult to cook beans like this.=
12. Rika: =It is.

From line 1 to line 5, the family members collaboratively retrieve the name of the chef that Natsuko could not recall. Then Natsuko begins to tell "the way it was" prefaced by "*mukashi wa*" ("in old times"). Rika supports and ratifies the story not only by telling her "that's the way it still is," but also by showing active involvement in lines 8 and 10. Such supportive actions are in contrast with Toshi's and Sumiko's respective reactions in lines 7 and 9, which may highlight the generational differences among family members. In addition to story-sharing, we can see that in line 4 Sumiko provides the name of the chef that Natsuko could not remember, helping Natsuko to continue the story. Thus, each family member's collaboration provides an opportunity to validate the voice of the elderly woman. This conversation exemplifies how cultural and family traditions are passed along intergenerationally.

The two examples above show that sharing similar stories in family conversation enables a family narrative to become not just a linear recounting of events, but something multidimensional and multigenerational. First, pieces of experiences, when added to the ongoing story, enrich the story itself. As shown in Example (2), the fact of cooking black beans is not told in a way that it is merely recounted as fact. In telling the story, the cooking method is transmitted across generations. It can be argued that sharing such knowledge and enabling the past and present to coexist in conversation instantiates and promotes family solidarity. In addition, the juxtaposition of the past and present assimilates the experiences, in turn strengthening family unity.

The next example is an intricate kind of co-constructing of the past and present. This kind of narrative performance is probably particular to family conversation. The excerpt is taken from Natsuko's life story. She is talking about her daughter's educational background. Based on what Natsuko is saying about her daughter Sumiko from a mother's perspective, Toshi joins the conversation to talk about her mother from a daughter's perspective. Toshi's involvement in storytelling manifests who she is, grounded in the lives of Natsuko and Sumiko. In this co-narration of Sumiko's life, re-created from two distant perspectives, the life stories of three women family members emerge:

(3)

1. Natsuko: sorekara Murasaki Ongaku Gakko: e itte
2. Toshi: nande mama piano- =

3. Natsuko: =datte mama ga do:shitemo piano ni ikitai tte iundamon

4. Toshi: he: mama chiisai koro kara piano yatteta no?

5. Natsuko: un sho:gakko: kara kana? yattetano yo? soide piano ni,

6. Toshi: ikitai tte?

7. Natsuko: Un, ikitai tte iunde, de dakara ima demo omenjo motten dashi oshiereba ii no yo ne?

8. Toshi: so:da yo ne

9. Natsuko: piano mo arun dashi ne?

10. Toshi: mukashi nanka kurutta yo:ni hiiteta yo

11. Natsuko: doko de?

12. Toshi: Hamadaoka no ouchi de.

13. Natsuko: Hamadaoka no ouchi de?

14. Toshi: un. Toshi sore de datte ironna kyoku oboetan damon.

15. Natsuko: aso:

16. Toshi: dakara kurutta yo:ni hiiteru kara sa?

17. Natsuko: ano nandattakke reko:do shotchu: kaketeta desho?

18. Toshi: un. soremo kini itta kyoku shika kakenai kara onnaji kyoku BAKKARI

19. Natsuko: maiban maiban onnaji no kikasarete oboechatta desho.

20. Toshi: so. onnaji no BAKKARI kiiteta kara sa: Toshi kurashikku ni wa tsuyoi no yo.

21. Natsuko: ha ha ha

22. Toshi: nandemo shittenno yo, kyoku toka sa dakedo dare no nandaka shiranai no.

(Natsuko and Toshi talk about piano lessons)

23. Natsuko: de mama honto: ni chitchai tokini ne nesshin dattano mainichi kaNARAzu okeiko shite ne?

24. Toshi: un

25. Natsuko: mo: iiwa tte iu to "mo:sukoshi!" tte itte jibun de okeiko shite

26. Toshi: ara imadattara kangae rarenai wa

27. Natsuko: so sonokurai nesshin datta no yo.

28. Toshi: nande ima wa hikanaku natchatta no kashira.

Translation

1. Natsuko: Then she went to the Murasaki School of Music.

2. Toshi: Why did Mom (study) the piano- =

3. Natsuko: =Because your mom said she wanted to study the piano no matter what.

4. Toshi: Really, did she start playing the piano when she was little?
5. Natsuko: Yes, since elementary school, I think, she started playing the piano. So the piano,
6. Toshi: (she) wanted to pursue that?
7. Natsuko: Yeah, wanted to pursue it, she said. So I think she should teach because she has the certificate.
8. Toshi: I think so, too.
9. Natsuko: She has the piano, too, y'know?
10. Toshi: She used to play (the piano) like crazy.
11. Natsuko: Where?
12. Toshi: At the house in Hamadaoka.
13. Natsuko: At the house in Hamadaoka?
14. Toshi: Yeah. That's why I learned so many classical pieces by heart.
15. Natsuko: Really?
16. Toshi: Because, like I said, (Mom) played (the piano) like crazy.
17. Natsuko: Uh, whatchamacallit, records, she used to play records so often, didn't she?
18. Toshi: Yeah, and she'd only listen to the ones she liked. [So I heard ONLY THE SAME ones!
19. Natsuko: [Every night, every night, you had to listen to the same ones, so you ended up memorizing them all, didn't you?
20. Toshi: Exactly! Since I heard nothing but the SAME ones, I am good at classical music.
21. Natsuko: ha ha ha!
22. Toshi: I know so many pieces, but I don't know who composed what.
(They keep talking about piano lessons.)
23. Natsuko: And when she was little, your Mom was really enthusiastic (about piano) she would practice EVERY SINGLE DAY.
24. Toshi: Uh huh.
25. Natsuko: If I told her, "That's enough (for today)," she would say "A little more!" and kept playing by herself.
26. Toshi: Wow, it's hard to imagine it nowadays.
27. Natsuko: I know. She used to be very enthusiastic.
28. Toshi: I wonder why she doesn't play (the piano) anymore.

The inaccessible history of her mother is made available to Toshi through her own participation in storytelling. In turn, Toshi's contribution makes her mother

Sumiko's life available to Natsuko. The life of a third person, which could easily be left unknown otherwise, can become visible via multigenerational contributions that reproduce a person's history: one from the past, the other from the present.

As a matter of fact, intergenerational story-sharing is common in conversation, as shown in the examples above. Downs (1989, 258) states, "When grandparents and grandchildren do interact, one of the most frequently reported forms of interaction is grandparents' sharing of experiences, events, or family history through stories." However, it is often reported in research on communication and aging that younger participants react negatively to stories told by older participants (Nussbaum and Bettini 1994). Although reciprocal storytelling has been noted to be advantageous among the elderly (Boden and Bielby 1983; 1986), story-sharing between different age groups, especially among families, is little documented. I argue that the production of family narratives, in which younger participants play an active role, is important. The mutual involvement of young and old must be given further attention in research on aging and communication.

Co-construction of Meaning

Research on the discourse of the elderly suggests that one of its prominent features, possibly to camouflage a loss of memory, is for the elderly speaker to use pronouns in place of nouns. Elsewhere in my previous studies on the co-construction of meaning in intergenerational family conversations (Hamaguchi 2001), I have observed the prominent use of the Japanese demonstrative pronoun *are* ("that") in Natsuko's discourse. Among the various uses of *are* that I discovered in my data, there are cases where *are* (that) does not seem to have any referent in the conversational context (e.g., "*that door* over there") or in the immediate knowledge of conversationalists (e.g., "*the accident* that happened yesterday").[1] Neurolinguist Morihiro Sugishita (quoted in Aoki 1994) notes that the frequent use of *are* (that) without a conversational referent is an indication of cognitive decline.

When *are* (that) falls into this category, the conversationalists begin to co-construct its meaning (Goodwin 1995). Either prompted by the younger member or the elderly one, the family members are able to retrieve the referent of *are* (that) most of the time, thus preventing conversational failure.[2] This conversational activity serves as a routine way of dealing with an aging individual in the family. This collaborative, everyday act also serves to manifest familial solidarity because it requires each member's involvement in sense-making. The elderly woman's use of *are* (that) demands the family members' involvement in conversation. At the same time, the younger members' requests for clarification invigorate the interaction because such requests urge clarification and ratification of meaning from the elderly person. In this chapter, I look at pronoun usage from a different perspective. The co-construction of meaning fills in the gap between family members in two ways. First, the knowledge gap is filled when the pronominal referent is retrieved. Second, the gap in experience is filled through the sharing of personal episodes. The latter happens when *are* (that) is a crucial piece of information in a narrative family conversation. Therefore, once the *are* (that) referent becomes clear, the story becomes a part of family history.

The first example of this kind involves an episode of story-sharing in which family members bridge the past and present collaboratively (see above). In Example (4) below, Natsuko incorporates the present in her story in order to minimize the knowledge gap between herself and her granddaughter. After successfully retrieving the pronominal referent, Natsuko uses that term for the referent as she continues to talk about her past experience. This phenomenon of using the present as a resource in elderly discourse is noteworthy because we usually expect younger persons to use the past as a resource for their present experiences.

Natsuko is talking about the cooking lessons she had in high school. Prior to this segment, she said that the teacher was a chef who worked in a hotel and came to her school to teach authentic French cuisine. She then talks about the lessons:

(4)

1.	Natsuko:	mazu ichiban hajime ni Ja:man bifute- bi:fu sute:ki tte iuno ga are yo a:
2.	Toshi:	teiban no menyu:?
3.	Natsuko:	e?
4.	Toshi:	menyu:?
5.	Natsuko:	are no koto yo ima iu
6.	Toshi:	Ja:man bi:fu sute:ki
7.	Natsuko:	dakara are yo=
8.	Toshi:	=sute:ki?
9.	Natsuko:	iie sute:ki ja nakute sa hikiniku no=
10.	Toshi:	=hamba:[gu?
11.	Natsuko:	[HAMBA:GU NANOYO! [laughter]
12.	Toshi:	fu:n

13. Natsuko: ichiban saisho ni narau no ga mo: maitoshi maitoshi hanba:gu.
14. Toshi: fu:n

Translation

1. Natsuko: First, at the very first time, what is called German befte- beef-steak is are, y'know, ah
2. Toshi: The regular menu?
3. Natsuko: Pardon?
4. Toshi: Menu?
5. Natsuko: It means are these days.
6. Toshi: [wondering] German beefsteak.
7. Natsuko: So, are, y'know?=
8. Toshi: =Steak?
9. Natsuko: No, not steak, (made) of ground meat=
10. Toshi: =Hamburger [steak?
11. Natsuko: [It's HAMBURGER STEAK! [laughter]
12. Toshi: I see.
13. Natsuko: The first thing we learned was always hamburger steak every single year.
14. Toshi: Uh-huh.

Here, Natsuko tries to make sense of her story to Toshi by using a word that should be comprehensible to her. At the same time, Toshi provides the missing element, hamburger steak, which was a crucial piece of information in Natsuko's story. With the piece of information collaboratively recovered, this story became part of their family history. Thus both participants' contributions are mutually meaningful. This is another way of strengthening family solidarity in conversation. As Ochs (1997, 191) states, "Narrative serves the important function of bringing the past into the present time consciousness. That is, narrative provides a sense of continuity of self and society." By nominalizing the pronominal element in the elderly woman's utterance, the younger speaker adds depth to the story. It is similar to adding color to a black-and-white movie; providing a concrete noun for the intended referent of the pronoun makes the past come alive. To some degree, elders' increased use of pronouns can be a burden, since such speech requires the family members to retrieve the intended referent. Nevertheless, *are* (that) gives caregivers or younger family members an opportunity to access the family history. A lack of interest in participating in such co-construction could result in the perpetuation of a knowledge gap.

More important, it could also lessen communication with the elderly. Hence I emphasize the importance of family conversation, not only for the elderly or families, but also for society as a whole.

In the following example, the retrieval of the referent leads to further elaboration of a past event. Natsuko, Sumiko, and Toshi are having dinner. After a period of silence, Natsuko begins to talk about an event that happened a few days before by referring to it by the pronoun *are* (that). With Sumiko's prompting, Natsuko retrieves the referent and elaborates on the story:

(5)

1. Natsuko: kono aida no atashi handobakku irete konakatta kana: kono
             aida no are ano hachinin gurai shika konakatta no yo ne
2. Sumiko: do:- =
3. Natsuko: = do:kyu:kai. Handobakku irete konakatta kana:

Translation

1. Natsuko: Of the other day, didn't I put it in my handbag? are of the other
             day. Uh only about eight people came.
2. Sumiko: The re- =
3. Natsuko: =The reunion. Didn't I put it in my handbag.

In line 2, Sumiko gives Natsuko a trigger for her self-retrieval of the referent, *"do:kyu:kai"* ("the reunion"). Sumiko, the daughter, may have known how many people had come to the reunion. She might have already heard about how it had gone. What is significant here, however, is that recovery of the intended referent, the reunion, was necessary for Natsuko to move to the next step in her story, i.e., showing a photograph of the party.

As stated earlier, a narrative can recount a present or future event. The pronoun *are* (that) can also refer to what will happen in the future. Example (6) will illustrate how the retrieval of the missing referents enables Toshi to introduce present and future events. This example is taken from a telephone conversation when Toshi was a graduate student at an American university:

(6)

1. Natsuko: ano are ga are de . . . are nandatte?
2. Toshi: nani ga nan de nannano?
3. Natsuko: ano . . . raishu:?
4. Toshi: a: konferensu ne?

Translation

1. Natsuko: Ah are is are and . . . are, right? ["Ah, that is that and . . . that, right?"]
2. Toshi: What is what and what?
3. Natsuko: Uhm . . . next week?
4. Toshi: Oh the conference, right?

What looks meaningless on the surface becomes an important prompt for revising the family history. Toshi was involved in organizing a conference at which she was also presenting. Having remembered that, Natsuko called her to wish her luck and asked her how she was doing. Roughly speaking, the interpretation of line 1 is "the conference is approaching. So you're busy, aren't you?" After this segment, Toshi was able to update Natsuko about the upcoming conference.

In this way, the same activity, co-construction of the referent of *are* (that), serves to co-construct not only the past, but also the present and the future. In so doing, family members become actively involved in revising family history while reconfirming family solidarity. Nevertheless, the frequent occurrence of this activity in everyday conversation makes the family realize the inevitable cognitive decline and memory loss of the elderly member. It can be a tedious task for younger family members if they have to request frequent clarification or elaboration of the referent. It can be face-threatening and could cause loss of face for the elderly member if told that what he or she said was incomprehensible. For this reason, ignoring the missing referent is also an option, although that strategy is rarely used. If family members start to reduce the time spent engaging in family conversation because of the aging of other family members, we stand to lose a way of demonstrating family identity, namely, who we are.

So far I have described how family members share past, present, or future experiences. Story-sharing and co-construction of meaning solidify familial closeness by bridging the knowledge gap between family members. Family conversation as narrative, however, is sometimes marked by the experience of aging.

Projecting the Future of Others

Ochs (1997) notes that the future in narratives concerns hypothetical events, such as scientific experiments or the uncertain future of the narrator. As seen above, however, family narratives can refer to events in the family's past as well as those that will happen in the near future. The future in intergenerational conversation occurs when the speaker alludes to the future of the other based on his or her own present state. More precisely, when younger family members mention or blame Natsuko's memory problem directly or indirectly, Natsuko avoids accepting responsibility by shifting the agent who has the memory problem to a future elderly person. For example, when her daughter tells her that she has asked what day it is four times in a couple of hours, Natsuko would say, "You will understand when you become 90!" or "Wait 30 years, and you will understand." This kind of reference to the future foresees what younger family members will face as a result of aging when they become the age of the elderly speaker. It also presents the overlap of the experienced and projected states of two members of the family. This projective positioning of others is a powerful device in elderly discourse since it ratifies and manifests their authority through their life experience. Only those who have subjective knowledge about aging can ratify "the aging self" and position others vis-à-vis this self. Alternatively, those who are so positioned are forced to envision their aging selves. Although it is hard to testify to its truth value, we can easily afford a great deal of credibility to what the elderly woman says. We will probably find out how meaningful elders' words were when we ourselves reach age 90.

Conclusion

Let me end this chapter by quoting Ochs (1997, 201):

> Narrative is a sense-making activity; it is also a primary vehicle for retaining experiences in memory. Entitlement to co-tell a narrative is then a powerful right, encompassing past, present, future, as well as imagined worlds.

This study has considered family conversation as narrative. Co-construction of the past, present, and future takes various forms in intergenerational family conversations, the overall function of which, I believe, is to reproduce the family identity. Reciprocal storytelling bridges the gap between "the way it was" and "the way it is." The pronoun *are* ("that") is used as a cue for mutual involvement in sense-making. These collaborative activities adjust and enrich the family history on the one hand, and re-create family solidarity on the other. Future projection in elderly discourse makes visible the power of the aged to highlight the inevitable processes of aging in conversation.

Co-construction of the past, present, and future is not always possible, especially when past events have become inaccessible to the elderly person. Organizing temporal matters has become extremely difficult for the elderly woman in this study following a series of unexpected hospitalizations in 2001. The family members found it hard to accept the apparent change in her cognitive ability, but dealing with it in everyday conversation proved even more difficult.

The way she refers to events, regardless of time, has become quite different from "the way it was." References to actual past events have decreased in her discourse. At the same time, keeping track of the present and future as "the way it is" is almost impossible for her. The elderly woman is no longer sure of what day it is even though she checks the date every day in the newspaper and crosses out the days passed and writes "today" in her agenda. Every day, she asks the date every few minutes until she becomes occupied with something else. In April 2005, she enjoyed her ninety-third birthday dinner with her family, and she was the only one who could finish the entire full-course French meal. Nevertheless, she did not remember the dinner after two days. Family conversation, however, is still an everyday activity through which we confirm our family identity. Dealing with aging *in* and *through* conversation provides innumerable hints for how a family should function in an aging society. This is a continuous challenge for the family, and respectful communication with the elderly is one of its major responsibilities.

Research on aging is interdisciplinary by nature. Nevertheless, qualitative and descriptive analysis of discourse *of* and *with* the elderly remains largely unknown. There were a surprising number of story-sharing episodes in my discourse data, and it is my hope that this story-sharing across generations can be used as one of the elicitation techniques for research on life stories or narratives of the elderly. I believe that both researchers and subjects benefit from finding otherwise inaccessible pieces of family history. A life without the elderly is a life without history.

Appendix: Transcription Conventions

A: [utterances
B: [overlapped
A: latched=
B: =utterances
    . . .   Pause longer than 1 second
CAPS   Emphatic stress
:   Prolonged vowel
-         Sound cut off
,   Clause final intonation

.   Sentence final falling intonation
?   Rising intonation, not necessarily indicating an interrogative
( )   Supplemented element that is omitted or unclear in the original
            text
[ ]   Nonverbal behavior

Notes

1. As long as the referent is in the shared knowledge of the conversationalists, the conversation goes smoothly, as in the following:

1.   Natsuko: are kiitano? mama.
2.   Sumiko: a mada kiitenai do:shitan desho:ne.

[Translation]

1.   Natsuko: Did you ask about *are*, Mom?
2.   Sumiko: Oh no, I haven't asked yet. I wonder what happened.

The referent does not appear in the context, but as can be surmised from the way Sumiko responds, it is clear to the participants what *are* means. The use of *are* that I consider significant in aging research is the case where co-construction of meaning is required in conversation.

2. I do not claim that the referent is retrieved at all times. However, it is extremely rare that conversationalists do not initiate co-construction or completely ignore *are*. For example, in 150 minutes of the family conversations, 91 tokens of *are* were found. Only five tokens failed to retrieve the referent as the result of either relinquishment or lack of knowledge on the part of the younger speaker (see Hamaguchi 2001).

References

Aoki, Y. 1994. *Hatago no kenkyū* (A study of Hata language). *Asahi Weekly Journal.* Tokyo: Asahi Shimbun, 22–25.

Boden, D., and D. D. V. Bielby. 1983. The past as a resource: A conversational analysis of elderly talk. *Human Development* 26: 308–319.

———. 1986. The way it was: Topical organization in elderly conversation. *Language and Communication* 6: 73–89.

Downs, V. C. 1989. The grandparent-grandchild relationship. *Life-span communication: Normative process*, ed. J. F. Nussbaum, 257–282. Hillsdale, NJ: Erlbaum.

Goodwin, C. 1995. Co-construction of meaning in conversations with an aphasic man. *Research on Language and Social Interaction* 28 (3): 233–260.

Hamaguchi, T. 2001. *Co-construction of meaning in intergenerational family conversations: A case of the Japanese demonstrative pronoun "are."* PhD diss., Georgetown University.

Jacoby, S., and E. Ochs. 1995. Co-construction: An introduction. *Research on Language and Social Interaction* 28 (3): 171–183.

Nussbaum, J. F., and L. Bettini. 1994. Shared stories of the grandparent-grandchild relationship. *International Journal of Aging and Human Development* 39: 67–80.

Ochs, E. 1997. Narrative. In *Discourse as structure and process*, ed. T. van Dijk, 185–207. London: Sage.

Tannen, D. 1989. *Talking voices: Repetition, dialogue, and imagery in conversational discourse.* New York: Cambridge University Press.

10 A Good Story Is Not Enough

Unmasking and Accommodating the
Social Meanings of Aging in Japan

Hiroshi Ota and Howard Giles

CHANGE IS A UNIVERSAL PHENOMENON. Be it at a molecular or societal level, change occurs at all times in some domains of our life, and it is as though the absence of change means the expiration of life. Change takes place at different velocities and proceeds in different directions. One change may beget another one and may lead to the creation of something different or new. To live a balanced life, we strive mindfully to find ways to adjust to various changes in and around us. In this way, the notion of change has spurred researchers in many academic disciplines to seek an understanding of its underlying mechanisms and ramifications.

Aging is one potent type of change. Against a backdrop of rapid population reconfigurations, it has recently garnered much scholastic and public attention. Aging, unfortunately, is likely to conjure up negative images. It is often viewed, one-sidedly, as a one-way developmental process, involving biological, psychological, physical, and social decrements. Various intervention measures and practices have already been adopted at both the societal and individual levels to help people successfully deal with aging-related changes (e.g., Kaplan, Henkin, and Kusano 2002). Nevertheless, *ageism* is a prevalent social phenomenon (Hendricks 2005; Kimmel 1988; Nelson 2005). Rather than being treated with respect, older adults in Western countries are likely to be discriminated against and avoided in many social domains (e.g., Braithwaite, Lynd-Stevenson, and Pigram 1993), and in extreme cases, suffer elder abuse (Brownell and Podnieks 2005) or commit suicide (McIntosh et al. 1994; Traphagan, this volume). This rather dismal picture of aging is, in fact, common to many cultures these days and is quite pronounced in rapidly aging nations like Japan (Giles et al. 2002).

In this chapter, we will examine aging in Japan through the issue of communication. Communication denotes a symbolic, transactional, and creative process (see also Bower, this volume). It is concerned with the notion of change and thus is a suitable vehicle for examining aging and intergenerational interactions. Specifically, we will take an intergroup communication perspective (see Harwood, Giles, and Ryan 1995; Tajfel and Turner 1986). This useful approach identifies macro- and microsocial factors to systematically explain the mechanisms of change and to suggest some possible strategies for achieving successful aging (see Giles and Dorjee 2004; Ryan et al. 1995).

In the sections that follow, the current status of aging in Japan will be briefly summarized, with particular attention to the negative and positive meanings people often attribute to aging in an exploration of the two seemingly contradictory faces of growing old. Second, we will review some major findings from our studies and supply more details about the aforementioned theoretical frameworks in which they are embedded. In concluding, some general theoretical and practical suggestions and some possible research directions will be proffered in order to improve views of aging and individuals' subjective well-being in Japan.

Aging and Communication between Younger and Older Adults in Japan

Japan has been one of the nations that have been regularly involved in our international research program from its initial stages (Gallois et al. 1999; Williams et al. 1997). Japan has experienced a remarkable change in its cultural makeup after World War II, due largely to its economic and industrial successes, as well as its oft-mentioned Western influences. Recent low birthrates (1.26 children per couple in 2005) and increased longevity (78.53 years for males, 85.49 years for females in 2005) have added a new face to the culture (Kōsei Rōdo Shō 2006), making Japan one of the fastest-aging countries in the world. According to the Statistics Bureau (Tōkei Kyoku 2007), people who are over 65 years of age constituted 20.8 percent of the entire population in 2006. Ailing, dependent, and despondent older adults, rather than healthy and strong ones, are a conspicuous presence, as exemplified by the ever-increasing number of bedridden elders (Imai 1998) and elderly suicides (Maeda et al. 1989; Traphagan, this volume). New aging policies, such as the long-term care insurance (*kaigo hoken*) and the National Health Promotion Plan for *ikigai* (source of value in living), have been recently implemented as ways of tackling these aging-related problems (e.g., Koyano 1999). As by-products, however, they appear to have brought public attention to a greater and more urgent need to successfully merge traditional and contemporary values regarding aging and elder care, as well as the imperative to tackle the shortage of care-provision facilities and personnel (e.g., Koyano 1996; Maeda 2000). Academic organizations, such as the Japan Geriatric Society (1959–present), the Japan Socio-Gerontological Society (1959–present), the Japan Society of Bio-Medical Gerontology (1981–present), the Japanese Society of Gerodontology (1986–present), the Japanese Psychogeriatric Society (1986–present), and the Japan Society of Care Management (2001–present), have been indispensable in highlighting and extending our understandings of many contemporary issues that pertain to aging in Japanese society.

Two faces or sides to aging dominate the public and academic discourse on growing old in Japan. First, aging has discernible negative connotations here, just as it does in Western societies. Indeed, "anti-aging" rhetoric is perceptible in the common vocabulary of everyday life (e.g., Shioya and Yoshida 2003), as seen in a number of advertisements for cosmetics, health care, and exercise. Shortages of care facilities for older adults and the scarcity of "barrier-free" facilities may represent a relative lack of societal attention to older adults. Other examples of the discourteous social treatment of older adults abound, as seen in younger people's condescending talk to older adults (Masataka 2000), elder-unfriendly new technology resources (Umeda and Yashiro 2003), age discrimination in employment opportunities (Genba 2005), blocks on college admission (*Fugōkaku* 2005), social segregation of the elderly (Nakazato 1990), and even elder abuse (Kobayashi 2004; Shibusawa et al. 2005), which has recently garnered wide public attention (Kiyokawa 2006). The recent inauguration of anti-elder-abuse associations and the promulgation of the Elder Abuse Prevention Law (*Kōreisha gyakutai bōshi hō*) are indicative of a growing awareness of how older adults can be maltreated (see Long, this volume).

A newspaper cartoon entitled "Kanshin suru dake ja" (A Good Story Is Not Enough; Kobayashi 2000) vividly reflects the precarious position of older adults in contemporary Japan. It sarcastically illustrates a scene on a train in which a young male is sitting with his head buried in the newspaper, much impressed by an engaging story he had found there. Hanging on to a strap beside him, an elderly female carries a large sack on her back and is standing with her eyes closed. The cartoon indicates that older adults are often viewed as an invisible social presence, and are neglected in real life. It is not surprising that a growing number of older adults express pessimistic views about aging, are unhappy with the label "old," and are reluctant to be affiliated with any informal institutions designated solely for their age group (see, for example, Iwabuchi and Naoi 2003; Traphagan 2000).

Obviously, seeing aging as a negative change alone does not sufficiently capture the complexities of aging in contemporary Japan. It is highly important to acknowledge that aging is a positive change that involves various social, psychological, and even material gains. For instance, elderly people still enjoy privilege in some social arenas, suggesting that the high social status and respect that they have traditionally been accorded have been preserved to some extent. Such an age-based hierarchy, originating in Confucianism and Shintoism (Kim and Yamaguchi 1995; Tachibana 1939), remains an important cultural norm that still prevails, albeit arguably to a lesser degree (e.g., Sung 2001). The government designates a special day in September as a national holiday called "Respect for the Aged Day." On this day, local communities and governments send congratulatory messages and gifts to older people. In another example, a special section on public transportation is reserved for elderly people as "priority seats." Moreover, it is often the case that one needs to be "sufficiently" old to be a full professor at a university. Professors tend to be over 40 years old (mean age = 57.2 years), and those under 40 years of age constitute only 0.4 percent of the total number of professors, according to statistics from the Ministry of Education, Culture, Sports, Science, and Technology (Monbukagaku Shō n.d.). These figures suggest a positive association between age, wisdom, and even power. Similarly, people are expected to consult and seek advice from older people and use honorific language when speaking with them (Sung 2001).

Aging is a double-edged sword. In the past, elder respect constituted an important foundation of Japanese culture (Sung 2001) and was used as a primary template for people's behavior during cross-generational interactions. The negative side of aging may have been "wrapped," masked, and made invisible, perhaps by *strategically* and *rhetorically* focusing attention on elder respect in society (e.g., Hendry 1995; Koyano 1989). However, the "wrapping" culture seems to be rapidly eroding, and what has been wrapped has been gradually unwrapped and unmasked. In this way, the duality of aging is now more easily observable, and, in particular, its negative side has been taken up in many more aspects of our social life than before. This coincides with what we gleaned from our empirical studies of intergenerational communication.

Intergroup Communication across Generational Lines

Social Identity and Communication Accommodation Theories

Our research enterprise has been unfolding since the mid-1990s and has explored various facets of intergenerational communication in countries around the Pacific Rim and elsewhere (e.g., Giles, Ballard, and McCann 2002; Giles, Makoni, and Dailey 2005). The set of theoretical frameworks we have adopted is referred to as the intergroup communication approach (see Harwood and Giles 2005; Hummert 2010). Theories that come under this umbrella, unlike some other human communication theories (see Gudykunst 2005), clearly situate social interactions in macrocultural contexts and regard people's behaviors therein as a reflection of power relationships perceived to exist among groups. Social identity theory (SIT: Tajfel and Turner 1986) is one of the major theoretical perspectives of this genre. It outlines a social psychological mechanism whereby people endeavor to enhance their social, rather than personal, identities through the utilization of various social strategies (e.g., social creativity and competition) (see Williams and Nussbaum 2001).

Social identity principles emerged as central to the development of communication accommodation theory (CAT: e.g., Giles, Coupland, and Coupland 1991). CAT affords special attention to how people can change their verbal and nonverbal behaviors (e.g., accommodate) as in- and out-group members, and how these changes affect the relationships among the communicators, as well as their views of themselves (for a history of CAT, see Gallois, Ogay, and Giles 2005). In acknowledging their importance, CAT specifies macrocultural factors (such as group vitality, see below) and contextual factors (e.g., social norms) as predictors of individuals' decisions (conscious or unconscious) as to whether and to what degree they can accommodate to their interlocutors.

Communication Predicament Model of Aging

CAT, a major behavioral and cross-disciplinary theory of communication (see Coupland and Jaworski 1997; Littlejohn and Foss 2005; Tracy and Haspel 2004), has spawned a further set of context-specific satellite models of accommodation (see Gallois, Ogay, and Giles 2005). One of these is the communicative predicament of aging model (CPA: Ryan et al. 1986), which has itself undergone further elaboration and refinement over the years (e.g., Barker, Giles, and Harwood 2004; Harwood et al. 1993). Following the CAT tradition, CPA sheds light on the powerful role of language in people's aging processes, especially vis-à-vis changes in older adults' psychological well-being.

The CPA specifies two possible routes toward psychological and physical changes arising from intergenerational communication. First, the aging process may proceed in a rather *negative* direction. Older adults themselves may collude and begin to act out unfavorable older adult stereotypes (Kite and Johnson 1988) when they receive age-alerting verbal and nonverbal messages from others, the consequences of which could be lowered elder-worth and lessened life satisfaction. Alternatively, they could try to communicatively defy others' ageist stances and remarks, although these assertive tactics could somehow backfire by consolidating and reinforcing negative elderly stereotypes (such as being perceived as complaining and grouchy).

Second, the negative spiral of aging may be impeded or counteracted, whereby positive change might be anticipated when an interaction is underpinned by shared beliefs regarding elder respect (e.g., Levy and Langer 1994). Younger adults' communicative accommodations (e.g., use of polite language) may send favorable and supportive messages to older adults when they are perceived to reflect respectful attitudes toward their older counterparts (Ryan et al. 1995). Awareness of positive meanings may work to safeguard against the loss of psychological and physical health for older adults (Levy and Langer 1994), while attention to respect norms for intergenerational contacts may bring about greater communicative satisfaction to younger adults (McCann et al. 2005).

Negativity and Positivity in Age Group Perceptions Surrounding Intergenerational Communication Contact in Japan

Collaborating with colleagues around the world (e.g., Australia, Canada, United States, Japan, South Korea, the Philippines), we used the above theories to investigate different aspects of intergenerational contact, including people's attitudes toward age groups in light of respect norms (Gallois et al. 1999; Ota 2004), age group vitality, and age group stereotypes (Ota, Giles, and Gallois 2002). Using a survey method, data were collected from both college-age younger adults (mostly 18–23 years old) and a community of older adults (over 60 years old) mostly residing in urban settings in central Japan. Findings from studies involving Japan not only provide adequate support for the major tenets of the theories, but also testify to the clear presence of positive and negative changes in various aspects of the aging process, as outlined below.

Respect Norms

Younger adults are expected to adhere to the norm of respect and, accordingly, speak politely and respectfully to elders by using a special register: honorifics. Our studies show that younger adults increase the amount of respect when their hypothesized interlocutors are their age-wise seniors: respect is more likely to be accorded to older than middle-aged and younger adults (Ota 2004). However, the norm is perceived to be obligatory, rather than voluntary, by the young (Ota et al. 1996), who, for this reason, may regard deferential behaviors toward their elders as default "ought-tos" (see also Triandis 1995). Arguably, "respect" may even have some negative connotations that arise from a deferent stance that is enacted very reluctantly and unenthusiastically (Hashimoto 2003; Ho 1994; Lawrence-Lightfoot 2000), and in ways that nonverbally communicate such dispositions to older people.

Age Group Vitality

Perceptions of group vitality, as a contextual variable, have been studied in many intergroup spheres, especially interethnic ones (e.g., Abrams, Eveland, and Giles 2003). Recently, this construct has been introduced into the domain of intergenerational relations (e.g., Barker, Giles, and Harwood 2004; Giles et al. 2000). Put simply, assessing one's (age) group as having high vitality indicates that an individual construes it as having strength in numbers, institutional support, and societal status over a contrastive other (age) group. Moreover, such a cognitive and affective state would likely promote feelings of identification with the in-group (see Giles, Bourhis, and Taylor 1977) and a heightened sense of positive age identity.

Both positive and negative changes characterized the younger respondents' perceptions of the vitality of young, middle-aged, and older adults. Ota, Giles, and Gallois (2002) found that, of the three age groups, while middle-aged people (40–53 years old) were judged to be the most powerful and high-status age group in many domains of life, older adults (over 60 years old) were considered to be the most politically powerful and the wealthiest homeowners, and were portrayed most positively in the mass media (see also Hagiwara et al. 2009 for positive images of older adults in Japanese TV commercials). Older adults were perceived more positively than younger adults (15–27 years old) across a number of dimensions, including power, status, and institutional support (see Ota, Giles, and Harwood 2002 for details). However, it is important to note that of the three groups, older adults received the *least* favorable ratings across dimensions such as future status, likelihood of media representation, involvement in education as students, and group strength.

Age Group Stereotypes

Age group stereotypes have implications for how age group members are judged in terms of their dispositional traits, which we assessed in terms of two stereotypic dimensions (Ota 2001; Ota , Giles, and Gallois 2002; see also Harwood et al. 1996). The so-called "benevolence" factor represents positive and moral personal traits, such as goodness, kindness, generosity, and wisdom, while the "personal vitality" factor is indicated by the degree to which members of age groups are deemed attractive, active, liberal, healthy, and flexible.

Our studies, again, indicate the dual processes of positive and negative changes. Younger adults perceived personal vitality to decrease linearly from young to older adults, while in contrast, benevolence, though in different proportions, was thought to *increase* from young to middle-aged to older adults (Ota 2001; 2004). The latter pattern of change is also seen in another study (Lu 2001), and it suggests a continuation of the traditional view of older adults as socially wise and venerable figures.

In sum, perceived dwindling social status and power, together with a perceived loss of physical health, are indicative of people's negative inclinations toward communication with older adults (e.g., Hummert and Shaner 1994). Such a stance, at least on the surface, may be counterbalanced by, on one hand, the enactment of respectful and polite communicative acts toward older adults based on images of their being kind, wise, generous, and powerful, and, on the other, elder respect norms (cf. feigned deference, McGee and Barker 1982). This duality was also seen in the way members of different generational categories reported on their communication among themselves.

Perceptions of Inter- and Intragenerational Communication Encounters

Through surveys, younger and older Japanese adults have reported on their experiences of communication with members of the same and different age groups in terms of four dimensions of communication (e.g., Giles et al. 2003; McCann et al. 2003; Williams et al. 1997). The four dimensions were: (1) others' accommodative (e.g., "told interesting story," "supportive") and non-accommodative (e.g., "closed-minded," "talk down") tendencies; (2) one's own respect-obligation (e.g., "felt obligated to be polite," "did not act like myself"); (3) age-irrelevant positivity (e.g., "age does not matter"); and (4) avoidance (e.g., "did not know what to say," "looked for ways to end conversation"). Older adults' communication experiences were subsequently examined to determine whether they could be used to predict older people's psychological health (Ota 2001; Ota, Giles, and Somera 2007) so as to test one of the central tenets of CPA outlined above.

The findings from those studies suggest the following. First, intergenerational contact is a complex communication process that requires effort to manage, as it simultaneously involves approach and avoidance; it is colored by favorable and unfavorable views of agewise in- and out-groups (see also Cai, Giles, and Noels 1998). To illustrate, older adults were found to receive mixed messages from younger adults. They judged younger adults, relative to their age peers, to be both *less* egocentric and negative (i.e., non-accommodative), and *less* allocentric and positive (i.e., accommodative) during intergenerational interaction. Nevertheless, they seemed to feel comfortable and to enjoy talking to younger adults, as they did not seem to show particularly high self-restraint or avoidance during communication with such agewise out-group members. In contrast, perhaps appreciatively, younger people often found older adults to be as accommodating as advisers and supporters, perhaps in the same way that peers are friends. At the same time, they judged their older counterparts to be more likely than themselves and their age group to speak in patronizing and controlling manners and to disregard their needs. In response, young people said they make some effort to restrain themselves and speak respectfully to older adults, while striving to distance themselves and end conversations when engaged in intergenerational encounters.

Second, it is safe to say that the findings presented in the previous section fit and represent the traditional cultural pattern of *intergenerational* communication often described in Confucian doctrine (Kim and Yamaguchi 1995). Age differences still appear to dictate how people communicate with one another (e.g., Takai and Ota 1994). Older adults are treated with respect during communication, so that younger adults maintain reserved and self-restrained communication with them, while the older adults may show less of such a tendency in return. Moreover, older adults seem to take on positive roles for younger adults by telling interesting stories and giving useful advice. These findings may suggest that culture is resistant to change at a deeper level (e.g., Samovar, Porter, and McDaniel 2006).

Third, as we indicated earlier, "old age" has rather negative meanings even to older adults (see also Cai, Giles, and Noels 1998). *Intra*generational communication experiences reported by older adults show a conspicuous level of communicative distance from their peers, as indicated in perceptions of others' non-accommodation and their own self-reported avoidance. (But see Taka-hashi, Tokoro, and Hatano; Hori; and Matsumoto, this volume, for a different perspective.) These findings are consistent with Traphagan's (2000) observa-tions of elderly adults dissociating themselves from the self-appellation "old" and their unwillingness to join "old people's clubs" in local communities (see also Iwabuchi and Naoi 2003). Koyano et al.'s (1997) study also reported that some negative views of older adults (especially vis-à-vis dynamism) are held by middle-aged and older adults.

Fourth, the salient presence of negative perceptions of aging does not nec-essarily mean that age peers (i.e., in-group members) are an unimportant pres-ence for older adults. This is observed in the significant positive association between perceived accommodation from other older adults and the latter's self-esteem and perceived life satisfaction (Ota, Giles, and Somera 2007). Attending to peers' needs while engaging in empathic and respectful communication (e.g., Harwood et al 2005) may confirm and strengthen positive social identities (see Fukukawa et al. 2004; and Takahashi, Tamura, and Tokoro 1994 for the rela-tionships between social interaction and psychological health). *Accommodation* from others in similar situations may convey identity-confirming and support-ive messages, while non-accommodation and a sense of avoidance of others can threaten one's sense of self-worth. In contrast, the absence of a significant impact from *intergenerational* communication on older adults' psychological health may very importantly indicate age segregation and a lack of meaningful social interaction between younger and older adults.

Aging, Change, and Changing Communication

Aging is a change that nobody can escape, as long as they continue to live. We have to accept it as a matter of fact. As with other changes that occur in our everyday lives, as unique individuals and members of a society, we are required to find constructive means to adjust to aging-related changes to maintain a positive sense of self. Our discussion has revolved primarily around positive and negative associations with aging, as illustrated in people's perceptions of age group vitality, age group stereotypes, and intergenerational communicative encounters. The duality of aging was also suggested in the nature of respect norms. We strongly contend that adroitly managing both of these social aspects is necessary for successful social interactions across and even within age groups, and that doing so will produce positive social and psychological consequences. In this sense, heeding "a good story" about the traditional respect for elders is important, but not enough. Nor is it sufficient to attend to the negative face of aging if we are to create a more balanced view. We need to appropriately and effectively *accommodate* both faces of aging that may occur in different social contexts. Further, such accommodation is necessary for *society* as well for individuals to achieve a positive sense of self. Our intergroup communication approach will offer some systematic and practical measures to help sustain and promote the positivity of aging, while carefully attending to its more negative aspects, at both the societal and individual levels. Mindfulness will help us keep the duality of aging in sight, and thereby facilitate effective communicative accommodation to others to bring about optimal results.

Mindfulness

Mindfulness (Langer 1985) is a state of mind that promotes the smooth flow of information, and thus contributes to people's performance of successful communication (Barker, Giles, and Harwood 2004; Burgoon, Berger, and Waldron 2000; Gudykunst 2005). It seems to easily align with the intergroup approach for its cognitive nature, in particular. Being mindful means to be "where you are with all your mind" (Weick and Putnam 2006, 276). It involves paying attention to the *internal* processes of mind, the *contents* of mind, and the *external* environment or context (Weick and Putnam 2006). Attention to the internal processes may help enhance one's awareness and understanding of the current situation surrounding the problem, and it may subsequently produce "penetrative insights or wisdom" (276) that help make better sense of the problem. It also helps people become aware of the worldviews or frames of reference that they use for analysis and interpretation of ongoing social issues. Mindfulness works as a safety net against mere reliance on a single perspective for the assessment of such problematic issues. In this way, it encourages the use of multiple modes of thinking in order to find suitable solutions.

Cognitive skills, such as differentiation and discrimination, the creation of new categories, and alternative conceptualizations of an object, constitute important components of being mindful. These skills may ultimately help call people's attention to and raise sensitivity not only to the immediate context in which problems have arisen (Burgoon, Berger, and Waldron 2000) but also to their relationships within the larger macrosociocultural context. A number of studies have reported the positive consequences (e.g., perspective taking, enhanced health) of being mindful in various facets of social life (e.g., Brown and Ryan 2003; Frable, Blackstone, and Scherbaum 1990; Langer 1985; Langer, Bashner, and Chanowitz 1985).

Besides the internal and external foci, we contend that mindfulness has important communicative implications at both the individual and *collective* levels. Individual communicators need to mindfully and appropriately interpret and generate messages to meet the needs of the personal and social identity that others bring to communicative interactions, as well as to attain certain levels of satisfaction in communication (e.g., Barker, Giles, and Harwood 2004; Langer and Moldoveanu 2000; Ting-Toomey 2005). Nevertheless, overall and perhaps long-term life satisfaction, happiness, and hopes of individuals may be difficult to achieve without a suitable environment (see Motohashi 2006 for the important role of society in a citizen's psychological well-being).

In this regard, some organizational communication scholars (Weick and Sutcliffe 2001) have argued that an organization itself has to be mindful to maintain a highly reliable and functional status. An organization, or perhaps any group, that is mindful—e.g., reluctant to simplify, committed to resilience, and aware of failure and success (Fiol and O'Conner 2003; Janis 1972)—may be, as a critical entity, ready to find appropriate ways to solve existing problems, and capable of successfully maintaining a healthy and functional status. A collectively mindful group may foster a positive interactional climate wherein the members can engage in *open* and *flexible* communication using possible alternative modes of thinking, and by which they can review and evaluate their current status for the better without losing sight of their own ways of thinking. Such a group may be open to initiating contact with other groups and exchanging information (or even material resources) to sustain and promote its well-being as a collective entity (cf. Kim 2001).

Mindfulness could, therefore, be an important factor in the accomplishment of successful communicative accommodation in our social lives. Mindfulness on the individual level will improve attention and facilitate subsequent communication behaviors, while collective mindfulness will help to promote a healthy and favorable communication climate. In this vein, the following sections offer some practical suggestions for the enhancement of more favorable inter- and intragenerational communication. Our discussion starts with issues at the societal level, in keeping with the social focus of the intergroup perspective.

Societal Level

To promote healthy and favorable intergenerational communication and thereby attain positive social identities for elders, society and its major institutions must be mindful of supporting and *accommodating* elders. Society needs to raise its consciousness in order to identify possible problems that hamper the emergence of better intergenerational relationships. In addition, it should be ready to assess and discuss these problems so as to devise and legislate, if need be, some appropriate and practical short- and long-term strategies to enhance intergenerational relationships.

Toward these ends, there are a number of intergroup practices that can be undertaken at the societal level. First, boosting age group vitality may help prepare the ground for favorable social identities to emerge for older as well as younger and middle-aged group members. Community agencies and national governments, besides nonprofit and nongovernmental organizations, could make greater and more genuine efforts to provide elderly people with support in various social contexts to promote healthy social lives. For instance, the creation of physical environments such as supportive housing and allied communities (Kochera and Bright 2006) will contribute to older adults' positive sense of self. City environments with "barrier-free" or universal design facilities, together with a walkable city layout, will send welcoming messages encouraging older adults of various health statuses to come out and participate in social activities (e.g., Yahagi 2005). At times, however, to enhance their group vitality in the longer term, it may actually be helpful for such an approachable living environment to include sections that involve challenges for them.

By the same token, through collaboration with nonprofit and nongovernmental organizations, communities may promote intergenerational contact programs (Kusano and Akiyama 2004; Kusano et al. 2009; see also Abrams and Giles 1999; Fox and Giles 1993). Such programs have already been implemented in some parts of Japan (Kusano and Akiyama 2004; Thang 2001) and are supported by local communities and government, with their importance stipulated in social policies aimed at promoting successful aging (Maeda 1996). Nevertheless, more programs would certainly be desirable. By sharing their stories and skills with younger adults through intergenerational contact programs (see also Hamaguchi, this volume), older adults may attain positive and enhanced social identities, insofar as they see their own contributions as providing valuable cultural and educational resources for members of other age groups. Importantly, older adults may find alternative sources of tangible and intangible social support in nonfamily relationships, especially with younger adults in their neighborhoods. Similar positive effects of intergenerational contact (e.g., learning traditions, changing perceptions of aging) are conceivable for people in younger age brackets as well (Yamamoto-Mitani and Wallhagen

2002). Undoubtedly, systematic research on intergenerational programs is necessary to create effective longitudinal programs (Kusano et al. 2009).

Another important way to increase older adults' vitality is to develop more healthy mass communication channels with which they can identify (see Abrams and Giles 2007; 2009). Positive and proportional portrayals of older adults in the media (e.g., Hagiwara et al. 2009; Holtzman and Akiyama 1985; Hori, this volume), including stories in books (see also Miyachi 1999), are an invaluable format to serve this purpose. As media consumers, people are significantly influenced by what they see in magazines, newspapers, books, and on TV. Positive media depictions of old age may contribute to perceptions of their high and positive age group vitality (Abrams, Eveland, and Giles 2003), leading to the enhancement of positive age group stereotypes, and, in turn, to positive communication (Ota, Giles, and Gallois 2002; see also McCann et al. 2005). Good stories about aging and intergenerational relationships should thus be generated, perpetuated, and shared in society.

Individual Level

Societal-level measures for positive intergenerational communication and successful aging must be complemented by efforts at the individual level. Given that social context can be an important factor in helping people to be mindful (Burgoon, Berger, and Waldron 2000), collective measures may encourage them to adopt mindful attitudes toward their social interactions. There are a number of specific skills and knowledge structures that may directly facilitate favorable communicative contact with members of different age groups, just as certain means have been found useful in communicating with members of different cultural groups (e.g., Gudykunst 2004). First and foremost, we should listen actively and attentively (therefore mindfully) to ourselves and others (Ting-Toomey 2005). At the same time, we should strive to find, in a sense, cognitive alternatives and avoid relying on a single perspective when processing information. When mindful, people may be better able to maintain higher cognitive flexibility, and engage in critical and divergent thinking when processing messages from others and assessing their current situations (Ting-Toomey 1999). In this way, mindful individuals may be able to successfully manage the dialectical tensions caused by the simultaneous coexistence of negative and positive meanings of aging in intergenerational communication. They may consider the two alternative and valenced perspectives on aging and prepare *contextually appropriate and effective accommodative strategies* to use when dealing with others in different age groups (Barker, Giles, and Harwood 2004), and they might respectfully provide a variety of social and practical supports to enhance their desired social identities (Williams et al. 1990).

Moreover, individuals, when mindful, may pursue different cognitive alternatives available to them in order to live a rewarding life. For example, individuals may actively strive to use various *social strategies* and adopt a self-enhancing stance by deliberately discerning positive meanings in messages that mainly convey negative meanings (see Major and Crocker 1993). An older adult may pay greater attention to the positive meanings of aging and try to act out such images to generate positive self-views (e.g., Langer 1985). For instance, fending off the negative stereotypes of aging, individuals may then strategically use certain nonverbal channels (e.g., cosmetics and dress styles) to maintain positive cognitive and affective states and dignity (e.g., Ishizuka and Ogawa 2006). Individuals may use various communicative (e.g., information-gathering) strategies to reduce age-related uncertainties and anxieties while trying, through constructive discussion, to gain an understanding of why negative or even positive messages have been sent to them, just as people may do in intercultural communication (Gudykunst 2005). In this way, the communication climate may be made less dismal or even changed for the positive.

Research Directions and Final Words

The communicative dimensions of intergenerational relations and successful aging have been grossly neglected in Japan and elsewhere until quite recently (Harwood 2007). Attention to these dynamics can have enormous payoffs, theoretically as well as practically. We would like to make some modest suggestions for living with and devising future research on aging and communication in Japan.

First, the refinement and elaboration of current theories of cross-generational communication is indispensable. In particular, the lack of intergenerational communication patterns for predicting elder subjective well-being as proposed by the original CPA, as well as the potency of *intra*generational experiences, has necessitated a new version of the model (see Barker, Giles, and Harwood 2004). Clearly, further research is necessary for understanding the complex dynamics and implications of intragenerational communication among different kinds of elderly people in Japan—particularly as it emerges in real-time peer-elderly encounters, which are both behaviorally coded and discursively analyzed. (See Hamaguchi, this volume, and Matsumoto, this volume, for analyses of discourse.)

Second, respect and mindfulness, although not concepts currently speci-fied in intergroup communication theory, are worthy of empirical scrutiny so as to disentangle their conceptual complexities and advance our under-standing of their roles in intergenerational contact. Such research should pay sufficient attention to younger adults, too, who once occupied the bottom of the power hierarchy in Japan according to Confucian principles. For instance, younger individuals there have been "disempowered" to be a powerless and silent presence, as illustrated by the archetype of the obedient and agreeable *ii ko* (good child), when being spoken to by someone older (Hashimoto 2003; see also Giles and Williams 1994). In order to view the "dark side" of respect when it comes to intergenerational communication, we should hear their voices, too, and study their view of cultural traditions, as reflected in respect and other Confucian norms.

Third, in addition to structural features (e.g., Ghorbani, Watson, and Weath-ington 2009), the role of mindfulness in intergenerational communication needs further investigation so that we can understand how it may facilitate accommo-dative communication between individuals of different age groups. Mindlessness may be associated with stereotype-based acts of communication and interpreta-tion (Barker, Giles, and Harwood 2004), while mindfulness may be an important precondition for satisfying relationships (e.g., Barnes et al. 2007).

In conclusion, individuals may be able to obtain a state of mindfulness through their own efforts, and from there perform accommodative com-munication. Encouragement and support from society is vital. In a sense, environment-individual consistency is critical. Nevertheless, people seem to be suffering as a result of their environment rather than extracting some-thing valuable from it. Our rapidly changing contemporary society often tends to be "mindless" and seems to have discouraged many people in Japan from being able to optimally think in mindful ways. Thus, they have no choice but to turn a blind eye to many issues that in fact warrant observa-tion and consideration. Things and people who are "slow" are wrongly left out. Things that are unchanged are wrongly left behind. On the other hand, it is interesting and contradictory that such a rapidly changing society seems to make people pursue stability.

In China, there is a movement that wishes to reinstate Confucianism as the backbone of Chinese culture in order to unite the country and regain harmony (Robertson and Liu 2006). Slow life and slow food have become buzzwords in Japan. While acknowledging the implications of change, it is important for us to take a moment and appreciate the lifestyle of traditional culture in Japan. Rapidity and change—the key underlining themes of modernism—were purposely advanced to constitute major cultural features of the world in the twentieth century (Gergen 1991). Perhaps we, individually and collectively, need to embrace aspects of romanticism a little more. Romanticism may simultaneously be a new and old value that encourages people to unwind so they can pay attention to, take interest in, and care about other people, including those who are different agewise. It should be an important value structure that drives people to look at and listen to various aspects of the self and others, and thus engage in communication with passion and love. It may help establish a climate where people go well beyond group differences and are willing to kindly and mindfully listen and accommodate to others so that they can live a more measured and fulfilling life together (e.g., Harwood et al. 2005). The intergroup communication perspective explicates, and thereby cautions us against, the dangerous processes of blind and mindless use of group membership to understand others (Langer and Moldoveanu 2000). In other words, this position may well encourage people to be slow and mindful lest they unduly impose categorical labels upon others and create rigid group boundaries. This may be an important philosophical and practical message that the intergroup communication perspective implicitly sends us when we explore the dynamics of aging and intergenerational communication.

References

Abrams, J. R., W. P. Eveland Jr., and H. Giles. 2003. The effects of television on group vitality: Can television empower? In *Communication yearbook* 27, ed. P. Kalbfleisch, 193–219. Mahwah, NJ: Erlbaum.

Abrams, J. R., and H. Giles. 1999. Epilogue: Intergenerational contact as intergroup communication. *Child and Youth Services* 20: 203–217.

———. 2007. Ethnic identity gratifications selection and avoidance by African Americans: A group vitality and social identity gratifications perspective. *Media Psychology* 9: 115–135.

———. 2009. Hispanic American television activity: Is it related to vitality perceptions? *Communication Research Reports* 26: 247–252.

Barker, V., H. Giles, and J. Harwood. 2004. Inter- and intragroup perspectives on intergenerational communication. In *Handbook of aging and communication research*, 2nd ed., ed. J. F. Nussbaum and J. Coupland, 139–166. Mahwah, NJ: Erlbaum.

Barnes, S., K. W. Brown, E. Krusemark, W. K. Campbell, and R. Rogge. 2007. The role of mindfulness in romantic relationship satisfaction and responses to relationship stress. *Journal of Marital and Family Therapy* 33: 482–500.

Braithwaite, V., R. Lynd-Stevenson, and D. Pigram. 1993. An empirical study of ageism: From polemics to scientific utility. *Australian Psychologist* 28: 9–15.

Brown, K. W., and R. M. Ryan. 2003. The benefits of being present: Mindfulness and its role in psychological well-being. *Journal of Personality and Social Psychology* 84: 822–848.

Brownell, P., and E. Podnieks. 2005. Long-overdue recognition for the critical issue of elder abuse and neglect: A global policy and practice perspective. *Brief Treatment and Crisis Intervention* 5: 187–191.

Burgoon, J. K., C. R. Berger, and V. R. Waldron. 2000. Becoming mindful in and through interpersonal communication. *Journal of Social Issues* 56: 105–127.

Cai, D., H. Giles, and K. A. Noels. 1998. Elderly perceptions of communication with older and younger adults in China: Implications for mental health. *Journal of Applied Communication Research* 26: 32–51.

Coupland, N., and A. Jaworski. 1997. Relevance, accommodation, and conversation: Modeling the social dimension of communication. *Multilingua* 16: 235–258.

Fiol, C. M., and E. J. O'Connor. 2003. Waking up! Mindfulness in the face of bandwagons. *Academy of Management Review* 28: 54–70.

Fox, S., and H. Giles. 1993. Accommodating intergenerational contact: A critique and theoretical model. *Journal of Aging Studies* 7: 423–451.

Frable, D. E. S., T. Blackstone, and C. Scherbaum. 1990. Marginal and mindful: Deviants in social interactions. *Journal of Personality and Social Psychology* 59: 140–149.

Fugōkaku: Riyū wa nenrei (Rejection: Age matters). 2005. *Yahoo Japan Online News*, July 1. http://headlines.yahoo.co.jp/hl?a=20050701-00000089-mai-soci (accessed July 2, 2005).

Fukukawa, Y., C. Nakashima, S. Tsuboi, N. Niino, F. Ando, S. Kosugi, and H. Shimokata. 2004. The impact of health problems on depression and activities in middle-aged and older adults: Age and social interactions as moderators. *Journal of Gerontology: Psychological Sciences* 59: 19–26.

Gallois, C., H. Giles, H. Ota, H. D. Pierson, S. H. Ng, T.-S. Lim, J. Maher, L. Somera, E. B. Ryan, and J. Harwood. 1999. Intergenerational communication across the Pacific Rim: The impact of filial piety. In *Latest contributions to cross-cultural psychology*, ed. J.-C. Lasry, J. Adair, and K. Dion, 192–211. Lisse, Netherlands: Swets and Zeitlinger.

Gallois, C., T. Ogay, and H. Giles. 2005. Communication accommodation theory: A look back and a look ahead. In *Theorizing about intercultural communication*, ed. W. B. Gudykunst, 121–148. Thousand Oaks, CA: Sage.

Genba, M. 2005. *Nenrei sabetsu: Shigoto no ba de naniga okotte iru ka* (Age discrimination: What is happening in workplaces?). Tokyo: Iwanami Booklet.

Gergen, K. J. 1991. *Saturated self: Dilemmas of identity in contemporary life.* New York: Basic Books.

Ghorbani, N., P. J. Watson, and B. L. Weathington. 2009. Mindfulness in Iran and the United States: Cross-cultural structural complexity and parallel relationships with psychological adjustment. *Current Psychology* 28: 211–224.

Giles, H., D. Ballard, and R. M. McCann. 2002. Perceptions of intergenerational communication across cultures: An Italian case. *Perceptual and Motor Skills* 95: 583–591.

Giles, H., R. Y. Bourhis, and D. M. Taylor. 1977. Towards a theory of language in ethnic group relations. In *Language, ethnicity, and intergroup relations*, ed. H. Giles, 307–348. London: Academic Press.

Giles, H., N. Coupland, and J. Coupland, eds. 1991. *The contexts of accommodation*. New York: Cambridge University Press.

Giles, H., and T. Dorjee. 2004. Communication climates and prospects for cross-cultural gerontology. *Journal of Cross-Cultural Gerontology* 19: 261–274.

Giles, H., S. Makoni, and R. M. Dailey. 2005. Intergenerational communication beliefs across the lifespan: Comparative data from West and South Africa. *Journal of Cross-Cultural Gerontology* 20: 191–211.

Giles, H., R. M. McCann, H. Ota, and K. A. Noels. 2002. Challenging intergenerational stereotypes across Eastern and Western cultures. In *Linking lifetimes: A global view of intergenerational exchange*, ed. M. S. Kaplan, N. Z. Henkin, and A. T. Kusano, 13–28. Honolulu: University Press of America.

Giles, H., K. A. Noels, H. Ota, S. H. Ng, C. Gallois, E. B. Ryan, A. Williams, T.-S. Lim, L. Somera, H. Tao, and I. Sachdev. 2000. Age vitality across eleven nations. *Journal of Multilingual and Multicultural Development* 21: 308–323.

Giles, H., K. A. Noels, A. Williams, H. Ota, T.-S. Lim, S. H. Ng, E. B. Ryan, and L. Somera. 2003. Intergenerational communication across cultures: Young people's perceptions of conversations with family elders, non-family elders, and same-age peers. *Journal of Cross-Cultural Gerontology* 18: 1–32.

Giles, H., and A. Williams. 1994. Patronizing the young: Forms and evaluations. *International Journal of Aging and Human Development* 39: 33–53.

Gudykunst, W. B. 2004. *Bridging differences: Effective intergroup communication*. 4th ed. Thousand Oaks, CA: Sage.

———, ed. 2005. *Theorizing about intercultural communication*. Thousand Oaks, CA: Sage.

Hagiwara, S., M. Prieler, F. Kohlbacher, and A. Arima. 2009. Nihon no terebi CM ni okeru kōreishazōno hensen (Changes in the portrayals of older adults in Japanese TV commercials). *Keiō University Media Communication Kenkyūjo Kiyō* 59: 113–129.

Harwood, J. 2007. *Understanding communication and aging: Developing knowledge and awareness*. Mahwah, NJ: Erlbaum.

Harwood, J., and H. Giles, eds. 2005. *Intergroup communication: Multiple perspectives*. New York: Peter Lang.

Harwood, J., H. Giles, S. Fox, E. B. Ryan, and A. Williams. 1993. Patronizing young and elderly adults: Response strategies in a community setting. *Journal of Applied Communication Research* 21: 211–226.

Harwood, J., H. Giles, H. Ota, H. D. Pierson, C. Gallois, S. H. Ng, T.-S. Lim, and L. Somera. 1996. College students' trait rating of three age groups around the Pacific Rim. *Journal of Cross-Cultural Gerontology* 11: 307–317.

Harwood, J., H. Giles, and E. B. Ryan. 1995. Aging, communication, and intergroup theory: Social identity and intergenerational communication. In *Handbook of communication and aging research*, ed. J. F. Nussbaum and J. Coupland, 133–159. Hillsdale, NJ: Erlbaum.

Harwood, J., M. Hewstone, S. Paolini, and A. Voci. 2005. Grandparent-grandchild contact and attitudes toward older adults: Moderator and mediator effects. *Personality and Social Psychology Bulletin* 31: 393–415.

Hashimoto, A. 2003. Culture, power and the discourse of filial piety in Japan: The disempowerment of youth and its social consequences. In *Filial piety: Practice and discourse in contemporary East Asia*, ed. C. Ikels, 182–197. Stanford, CA: Stanford University Press.

Hendricks, J., ed. 2005. Ageism in the new millennium. *Generations* 24.

Hendry, J. 1995. *Wrapping culture: Politeness, presentation, and power in Japan and other societies.* Oxford: Clarendon Press.

Ho, D. Y.-F. 1994. Filial piety, authoritarian moralism, and cognitive conservatism in Chinese societies. *Genetic, Social and General Psychology Monographs* 120: 347–365.

Holtzman, J. M., and H. Akiyama. 1985. What children see: The aged on television in Japan and the United States. *Gerontologist* 25: 62–68.

Hummert, M. L. 2010. Age group identity, age stereotypes, and communication in a life span context. In *The dynamics of intergroup communication*, ed. H. Giles, S. A. Reid, and J. Harwood, 41–52. New York: Peter Lang.

Hummert, M. L., and J. Shaner. 1994. Patronizing speech to the elderly as a function of stereotypes. *Communication Studies* 45: 145–158.

Imai, K. 1998. Bed-ridden elderly in Japan: Social progress and care for the elderly. *International Journal of Aging and Human Development* 46: 157–170.

Ishizuka, A., and T. Ogawa. 2006. The interest and motivation for good appearance on the part of the elderly in nursing homes. *Journal of Health Care and Nursing* 2: 11–16.

Iwabuchi, A., and A. Naoi. 2003. Aged society images as a perspective on our society and some characteristics of those images. *Osaka Daigaku Daigakuin Ningenkagaku Kenkyūka Kiyō* 29: 69–98.

Janis, I. L. 1972. *Victims of groupthink.* New York: Houghton Mifflin.

Kaplan, M., N. Henkin, and A. Kusano, eds. 2002. *Linking lifetimes: A global view of intergenerational exchange.* Lanham, MD: University Press of America.

Kim, U., and S. Yamaguchi. 1995. Cross-cultural research methodology and approach: Implications for the advancement of Japanese social psychology. *Research in Social Psychology* 10: 168–179.

Kim, Y. Y. 2001. *Becoming intercultural: An integrative theory of communication and cross-cultural adaptation*. Thousand Oaks, CA: Sage.

Kimmel, D. C. 1988. Ageism, psychology, and public policy. *American Psychologist* 43: 175–178.

Kite, M. E., and B. T. Johnson. 1988. Attitudes toward older and younger adults: A meta-analysis. *Psychology and Aging* 3: 233–244.

Kiyokawa, T. 2006. *Tokuyō nyūkyosha ni seiteki bōgen* (Using sexually abusive language to an elder home resident). *Asahi Shimbun*, August 6: 31.

Kobayashi, A. 2004. *Kōreisha gyakutai: Jittai to bōshisaku* (Elder abuse: Reality and preventive measures). Tokyo: Chūkōshinsho.

Kobayashi, M. 2000. Kanshin suru dake ja (A good story is not enough). *The Chūnichi Newspaper*, July 26: 5.

Kochera, A., and K. Bright. 2006. Livable communities for older people. *Generations* 24: 32–36.

Kōsei Rōdo Shō (Ministry of Health, Labor, and Welfare). 2006. *Nihonjin no heikin jumyō* (Longevity of the Japanese people). www.mhlw.go.jp/toukei/saikin/hw/life/life05/index.html (accessed August 30, 2007).

Koyano, W. 1989. Japanese attitudes toward the elderly: A review of research findings. *Journal of Cross-Cultural Gerontology* 3: 335–345.

———. 1996. Filial piety and intergenerational solidarity in Japan. *Australian Journal of Aging* 15: 51–56.

———. 1999. Population aging, changes in living arrangement, and the new long-term care system in Japan. *Journal of Sociology and Social Welfare* 26: 155–167.

Koyano, W., Y. Kodama, T. Ando, and T. Asakawa. 1997. Images of the elderly held by middle-aged persons: Studied with the SD method. *Japanese Journal of Gerontology* 18: 147–152.

Kusano, A., and H. Akiyama. 2004. *Intergeneration: Komyunitii o sodateru sedai kankō ryū* (Intergeneration: Developing community through cross-generational exchange). *Gendai no Esupuri* 444. Tokyo: Shibundō.

Kusano, A., T. Kaneda, Y. Mano, and S. Kakinuma. 2009. *Sedai kankō ryūkōka: Ningen hattatsu to kyōsei shakaizukuri no shiten kara* (Effects of intergenerational exchange: From the viewpoint of human development and community building). Tokyo: Sangakusha.

Langer, E. J. 1985. *Mindfulness*. Reading, MA: Addison Wesley.

Langer, E. J., R. S. Bashner, and B. Chanowitz. 1985. Decreasing prejudice by increasing discrimination. *Journal of Personality and Social Psychology* 49: 113–120.

Langer, E. J., and M. C. Moldoveanu. 2000. The construct of mindfulness. *Journal of Social Issues* 56: 1–9.

Lawrence-Lightfoot, S. 2000. *Respect: An exploration.* Cambridge, MA: Pegasus.

Levy, B., and E. J. Langer. 1994. Aging free from negative stereotypes: Successful memory in China and among the American deaf. *Journal of Personality and Social Psychology* 66: 989–997.

Littlejohn, S. W., and K. A. Foss. 2005. *Theories of human communication.* 8th ed. Belmont, CA: Wadsworth.

Lu, H.-I. 2001. Older adults' wisdom on a "life-planning task": Characteristics and relation to life experiences. *Japanese Journal of Educational Psychology* 49: 198–208.

Maeda, D. 1996. Social security, health care, and social services for the elderly in Japan. In *Aging in Japan.* http://nippon.zaidan.info/seikabutsu/1996/00147/contents/081.htm (accessed April 26, 2006).

———. 2000. The socioeconomic context of Japanese social policy for aging. In *Caring for the elderly in Japan and the United States: Practice and social policies,* ed. S. O. Long, 28–51. New York: Routledge.

Maeda, D., K. Teshima, H. Sugisawa, and Y. S. Asakura. 1989. Aging and health in Japan. *Journal of Cross-Cultural Gerontology* 4: 143–162.

Major, B., and J. Crocker. 1993. Social stigma: The consequences of attributional ambiguity. In *Affect, cognition, and stereotyping: Interactive processes in group perception,* ed. D. M. Mackie and D. L. Hamilton, 345–370. San Diego: Academic Press.

Masataka, N. 2000. *Oi wa kōshite tsukurareru* (How people age). Tokyo: Iwanami.

McCann, R. M., R. M. Dailey, H. Giles, and H. Ota. 2005. Beliefs about intergenerational communication across the lifespan: Middle age and the roles of age stereotyping and respect norms. *Communication Studies* 56: 293–311.

McCann, R. M., H. Ota, H. Giles, and R. Caraker. 2003. Perceptions of intra- and intergenerational communication among adults in Thailand, Japan, and the USA. *Communication Reports* 16: 1–23.

McGee, J., and Barker, M. 1982. Deference and dominance in old age: An exploration in social theory. *International Journal of Aging and Human Development* 15: 247–262.

McIntosh, J. L., J. F. Santos, R. W. Hubbard, and J. C. Overholser. 1994. *Elder suicide: Research, theory, and treatment.* Washington, DC: APA.

Miyachi, T. 1999. *Tsutaetai mono, tsutawaru mono ehon, jidō bungaku ni okeru rōjinzō* (What we want to and can share: Images of older adults in picture books and children's books). Tokyo: Grand Mama Publishing.

Monbukagaku Shō (Ministry of Education, Culture, Sports, Science, and Technology). n.d. *Gakkō kyōin tōkei chōsa dai 2bu: Kyōin kojin chōsa, daigaku* (Statistics on teachers. Second chapter: Colleges and universities). www.mext.go.jp/b_menu/toukei/001/002/2004/003/023.htm (accessed April 26, 2006).

Motohashi, Y. 2006. *Jisatsu ga hetta machi: Akitaken no chōsen* (A city saw a reduced rate of suicide: The case of Akita Prefecture). Tokyo: Iwanami Shoten.

Nakazato, K. 1990. Shakai kara no danzetsu ni yoru komyunikeeshon shōgai: Rōjin no shiten kara (Alienation from society and communication problems: Older adults' perspectives). *Kyōiku to Igaku* 38: 581–587.

Nelson, T. D., ed. 2005. Ageism. *Journal of Social Issues* 6 (2).

Ota, H. 2001. *Intergenerational communication in Japan and the United States: Debunking the myth of respect for older adults in Japan*. PhD diss., University of California, Santa Barbara.

————. 2004. *Younger adults' communication experiences with older adults in Japan*. Paper presented at the Annual Convention of the National Communication Association in Chicago.

Ota, H., H. Giles, and C. Gallois. 2002. Perceptions of younger, middle-aged and older adults in Australia and Japan: Stereotypes and age group vitality. *Journal of Intercultural Studies* 23: 253–266.

Ota, H., H. Giles, J. Harwood, H. D. Pierson, C. Gallois, S. H. Ng, T.-S. Lim, E. B. Ryan, J. Maher, and L. Somera. 1996. *A neglected dimension of communication and aging: Filial piety across eight nations*. Paper presented at the Annual Convention of the Speech Communication Association, San Diego, CA.

Ota, H., H. Giles, and L. Somera. 2007. Beliefs about intra- and intergenerational communication in Japan, the Philippines, and the United States: Implications for older adults' subjective well-being. *Communication Studies* 58: 173–188.

Robertson, B., and M. Liu. 2006. Can the sage save China? *Newsweek International Edition*, March 20: 20–24.

Ryan, E. B., H. Giles, G. Bartolucci, and K. Henwood. 1986. Psycholinguistic and social psychological components of communication by and with the elderly. *Language and Communication* 6: 1–24.

Ryan, E. B., S. D. Meredith, M. J. MacLean, and J. B. Orange. 1995. Changing the way we talk with elders: Promoting health using the communication enhancement model. *International Journal of Aging and Human Development* 41: 89–107.

Samovar, L. A., R. E. Porter, and E. R. McDaniel. 2006. *Communication between cultures*. 6th ed. Belmont, CA: Thomson Wadsworth.

Shibusawa, T., M. Kodaka, S. Iwano, and K. Kaizu. 2005. Interventions for elder abuse and neglect with frail elders in Japan. *Brief Treatment and Crisis Intervention* 5: 203–211.

Shioya, N., and A. Yoshida. 2003. *Anti-eijingu no kagaku: Oi ni makenai* (Science of Anti-aging: Defying to be old). *Gendai no Esupuri* 430. Tokyo: Shibundō.

Sung, K. T. 2001. Elder respect: Exploration of ideals and forms in East Asia. *Journal of Aging Studies* 15: 13–26.

Tachibana, K. 1939. The origin of respect for the aged in Japan. *Japanese Journal of Psychology* 14: 307–314.

Tajfel, H., and J. C. Turner. 1986. The social identity theory of intergroup behavior. In *Psychology of intergroup relations*, ed. S. Worchel and W. G. Austin, 7–17. Chicago: Nelson-Hall.

Takahashi, K., J. Tamura, and M. Tokoro. 1994. Patterns of social relationships and psychological well-being among the elderly. *International Journal of Behavioral Development* 21: 417–430.

Takai, J., and Ota, H. 1994. Assessing Japanese interpersonal communication competence. *Japanese Journal of Experimental Social Psychology* 33: 224–236.

Thang, L. L. 2001. *Generations in touch: Linking the old and young in a Tokyo neighborhood.* Ithaca, NY: Cornell University Press.

Ting-Toomey, S. 1999. *Communicating across cultures.* New York: Guilford.

———. 2005. The matrix of face: An updated face-negotiation theory. In *Theorizing about intercultural communication*, ed. W. B. Gudykunst, 71–92. Thousand Oaks, CA: Sage.

Tōkei Kyoku (Statistics Bureau). 2007. *Nenrei danjobetsu jinkō oyobi wariai* (Population and its proportion by age and gender). www.stat.go.jp/data/jinsui/2006np/zuhyou/05k18-03.xls (accessed on August 30, 2007).

Tracy, K., and K. Haspel. 2004. Language and social interaction: Its institutional identity, intellectual landscape, and discipline-shifting agenda. *Journal of Communication* 54: 788–816.

Traphagan, J. W. 2000. *Taming oblivion: Aging bodies and the fear of senility in Japan.* New York: State University of New York Press.

Triandis, H. C. 1995. *Individualism and collectivism.* Boulder, CO: Westview.

Umeda, Y., and S. Yashiro. 2003. La recherche littéraire (III): Du caractère d'inter-texte du RPG. *Shizuoka kenritsu Tankidaigakubu Kenkyū Kiyō* 17: 1–22.

Weick, K. L., and T. Putnam. 2006. Organizing for mindfulness: Eastern wisdom and Western knowledge. *Journal of Management Inquiry* 15: 275–287.

Weick, K. L., and K. M. Sutcliffe. 2001. *Managing the unexpected: Assuring high performance in an age of complexity.* San Francisco: Jossey-Bass.

Williams, A., H. Giles, N. Coupland, M. Dalby, and H. Manasse. 1990. The communicative contexts of elderly social support and health: A theoretical model. *Health Communication* 2: 123–143.

Williams, A., and J. F. Nussbaum. 2001. *Intergenerational communication across the lifespan.* Mahwah, NJ: Erlbaum.

Williams, A., H. Ota, H. Giles, H. D. Pierson, C. Gallois, S. H. Ng, T.-S. Lim, E. B. Ryan, L. Somera, J. Maher, D. Cai, and J. Harwood. 1997. Young people's beliefs about intergenerational communication: An initial cross-cultural analysis. *Communication Research* 24: 370–393.

Yahagi, H. 2005. *Ōgataten to machizukuri—Kisei suru Amerika, mosaku suru Nihon* (Large-scale shopping centers and community development: Restrictions in the United States and exploration in Japan). Tokyo: Iwanami.

Yamamoto-Mitani, N., and M. I. Wallhagen. 2002. Pursuit of psychological well-being (*ikigai*) and the evolution of self-understanding in the context of caregiving in Japan. *Culture, Medicine, and Psychiatry* 26: 399–417.

Afterword

Successful Aging and Communication Wellness: A Process of Transition and Continuity

Jon F. Nussbaum and Carla L. Fisher

COMMUNICATION IS CENTRAL to wellness across the entirety of the life span. As such, communication is at the core of successful aging. Even though older adults' aging-related experiences vary somewhat across cultures, the link between communication patterns and wellness can be found cross-culturally, in both Western and Eastern cultural traditions (Pecchioni, Ota, and Sparks 2004). It is a human desire—a biological need—to interact and relationally bond with others to survive and to remain vibrant. A wealth of research shows that communication influences older adults' psychological well-being and their social quality of life, as well as their physical and mental health. Hence, communication, at any point in the life span and in any culture, is a human mechanism for achieving and maintaining wellness.

Successful aging and communication are central themes radiating throughout this book. Collectively, these themes bind each individual piece together. The chapters frequently use the lens of communication to collectively explore and challenge what it means to successfully age. In the first half of this book, the authors identify significant social factors that are critical to understanding aging. These social factors can also lead to misunderstandings or misconceptions about what it means to age. In so doing, they highlight the influential role that communication plays in the ability of older adults to successfully age. In the second half of the book, the authors further examine communication wellness and its role in how we navigate the aging process.

In this afterword, we reflect on the positions offered by the book's authors regarding successful aging and communication, particularly in terms of interpersonal connection. Additionally, we make clear various pathways in which we can continue this conversation in future research and practice involving older adults in an effort to enrich their lives as well as those of generations to come.

Aging: A Process of Transition and Continuity

In Chapter 5, Hori reviews a film (*Lily Festival*) that highlights how "aging involves both transition and continuity." While aging does involve many changes, both positive and negative, it can also be characterized by ongoing independence, vivaciousness, and life. It is through communication that we necessarily navigate the new in older adulthood while maintaining stability. Still, it is also through unhelpful communication that we may impede this process and in effect negate successful aging. The authors point us to important social situations in which older adults can successfully age but at the same time challenge societal assumptions and structures, as well as communicative practices, that can inhibit older adults' ability to achieve lifelong wellness.

Challenging Social Factors and Enhancing Communication Wellness

We must reframe social assumptions about aging across cultures. Too often, universal presumptions and practices tend to fixate on aging as morbid and awkward, as a debilitating decline. As Doba and colleagues point out in Chapter 2, societies at times only concern themselves with the "dark side" of aging. For instance, many authors in the first half of this book challenge global misconceptions and stereotypes about aging, including stereotypes that all older adults are inactive, suffer inevitable cognitive decline, are unable to learn, have stagnant unidimensional identities, are burdensome to families, become completely dependent, and live asexually. Social assumptions like these can ultimately narrow our perspectives and expectations about what it means to age, thereby limiting our understanding of what it means to *successfully* age.

Yet, these first five chapters demonstrate that by challenging the social structures, assumptions, and attitudes that promote ageist stereotypes, we can change misconceptions about aging and the old and actively strengthen the social environment in which we age. These chapters depict successful aging as defined by activity, generativity, identity development, emotional connection and intimacy, vibrant energy, independence, and purpose. Thus, even though aging involves transition and adaptation, it also involves processes that span our life course—processes of continuity. Moreover, the aging process of transition and continuity manifests through changes and consistencies in our communicative practices and conceptions, particularly through interpersonal connections generated via social activity.

It is important that we not only challenge misconceptions about aging on a societal level but that we understand the communicative practices that are central to successful aging, and that we understand these in various social contexts, as the authors of this book vividly portray. For instance, in Chapter 1 Takahashi and colleagues examine what it means to successfully age in a post-retirement phase of life. They demonstrate the value of continued learning in older age within the social context of peer activity. In doing so, they show how older adults expand their social networks, receive social support, and engage in experiences that enhance their identity. Their work further breaks down the misconception that aging is pure decline. The work of so-called activity theorists is in line with these assertions, in that they suggest that activity, including social interaction, is positively related to older adults' well-being (Adams 1969; Bley et al. 1972; Lemon, Bengtson, and Peterson 1972; Nussbaum 1983). From this viewpoint, older adults successfully age when they maintain high levels of activity. This theory predicts that "successfully aging" older adults will interact frequently and maintain close bonds. In other words, activity is experienced communicatively through social activity.

We see this further extended in Doba and colleagues' work on the "New Elder Citizen Movement." According to activity theorists, successfully aging adults' conversations will involve concern for others as well as the community. Doba et al. provide a social situation in which this can occur. As Chapter 2 indicates, older adults need to be involved in influencing our larger social structures, our society, and its governing practices and policies on a broader social level. Such active involvement can occur through intergenerational exchange, a practice advocated by the United Nations as central to the International Plan of Action on Ageing. The New Elder Citizen Movement engages later adulthood in an active, purposeful, and meaningful manner. Intergenerational communication that is also community changing is one key to older adults' successful aging, as it enhances their self efficacy, autonomy, and sense of purpose in society. Moreover, intergenerational exchange is a communicative process that we continuously experience across the life span. Like Japan, many other places across the globe are facing an unprecedented increase in the population of older adults. Japan's New Elder Citizen Movement of intergenerational connection and generativity can serve as a model for other countries to adopt similar practices or policies to improve the experiences of the old around the world, as well as the lives of future generations by integrating them more significantly (and influentially) within our social structures.

In the subsequent chapters, we have the opportunity to take a deeper look at successful aging and communication wellness in another important social context: the family. These chapters show how older adults' successful aging is tied to intimate connections forged through healthy communication in familial environments. According to Laura Carstensen's (1991; 1992) socioemotional selectivity theory, as we age our social networks dwindle and our intimate ties, particularly our long-term relationships with our loved ones like friends and family, become increasingly important to our ability to attain a high socioemotional quality of life. Yet, as we can see in these chapters, communication in the family dynamic is not always healthy. We need to refine our communicative practices not only within our intimate networks but also on a larger scale. For instance, in Chapter 5, Hori challenges the idea that older adults, particularly women, are not intimate, sexual beings. She questions the stereotypes perpetuated by the media that old age is ugly, sterile, unromantic, and asexual. Intimacy, both in romantic terms and in terms of emotional connection, is critical to successful aging (Nussbaum, Miller-Day, and Fisher 2009; Nussbaum et al. 2005). Older adults can more successfully age through intimate relationships with family caregivers, friends, romantic partners, parents and children, and other loved ones. Socially negative assumptions that deny this need or remove intimacy from the aging process must be overturned in the media if we are to begin to cultivate a social environment that is fit for successful aging.

Such changes in social assumptions are warranted not only in far-reaching social platforms like the media but also in our own homes, as evidenced in Chapters 3 and 4. Long and Traphagan bring to light ominous experiences in aging that often occur in the home (and too often go unnoticed or ignored) in their examinations of spousal caregiving abuse and suicide among older Japanese generations. Traphagan demonstrates the importance of healthy interpersonal communication and connection in successful aging in his examination of motives for suicide in older generations. He considers such factors as loneliness, isolation, and feelings of dependency, or becoming a burden. Long brings to the forefront abusive communication that can occur between spouses as one provides care for the other. Furthermore, she reveals that such abusive communication is not typically visible on the surface and therefore goes unaddressed by our larger social structures and services. These chapters capture the difficulty of any type of caregiving. Families are a significant source of social and instrumental support for the elderly, and, in turn, social structures need to attend to the family's role in providing elder care. Caretaking is a responsibility that many family members will take on at some point. Adjusting to caretaking often involves intense scenarios that can entail conflict, as relational roles are redefined and power struggles are likely to occur (Nussbaum et al. 2000). As Long shows us, negative communication can be "masked" or invisible to those outside the boundaries of the family or, as Traphagan demonstrates, it may simply go unaddressed because of a lack of knowledge and understanding that this problem exists in older adulthood. Both authors stress that scholars and practitioners must understand that there is more than one side to the aging story—more than one face.

A life-span perspective is an important framework for further exploration. A life-span approach allows us to capture and understand the communicative and relational changes that are necessary for older adults to adapt to aging and maintain wellness across time, especially within the family. Communication and relationships are both developmental phenomena (Nussbaum et al. 2000; Pecchioni, Wright, and Nussbaum 2005). As we age, our relationships change as well. As we move across the life span, our communication behaviors also change as we renegotiate our social environments, redefine our relationships, and adapt to age-related changes associated with cognition and language. In light of this, communication and relationships are not static. Rather, they are ever-changing as we are constantly evolving.

As we age and our lives evolve, we must learn to communicatively adapt to these changes (Nussbaum et al. 1996). To do so, it is vitally important that we understand how our relationships transform and demand new communication competencies; such an understanding will enable us to sustain these bonds. As we saw in these chapters, various transitions, such as identity issues, family caregiving, and the risks of suicide, all challenge older adults' abilities to successfully age in any culture. Such events require relational redefinition that must be negotiated via communication. At the same time, we need to be talking about these issues on a broader, more influential societal level to ensure they are unveiled, addressed, and not forgotten. In the second half of this book, we have the opportunity to extend this conversation in a more detailed fashion by examining how communication is key to navigating the aging process.

Successful Aging *Is* Communication Wellness

While biologists examine the processes and causes of aging from a physiological stance, social scientists examine how people cope with and adapt to aging-
related changes. A communication perspective on aging focuses on the social
interaction of older individuals and, hence, centers on the importance of communication and social relationships in the aging experience. From this stand-
point, communication is examined as behavior that can facilitate successful
adaptation to aging-related life changes. According to Nussbaum et al. (1996),
studies that utilize a communication focus further confirm that "communication lies at the core of the aging process."

The final chapters of the book more closely examine both verbal and nonverbal communicative behavior and reveal the complexities of their role in successful aging as experienced in a variety of social contexts, including health-care,
family, intergenerational, and peer communication. For instance, as Morita discusses in Chapter 7, the well-being of older adults is greatly affected by relationships and social encounters with health care professionals (see also Nussbaum
et al. 2000). Health care across the world has evolved over the years and these
changes have altered the interactive experiences that older adults have in relation to their care (Nussbaum et al. 2000; Nussbaum, Pecchioni, and Crowell
2001). As non-Western countries, including many in Asia, are turning to West-
ernized formal care services for support of aging family members (Koyano 1999;
Phillips 2000; Sung 1995), these interactive experiences are becoming more of
a concern across cultures. Like Morita's chapter, recent studies of health care
in both Western and Eastern cultures reveal how these changes heighten the
need for relational and communication skills that better attend to older adults'
psychosocial needs.

Yet, we must also consider cultural biases in our assumptions about aging
and communication wellness. As Bower asserts in Chapter 6, Western and Eastern perspectives on communicative behavior differ. Accordingly, to be fully
understood and to eliminate presumptive biases, communication must be explored using a sociocultural lens. For example, Bower notes that Americans
tend to talk more than Japanese. Relatedly, in comparison to Japanese older
adults, Americans place more value on quantity of talk, as well as the continu-
ance of talk, and have negative conclusions about the implications of silence for
successful aging. As Bower advocates, we need to better understand culturally
embedded assumptions about talk if we are to fully understand communication practices that are key to successful aging. We must appreciate how com-

munication is made meaningful within the cultural and social contexts of such behaviors.

In addition, age can be a cultural variant contributing to different social experiences and perceptions across generations. In Chapter 8, we see this assertion being further addressed in Matsumoto's examination of "painful self-disclosure" communication. While such behavior tends to have negative implications in intergenerational interaction, it appears to function differently in the overlooked social context of peer interaction. Matsumoto reveals that such behaviors are understood to be socially meaningful in friendship interaction, especially among women, by fulfilling social support needs.

Still, intergenerational communication is a complex and often everyday experience for older adults. Competent intergenerational communication is, therefore, critical to successful aging, as Ota and Giles articulate in Chapter 10. The literature and theory to date can offer communication-focused insight on what it means to successfully age, particularly within the intergenerational context. Theoretical perspectives on communication and aging view older adults as active, social participants in relational networks who use communication to constantly adapt and maintain relational and emotional stability (Nussbaum et al. 2000). Communication frameworks grounded in intergroup theories such as Communication Accommodation Theory (CAT), Social Identity Theory, the Communication Predicament of Aging Model (CPA), and the Communication Enhancement Model of Aging (CEM) allow scholars to focus on communication and relational competencies that are necessary to successful aging. Moreover, they are instrumental in highlighting the relational and communication challenges that older adults encounter within their social networks.

Intergenerational communication has the potential to either threaten or maintain older adults' social identity. As we saw in Chapter 2, the New Elder Citizen Movement in Japan is an innovative step toward facilitating communication wellness through intergenerational exchange. The driving force behind this movement seems to align with Ota and Giles' advocacy for "mindfulness" in aging experiences. In Chapter 9, Hamaguchi again considers intergenerational communication, particularly in terms of being mindful in family conversations as kin members interactively create their histories, make sense of lived experiences, and together cultivate a shared identity through family narratives. Yet, scholars, health professionals, and practitioners across the globe must develop ways to nurture social environments in which intergenerational relationships can thrive and communication can facilitate successful aging.

Cultural considerations in intergenerational interaction are important. According to Pecchioni, Ota, and Sparks (2004), there is very little variation in cross-cultural comparisons of intergenerational communication outcomes due to ageist attitudes. These attitudes ultimately manifest in communicative behaviors and impact individuals' quality of life. In the United States and Australia, intergenerational communication significantly affects older adults' psychological well-being, including self-esteem and cohesion (see Pecchioni, Ota, and Sparks 2004). Yet, in the People's Republic of China, Hong Kong, and Japan, studies show that it is primarily intragenerational communication—or communication between older adults—that impacts their psychological health (Cai, Giles, and Noels 1998; Noels et al. 2001; Ota, Giles, and Gallois 2002). Regardless of this differentiation, these findings support one conclusion: older adults' communicative experiences—both in intergenerational and intragenerational social contexts—are an important consideration in understanding how to maximize quality of life.

Communication Lessons to Enhance Successful Aging

Collectively, the authors of this book offer communication-focused lessons on what it means to successfully age. First, older adults should maintain active engagement in social interactions. Their interactions with those close to them, such as family and friends, are most influential in affecting their well-being, as these are older adults' primary source of emotional and instrumental support. Yet, at the same time peer communication is not to be undervalued, as it can be a source of support, identity formation, and emotional connection for older adults. Second, to maintain relationships and maximize wellness in later life, our communication skills, particularly in terms of managing conflict, making decisions, and effectively listening, must be consistently utilized. These competencies are vital in navigating various life challenges and ultimately necessary to appreciate and adapt to the changing nature of our relational bonds and the aging experience itself. Third, we must value intergenerational communication and the multiple purposes it can serve in older adults' abilities to age successfully; and at the same time, younger generations must adjust their communicative behavior in accordance with the needs of the older adults they are interacting with. Fourth, everyone needs to be aware of his or her individual social biases, assumptions, and overgeneralizations about people who do not "fit" within one's social groups. By becoming more aware, we can begin to eliminate ageism and, in effect, minimize negative social experiences that are shaped by age-related stereotypes. Furthermore, we can begin to break down social structures that promote ageist attitudes, and begin to nurture global understanding and cultural diversity in what it means to successfully age. Finally, to maximize well-being and achieve quality care, older adults must become proactive in their communicative behavior. Accordingly, their family members and allied health practitioners must become effective listeners and negotiators to aid older adults in serving their vital psychosocial needs.

As they age, older adults' communication and relational skills enable them to maintain a sense of well-being and maximize wellness across the life span. These competencies are equally important across cultures, as comparable aging experiences can be found cross-culturally. Older adults across the globe encounter similar challenges during interactions, from social stigmas to the difficulties of sustaining close ties. They experience similar aging processes of transition and continuity. In essence, communication is a universal part of life and is thus found at the core of successful aging.

References

Adams, D. 1969. Analysis of life satisfaction index. *Journal of Gerontology* 24: 470–474.

Bley, N. B., M. Goodman, D. Dye, and B. Haiel. 1972. Characteristics of aged participants in age segregated leisure programs. *Gerontologist* 12: 368–370.

Cai, D., H. Giles, and K. Noels. 1998. Elderly perceptions of communication with older and younger adults in China: Implications for mental health. *Journal of Applied Communication Research* 26: 32–51.

Carstensen, L. L. 1991. Selectivity theory: Social activity in life-span context. *Annual Review of Gerontology and Geriatrics* 11: 195–217.

———. 1992. Social and emotional patterns in adulthood: Support for socioemotional selectivity theory. *Psychology and Aging* 7: 331–338.

Lemon, B. W., V. L. Bengtson, and J. A. Peterson. 1972. An exploration of the activity theory of aging: Activity types and life satisfaction among in-movers to a retirement community. *Journal of Gerontology* 27: 511–523.

Koyano, W. 1999. Population aging, changes in living arrangement, and the new long-term care system in Japan. *Journal of Sociology and Social Welfare* 26: 155–167.

Noels, K. A., H. Giles, C. Gallois, and S. H. Ng. 2001. Intergenerational communication and psychological adjustment: A cross-cultural examination of Hong Kong and Australian adults. In *Aging, communication, and health: Linking research and practice for successful aging*, ed. M. L. Hummert and J. F. Nussbaum, 249–297. Mahwah, NJ: Erlbaum.

Nussbaum, J. F. 1983. Relational closeness of elderly interaction: Implications for life satisfaction. *Western Journal of Speech Communication* 47: 229–243.

Nussbaum, J. F., M. L. Hummert, A. Williams, and J. Harwood. 1996. Communication and older adults. In *Communication yearbook 19*, ed. B. R. Burleson, 1–47. Thousand Oaks, CA: Sage.

Nussbaum, J. F., M. Miller-Day, and C. L. Fisher. 2009. *Communication and intimacy in older adulthood.* Madrid: Aresta.

Nussbaum, J. F., L. Pecchioni, and T. Crowell. 2001. The older patient–health care provider relationship in a managed care environment. In *Aging, communication, and health: Linking research and practice for successful aging*, ed. M. L. Hummert and J. F. Nussbaum, 23–42. Mahwah, NJ: Erlbaum.

Nussbaum, J. F., L. Pecchioni, J. D. Robinson, and T. Thompson. 2000. *Communication and aging.* 2nd ed. Mahwah, NJ: Erlbaum.

Nussbaum, J. F., M. J. Pitts, F. N. Huber, J. R. Krieger, and J. E. Ohs. 2005. Ageism and ageist language across the life span: Intimate relationships and non-intimate interactions. *Journal of Social Issues* 61: 285–303.

Ota, H., H. Giles, and C. Gallois. 2002. Perceptions of younger, middle-aged, and older adults in Australia and Japan: Stereotypes and age group vitality. *Journal of Intercultural Studies* 23: 253–266.

Pecchioni, L. L., H. Ota, and L. Sparks. 2004. Cultural issues in communication and aging. In *Handbook of communication and aging research*, ed. J. F. Nussbaum and J. Coupland, 167–207. Mahwah, NJ: Erlbaum.

Pecchioni, L. L., K. Wright, and J. F. Nussbaum. 2005. *Life-span communication.* Mahwah, NJ: Erlbaum.

Phillips, D. R. 2000. *Ageing in the Asia-Pacific region: Issues, policies and future trends.* London: Routledge.

Sung, K. T. 1995. Measures and dilemmas of filial piety. *Gerontologist* 35: 240–247.

Contributors

ANNE R. BOWER is CEO of Tyler Research Associates, a qualitative health care research consulting service. She is also adjunct assistant professor in the Department of Medicine, New Jersey Institute for Successful Aging at the University of Medicine & Dentistry of New Jersey School of Osteopathic Medicine. Her recent publications include *Redefining Dementia Units: A Roadmap for Culture Change* (2008), coauthored with William Senders.

NOBUTAKA DOBA (MD and PhD, Chiba University School of Medicine) had a long career in clinical medicine in cardiology. After retiring as the head of Teikyo University Ichihara Hospital, he has devoted himself to encouraging the evolution of a new lifestyle for the elderly. His current interests focus on frailty among the elderly, especially its progression and prevention, and he has been carrying out an observational cohort study at the Life Planning Center as a senior medical consultant. He is the author of *A Handbook of Clinical Geriatrics for All Health Care Professionals* (Igaku-shoin, 2005).

CARLA L. FISHER (PhD, Penn State University, 2008) is an assistant professor of communication studies at Arizona State University. She is a former predoctoral fellow with the National Institute on Aging and completed the advanced training institute on health behavior theory cosponsored by the National Cancer Institute. Her research focuses on the centrality of family communication to wellness across the life span, particularly during health and aging transitions. Her research has been published in books and journals including *Health Communication* and the *Journal of Language and Social Psychology*. Her recent work on how women diagnosed with breast cancer adapt through mother-daughter communication will be published in Hampton Press's health communication book series.

HOWARD GILES is professor of communication at the University of California, Santa Barbara. Prior to that he was head of psychology and chair of social psychology at the University of Bristol, England, where he also obtained his doctorates. His interests revolve around many domains in the study of intergroup communication and he has had a long-standing investment in cross-cultural studies of aging and intergenerational communication. He has over 400 publications (including 20 books), dozens in the area of cross-cultural gerontology.

TOSHIKO HAMAGUCHI (PhD, linguistics, Georgetown University) is lecturer in the Department of English Language and Literature at the University of the Sacred Heart, Tokyo. Her research interests include aging and communication, intergenerational family discourse, the discourse of people with Alzheimer's disease, and multimodal discourse.

GIYOO HATANO, PhD, who passed away in January 2006, was an internationally well-known researcher in cognitive development. He was involved in research on naïve biology, conceptual changes, and classroom learning. His publications include *Young Children's Naïve Thinking about the Biological World* (with K. Inagaki; Psychology Press, 2002) and "When Is Conceptual Change Intended? A Cognitive-Sociocultural View" in *Intentional Conceptual Change* (with K. Inagaki; Erlbaum, 2003).

SHIGEAKI HINOHARA (MD, Kyoto Imperial University, 1937; PhD, Kyoto University, 1941) began working as an internist at St. Luke's International Hospital in 1941, and later became head of the department of internal medicine and deputy director and then director of the hospital. He is currently chairman of the board of trustees and honorary president of the hospital. He established the Life Planning Center, a foundation that seeks to reform medical care with a focus on patient education, in 1973, and continues to serve as its president. In 2000, he founded the Association of the New Elderly. Hinohara remains active as the elder statesman of clinical medicine in Japan. His numerous publications include *Jūdai no kimi e: 95-sai no watashi kara* (Advice from myself at 95 to you as a teenager) (Toyamabō International, 2006) and *Kōreisha no kenkōgaku* (Health science for the elderly) (Sōeisha/Sanseidō Shoten, 2007), coauthored with Nobutaka Doba.

HIKARI HORI (PhD, visual culture and gender studies, Gakushin University, 2004) is Assistant Professor of Japanese film and visual culture, East Asian Languages and Cultures Department at Columbia University. She has worked as a research associate at the National Film Center, Tokyo, and also as a film program coordinator at the Japan Society, New York. Her publications include "Oshima Nagisa's 'Ai no korida' Reconsidered: Law, Gender, and Sexually Explicit Film in Japanese Cinema," in Creekmur and Sidel, eds., *Cinema, Law and the State in Asia* (Palgrave, 2007), and "Migration and Transgression: Female Pioneers' Documentary Filmmaking in Japan," *Asian Cinema Journal* 11 (2005).

SUSAN ORPETT LONG (PhD, University of Illinois at Urbana-Champaign) is professor of anthropology and founding coordinator of the East Asian Studies program at John Carroll University. Her ethnographic research has focused on bioethics and culture, gender and family, and aging and elder care in Japan. She is the author of *Final Days: Japanese Culture and Choice at the End of Life* (University of Hawaii Press, 2005) and numerous book chapters and articles. She also edited *Caring for the Elderly in Japan and the US: Practices and Policies* (Routledge, 2000) and *Lives in Motion: Composing Circles of Self and Community in Japan* (Cornell East Asia Series, 1999).

YOSHIKO MATSUMOTO (PhD, linguistics, University of California at Berkeley) is associate professor of Japanese in the Department of East Asian Languages and Cultures and by courtesy, in the Department of Linguistics, at Stanford University, as well as an affiliate of the Stanford Center on Longevity and the Clayman Institute for Gender Research. Her research interests include linguistic pragmatics, in particular, how certain meanings are conveyed and construed by the speaker and the listener. Her publications include *Noun-Modifying Constructions in Japanese: A Frame Semantic Approach* (1997), "Discourse of the Elderly from the Speaker's Point of View" (2008), and "Dealing with Changes—Humorous Self-Disclosure by Elderly Japanese Women" (2009).

NATSUMI MORITA (PhD, St. Luke's College of Nursing, Tokyo) is associate professor of nursing and medical care at Keio University. Her publications include *Shinpan: Kango no tame no wakariyasui keesu sutadii* (Case study: From theme-setting to report writing for nursing, new edition) (Tokyo: Shorinsha), and "Ketsueki tōseki ryōhō o ukete seikatsu suru mansei jinfuzen kanja no "kimochi" no kōzō" (The structure of *kimochi* in patients living with hemodialysis of end-stage renal disease), *Journal of St. Luke's Society for Nursing Research* 12 (2) (2008).

JON F. NUSSBAUM (PhD, Purdue, 1981) is professor of communication arts & sciences and human development & family studies at Penn State University. He was formerly president of the International Communication Association, editor of the *Journal of Communication*, and a Fulbright Research Fellow in the UK. He is currently a fellow of the International Communication Association and a fellow within the Adult Development and Aging Division of the American Psychological Association. Nussbaum has published 13 books and over 80 journal articles and book chapters on communication behaviors and patterns across the life span, including research on family, friendship, and professional relationships with older adults. Among his recent books are *Brain Health and Optimal Engagement for Older Adults* and *Communication and Intimacy for Older Adults*. His current research centers on quality health care for older adults, health care organizations, and intimacy across the life span.

HIROSHI OTA (PhD, University of California, Santa Barbara, 2001) is professor of communication at Aichi Shukutoku University. His research interests revolve around the social psychological processes involved in intergroup communication between age and cultural groups. His recent works include "Investigating Cancer and Aging in Cultural Perspective" (coauthored with Loretta Pecchioni and others) and "Beliefs about Intra- and Intergenerational Communication in Japan, the Philippines, and the United States: Implications for Older Adults' Subjective Well-Being" (coauthored with Howard Giles and Lilnabeth Somera).

KEIKO TAKAHASHI, PhD, is professor emeritus at University of the Sacred Heart, Tokyo. Her work focuses on the life-span development of social relationships and its relation to culture, and the development of social cognitions. Her publications include "Toward a Lifespan Theory of Close Relationships," *Human Development* 48 (2005); "Japan" in *International Encyclopedia of Adolescence* (Routledge, 2006); and *Human Relationships: Life Span Development of Affective Networks* (Tokyo University Press, 2010).

MAKIKO TOKORO, PhD, is a lecturer at Toyo Gakuen University. She is working on successful aging among older adults through participation in sociocultural activity.

JOHN W. TRAPHAGAN is associate professor of religious studies at the University of Texas at Austin. He is the author of numerous articles and books including *Taming Oblivion: Aging Bodies and the Fear of Senility in Japan* and *The Practice of Concern: Ritual, Well-Being, and Aging in Rural Japan*. His work has appeared in journals such as *Alzheimer Disease and Associated Disorders*, the *Journal of Adult Development, Ethnology,* the *Journal of Anthropological Research, Research on Aging,* and the *Asia Pacific Journal of Anthropology.* He is currently secretary general of the Japan Anthropology Workshop.

Index

Page numbers in boldface refer to figures and tables.